# A Handbook for the Teaching of Social Studies

## Second Edition

The Association of Teachers of Social Studies
in the City of New York /
United Federation of Teachers

*Edited by*
William S. Dobkin
Joel Fischer
Bernard Ludwig
Richard Koblinger

**Allyn and Bacon, Inc.**
Boston • London • Sydney • Toronto

Library of Congress Cataloging in Publication Data

Main entry under title:

A Handbook for the teaching of social studies.

Bibliography: p.
Includes index.
1. Social sciences — Study and teaching.   I. Associa-
tion of Teachers of Social Studies in the City of New
York.   II. United Federation of Teachers.   III. Dobkin,
William S.
H62.H2453   1985        300'.7        84-6278
ISBN 0-205-08149-5

Printed in the United States of America

10 9 8 7 6 5 4 3     89 88 87 86

# Contents

# Foreword

The contributors—supervisors and teachers of the Association of Teachers of Social Studies in the City of New York—are to be congratulated. They have succeeded in combining the best features of the previous edition with updating and additional chapters to reflect the trends and priorities of the 80s. For those who work in the field, in both training and teaching, the *Handbook* provides a valuable tool. Its authors, successful practitioners themselves, have considered the problems confronting both pre- and inservice teachers. Within the various chapters, the authors admit their unified conviction that there is no single best method, strategy, technique, or medium to achieve social studies learning. The emphasis is on many approaches as indicated by the material on goals and objectives in Chapter 1; procedures for planning effective social studies in Chapter 2; the art of questioning in Chapter 3, where the authors illustrate the maxim "to teach well is to question well"; individuation of instruction in Chapter 4; the role of values in education as developed in Chapter 5; and basic skills including reading, use of a map and globe, research, and thinking in Chapter 6.

This edition devotes an entire new chapter (Chapter 7) to an emphasis on writing skills. As in other chapters, numerous "how to" exhibits are provided. The section on media, Chapter 8, has been greatly strengthened and enhanced by the inclusion of the role of computers in social studies learning. Gaming and simulations are dealt with in Chapter 9, and evaluation, in Chapter 10, is delineated as an integral part of instruction. Chapter 11 points out opportunities and strategies for curriculum and electives development in junior and senior high schools. Teachers in training, novice teachers, and experienced teachers will be made more secure by the new Chapter 12 on mainstreaming in the social studies classroom. Chapter 13 deals with professional growth.

The new edition of the *Handbook* not only urges teachers in junior and senior high schools to make social studies meaningful, relevant, alive, and useful to students but also gives specific suggestions drawn from classroom-tested experiences. Means are presented with which the teacher can counter student mistrust and indifference in citizenship education programs. These are difficult times for teachers of social studies. They have more responsibilities than can be met satisfactorily. The new volume emphasizes the promotion of learning through effective teaching—helping students "learn how to learn"—and establishes a new role for the teacher as facilitator, planner, manager, stage-setter, and trouble-shooter. For the learner, the book outlines a new responsibility – the self-guiding investigator.

Social studies teachers cannot hope to prepare students fully to meet the explosion of knowledge. We do not know what is going to explode next. Also, we cannot be sure about the world of the 1980s and beyond. Yet we feel an obligation to prepare young people for citizenship responsibilities in a global arena. They should be well-informed, know how to use a variety of skills, be able to employ problem-solving methods, come to decisions, and act on them. Tomorrow's citizen must be informed and fortified.

The content of this edition of the *Handbook* has been designed to help build this fortification. Teachers are given practical and varied strategies for implementation. Preservice and inservice teachers with social studies responsibilities receive much support in the *Handbook* in how to deal with current problems and trends such as mainstreaming, including the basics of reading and writing, and teaching computer literacy.

Our democratic society demands that citizens be able to make decisions and shape public policy by active participation in the society. America's future depends on the civic and political involvement and competence of its citizens. The authors have put forth a strong case for social studies as one of the "basics" in education.

The contributors have fulfilled their objectives in this well-planned, pupil-tested, and updated *Handbook*. It is especially valuable for the teaching of social studies in college programs as well as in elementary and secondary schools. Thus it is a vital means to the goal of preparing and fortifying the coming generation to meet their global obligations. Forthcoming editions of the *Handbook* should continue to be a bulwark against the challenges of the future.

*Leonard W. Ingraham, Ed. D.*

Director, Bureau of Social Studies
New York City Public Schools (retired);

Professor of Social Studies Education
Arizona State University

# Foreword

I was president of the Association of Teachers of Social Studies in the city of New York thirty years ago (1951–52). If my memory serves me well, four general membership meetings were held that year. The first dealt with the banning of the *Nation* magazine from school libraries, and the second focused on the rise of Neo-Nazism in Germany. The third meeting explored ways of improving the teaching of economics, while the fourth concentrated on teaching strategies for the slow learner—a term in general use at that time.

Despite Paul Valery's perceptive observation that "the trouble with the world today is that the future is not what it used to be," for social studies teachers, the more things change the more they tend to remain the same. A glance at the contemporary scene reminds us that as a profession, social studies teachers seem doomed to relive the persistent issues of the past: censorship and academic freedom, democracy and authoritarianism and totalitarianism, the appropriate goals and content of civic education, and the uses of methodology to translate sophisticated ideas into comprehensible materials for all students, including those with learning disabilities.

Each generation of social studies teachers faces the same basic daily challenge: what to teach and how to teach it. While the content of what to teach is often determined by state mandates and administrative fiat, the province of how to teach seems to belong to the professional educator in many, but not in all, parts of the country.

Since the first edition of this *Handbook*, the ATSS, to its credit, has assumed a role of leadership in the social studies by sharing with the profession the creative lesson plans of its members. This edition, like its predecessor, continues to be a valuable guide through the tangled web of methodologies. This extraordinary collaborative effort on the part of many teachers, supervisors, and college instructors is based on John Dewey's conviction that method is a way of organizing subject matter. Practicing Talleyrand's admonition of "no zeal," the editors and contributors offer us a multiplicity of teaching ideas, techniques, and activities without sanctifying any one of them. This rich agenda of valuable and imaginative suggestions should enable teachers to transform their classroom time from the daily doldrums to adventures of the mind and of the spirit.

Since we have entered the bicentennial decade with two historic celebrations on the horizon (the drafting of the United States Constitution in 1987 and the ratification of the Bill of Rights in 1991), the ATSS should undertake another pioneering effort. Marshalling the talents of its members, it could produce a *Handbook on the Teaching of the United States Constitution and the Bill of Rights.* What a contribution that would be!

Even in retirement, a social studies educator, like myself, cannot refrain from giving assignments.

*Isidore Starr*

Professor Emeritus of Education
Queens College
City University of New York

# Preface

Whereas "innovation and experimentation" were the catchphrases of the early 1970s when the last edition of this *Handbook* was produced, "back-to-basics" became the catchphrase of the 1980s, as this edition goes to print. All the perceived failures of the educational establishment to produce scientific, mathematical, and "useful-to-business" geniuses were neatly explained away by education's emphasis on so-called fluff courses and "cutesy" teaching techniques. Fond memories of the good old days, when teachers really "taught" (i.e., lectured, held rote recitations, and piled on the homework) were invoked to challenge the efficacy of the "new social studies" courses and techniques.

This revised edition answers the challenge of those who would return us to the times of limited and confining methodologies; it is a response to those who would wish to define the meaning of "basics" very narrowly. A variety of techniques, used in a variety of subject matters, is a "basic" trait of social studies teaching. The basics of good teaching, as we see it, lie not in going back to a stress on facts, but in realizing that students must be given a variety of tools, in a variety of ways, with which to obtain, examine, and analyze those so-called facts.

We have endeavored to retain (with updating) as much of the previous edition's approaches as possible while also addressing some of the concerns (e.g., mainstreaming and writing in the social studies) that have arisen since the last printing.

This book is evidence of the creativity interested teachers can generate. It was, and still is, a methods book generated by teachers for teachers in a collaborative effort. A glance at the long list of contributors gives evidence of its origins, but special thanks must go to Richard Kobliner as the liaison to the publisher from the Association of Teachers of Social Studies/United Federation of Teachers and to Bill Sigelakis, under whose presidency of the ATSS/UFT this revision was initiated.

# Acknowledgments

We would like to thank the following people for their contributions:

George Altomare
Alan Argoff
Linda Beimer
Michael Berger
Amelia Brown
John Bunzel
Don Cody
Martin Cohen
Robert Consigli
William Dobkin
Ira Epstein
Sybil Evans
Arnold Feinblatt
Joel Fischer
Philip Freedman
Edward Fry
Anthony Gallo
Melvyn Garskof
Arthur Genen
Michael Gerber
Lester Golden
Claire Goodman
Vivian Grano
Harold Greenberg
Robert Gumerove
Fred Haines
Joel Heffner
Thomas Hennessy
Carolyn Herbst
Lawrence Herstik
Bernard Hirschorn
Kenneth Hodgins
Florence Jackson
Arthur Keiselman
James Killoran
George Kirsch
Alan Kitt
Sheldon Lazarowitz
Neil Lefkowitz
Philip Lefton

Peter Lerner
Bert Linder
Roy Longarzo
Bernard Ludwig
Michael Lustig
Margaret MacNamara
Janet McAuley
Muriel Mandell
Harris Nierman
Isador Olicker
Julius Perlman
JoAnn Piazzi
Albert Post
Carol Raphael
Harry Rice
Sylvia Rose
Ronald Rosenberg
Harold Rosenbloom
Erwin Rosenfeld
Walter Sadowski
Elliot Salow
Richard Schiff
Michael Schoenfeld
Derek Schuster
Harvey Seligman
Ron Shafran
Victor Shapiro
Seymour Siegel
William Sigelakis
Stephen Spector
George Staples
Harvey Steinerman
Henry Stern
Maurice Tandler
Leonard Wechsler
Dana Willens
Jesse Witchell
Dennis Young
Jack Zevin
Richard Zuckerman

# 1

●●●●●●●●●●●●●●●●●●●●●●●●●●●●●●●●●●●●●●●●●●●●●●●●●●●●●●●●●●●●●●●●●●●●●●●●●

# Goals and Objectives

●●●●●●●●●●●●●●●●●●●●●●●●●●●●●●●●●●●●●●●●●●●●●●●●●●●●●●●●●●●●●●●●●●●●●●●●●

It is important for social studies teachers to understand the special role they play in society. Those who attempt to define the role of other individuals should certainly know their own. Defining the social studies teacher is complicated by the encompassing nature of social studies as a learning discipline. The subject content varies from areas of high skill concentration, such as geography, to consciousness-raising electives, such as "The American Woman." Curriculum goals help to establish the role.

The task of writing the overall goals for a course of study and of writing the specific central question (or *aim*) on which the daily lesson will focus, is where teachers must begin if they are to give direction to the learning experiences they wish their students to have. Many teachers have difficulty in getting started. Once started, they frequently bog down in a morass of unrelated or unsorted information. This is usually attributable to a false start resulting from the teacher's lack of direction. A teacher obtains direction through an understanding of *goals* and *objectives*.

We will use these two terms, goals and objectives, to describe two different considerations. We define *goals* as the broad purposes of social studies. These purposes are the basic rationale for the position of social studies in the school curriculum. They are the main charge that society places on social studies teachers and define their role more than anything else does. Goals are pervasive and transcend any daily lesson aim, no matter what it might be. An *objective*, on the other hand, represents the specific change or changes that take place in students on a daily basis, as they are exposed to social studies learning. We will deal first with the goals of social studies.

In searching for purpose, the social studies teacher faces three basic alternatives: content, individual needs, or societal role. A stress on content takes place when the teacher reacts to *disciplinary* pressures. Emphasis on *individualistic* pressures accents how he or she can assist each student as to personal needs, while *societal* pressures help to integrate the individual into society.

"Why are we taking a trip to the stock market?" the teacher might ask in order to elicit an aim for a field trip. These might be some of the responses, labeled in parentheses according to the three basic alternatives:

1. To learn how stocks and bonds are sold (disciplinary).

2. To learn how to become investors and become rich (individualistic).

3. To understand how the investor makes decisions that influence all of us (societal).

While there is no correct answer, because the answer could be any combination of the three responses, the teacher should decide where the emphasis ought to be. It is generally agreed that social studies teachers should stress societal goals, which are represented by the third choice. This is agreement by definition. The social studies teacher's role in society is, by definition, to establish the interrelationship of responsibilities between the individual and the community.

With this in mind, let us examine those goals of social studies instruction that have remained relatively constant in American educational history. For despite new scholarship in history and in the social sciences, despite changes in teaching methods, strategies, and techniques, and despite a continual series of social, political, and economic upheavals, certain traditional objectives seem still to be fundamental for all school systems. Individual communities, with different needs and values, may vary in the relative weight given to each objective, the sequence in which they are achieved, and the procedures developed for implementation. However, these traditional goals are as valid as ever and are likely to remain so:

1. *Development of critical thought.* Reason dictates that human progress and survival rest upon understanding, tolerance, and knowledge. The best hope for achievement of these characteristics lies in the victory of rational thought over the passions of emotion.

2. *Broad acceptance of, and respect for, other peoples' cultures.* This does not mean passing judgment on other peoples' value systems according to our own standards. It does mean respecting their right to exist and to flourish, and to live in accordance with their values, as long as they do not interfere with anyone else's right to exercise the same privilege.

3. *Enlightened patriotism.* The psychologically healthy person must feel a sense of belonging to society, and a viable society must command a degree of commitment and loyalty from its members. The social studies teacher must help the student to achieve a sensible balance between the objectives of loyalty and critical thought.

4. *Good citizenship.* Active, informed participation by all citizens is the best guarantee of a healthy democracy. History shows that corrup-

tion flourishes in an atmosphere of apathy and neglect on the part of the citizenry. If the tools of democratic government are utilized, the entire populace becomes a watchdog and the possibility of illegal and/or corrupt behavior on the part of public officials is substantially reduced.

5. *Knowledge of significant developments in human history.* It is impossible to understand the modern world and to act intelligently upon the problems which confront it without an appreciation of those events of the past that have shaped the present. This does not mean the memorization of dry, unrelated lists of happenings. Rather, it means the understanding of certain historical events which are generally recognized as key elements in the development of important social, political, and economic orders and patterns.

6. *Acquisition of fundamental skills.* To pursue learning beyond the structure of a classroom and a course, an individual must be furnished with the research skills to do so. In addition, a true understanding of geopolitical factors requires mastery of certain geographic skills. Geology, topography, and territorial relationships affect domestic and foreign concerns.

7. *Understanding of fundamental concepts.* Given the vast amounts of information in social studies, it is imperative that people be able to sort it out and to order it in a logical and comprehensive manner. A grasp of concepts allows students to organize tremendous quantities of content in a meaningful fashion, whether during their school years or later in life.

8. *Appreciation of the interrelationship of all disciplines.* Academic subjects are artifacts of scholarly organization. Too many people learn about a content area as if it existed in a vacuum, without being affected by or having an effect upon other aspects of human striving. All aspects of human endeavor are interrelated, and this fact ought to be recognized in schools.

While there is general agreement on the broad goals of social studies, there is considerable variety regarding their implementation in the schools. Several factors seem to determine the method and the extent to which these objectives are pursued. First, there is the student population. How old are the students in the target group? What are their socioeconomic backgrounds? What are their interests? What attitudes do they possess? Second, the composition of the community exerts a force. What is/are the primary ethnic group(s)? What is the socioeconomic distribution of those living there? How are they geographically situated? What are the history, economy, and politics of the community? Third, the financial and physical resources affect the curriculum. How large is the school budget? What are the number and quality of school facilities available? What type of contribution do adults in the community make to school functions? Finally, law and tradition must be considered. How do state and local laws determine and/or limit what can be taught? What has been the historical role of the school in the community? Are there pressure groups that try to exert influence on the community? Do law and tradition refer only to what should be included in the curriculum, or to *how* it should be taught, as well?

## COGNITIVE AND AFFECTIVE LEARNING

Attempts to define more concisely what and how teachers should teach have been explored in great depth in recent years.[1] Many of the educational researchers and theorists who have been involved have addressed themselves to the question of whether or not content objectives have their counterparts in the behavior of individuals. One result of these investigations has been the development of *taxonomies* or hierarchies for the cognitive and affective domains of knowledge and the behaviors associated with them. For instance, cognitive objectives vary from simple recall of material to highly original and creative ways of analyzing, synthesizing, and evaluating new ideas and materials. In all cases, however, emphasis is on the development of intellectual skills.

The affective domain, on the other hand, is concerned with the development and clarification of attitudes and values. While the public school curriculum has always dealt, at least indirectly, with this area, recently there has been a growing realization that achievement of all cognitive objectives requires the parallel, concomitant achievement of affective objectives. For example, putting a book or a teacher in front of a pupil will not result in the desired cognitive gains unless the pupil is *aware* of the book or the teacher and *absorbs* what is presented. What this means for the educational experience is that "teaching" does not necessarily result in learning. Certain attitudes and/or values must be present if the student is actually to learn something. Conversely, attitudes and/or values devoid of substantive backing are ill-founded and immensely changeable. In sum, the cognitive and affective domains are interdependent and follow a parallel hierarchy.

The following comparative table illustrates this last point. The italicized terms are shorthand for the hierarchical levels in each taxonomy:*

| Cognitive domain | Affective domain |
| --- | --- |
| 1. The cognitive continuum begins with the student's recall and recognition of *knowledge*, | 1. The affective continuum begins with the student's merely *receiving* stimuli and passively attending to them. It extends through his more actively attending to them, |

---

*From *Taxonomy of Educational Objectives: Handbook II, Affective Domain* by David R. Krathwohl et al. Copyright © 1964 by Longman Inc. Reprinted by permission of Longman Inc., New York.

2. it extends through his *comprehension* of the knowledge,

3. his skill in *application* of the knowledge that he comprehends,

4. his skill in *analysis* of situations involving this knowledge and his skill in *synthesis* of this knowledge into new organizations,

5. his skill in *evaluation* in that area of knowledge to judge the value of material and methods for given purposes.

2. his *responding* to stimuli on request, willingly responding to these stimuli, and taking satisfaction in this responding,

3. his *valuing* the phenomenon or activity so that he voluntarily responds and seeks out ways to respond,

4. his *conceptualization* of each value, to

5. his *organization* of these values into a system and finally of the value complex into a single whole, a *characterization* of the individual.[2]

Thus, it is possible to utilize an objective in one domain to achieve an objective—or a change—in the other domain. For example: a pupil can be given information (cognitive) for the purpose of helping him or her to change an attitude; or he or she can be helped to develop an affective interest in certain material so that he or she will learn to use it. In the same way, as a teacher plans which material to include in a lesson, it can be seen that a single objective in one domain can be used as a catalyst for the purpose of developing multiple objectives in the other domain: teaching about the Compromise of 1850 involves the complex question of values as reflected in differing cultures.

In general, a major danger for the teacher of social studies is the tendency to stress subject matter mastery at the possible expense of affective objectives. Such a mistaken emphasis can result only in obviating the purposes inherent in the concept of social studies, even if done inadvertently. Considering the scope, complexity, and seriousness of the problems that a citizen must face today, the importance of the social studies teacher's obligation is clear.

Not surprisingly, the interest of educational researchers and theorists in the different levels of cognitive and affective learning, and in the interaction of the two domains, has led to a change in what constitutes a valid objective for social studies instruction. As Doll observes, "Learning experiences for pupils may be defined as interactions between learners and their environments which create behavioral changes in the learners."[3] The emphasis, accordingly, is now on structuring lesson and course objectives in terms that specify a particular change in behavior.

### OBJECTIVES

Social studies teachers, in particular, have been searching for a concrete method of communicating specific social studies objectives. The search has concentrated on behavioral objectives. The adoption of the behavioral objective format was given impetus from two sources: the clamor for *accountability* and governmental requirement that those receiving grants must state their objectives in a manner that can be objectively evaluated. Many teachers balk at outside interference that imposes rigid guidelines on a subject area requiring latitude in teacher and student options. Other teachers welcome a technique that encourages them to communicate to students, colleagues, and the public in concrete terms. If for no other reason, teachers can benefit from considering behavioral objectives as a means of correlating learning objectives with evaluation. Students ought to know exactly what is expected of them before they embark on a learning experience and are judged by an instrument which taps these expectations. A discussion of the relationship between behavioral objectives and evaluation is resumed in Chapter 10 of this handbook.

On page 2 we described outcomes in terms of *learning* and *understanding*. While these constitute legitimate social studies *goals*, they do not describe a breakdown into recognizable *steps*, or what is happening to the student in the learning process. The purpose of writing behavioral objectives is to define specific *terminal traits* to be observed in students.

A behavioral objective usually contains three elements concerned with learning:

1. What must be done (action verb).
2. How it will take place (environment).
3. How well it must be done (acceptance level).

These are examples of social studies behavioral objectives for specific learning activities:

1. Given the symbols representing familial members, the students will diagram two family lineage patterns.
2. After viewing the film *Say Goodbye,* the students will describe the plight of three endangered species.
3. By examining the graph on the Federal Budget, the students will identify the three major expenditures and will express their opinions on national priorities.

Consider the above statements. Is the learning environment apparent? Are you clearly able to identify the learning activity? Will it be easy or difficult to evaluate the expected outcomes? Notice the utilization of the action verbs "diagram," "identify," and "describe." While these verbs stress cognitions, the phrase "express their opinion" in the third objective, illustrates that it is possible to adapt the behavioral format to the affective domain.

These verbs, in addition to those used in the examples, are particularly useful in writing social studies objectives:

| | |
|---|---|
| categorize | group |
| classify | label |
| demonstrate | list |
| design | match |
| select | |

Some of the verbs that represent a level of learning which combines the affective and cognitive domains are as follows:

| | |
|---|---|
| express | judge |
| debate | interpret |
| evaluate | contrast |

A behavioral objective written in the affective domain does not specify how a student "feels"; it does specify that a student will perform an act which shows "feeling." Teachers can avoid the criticism that they are imposing objectives on students by arriving at these objectives, no matter what format is used, through a process of interaction with the class and the individual students. Behavioral objectives are particularly useful when arrived at with an individual student who "contracts" to achieve some specific undertaking.

In this chapter we have offered two basic recommendations for the teacher's journey through a career in social studies. Take the high road. This is represented by the broad and idealistic goals of social studies. Take along a good road map. This is represented by the technique of writing specific learning objectives.

## ENDNOTES

1. Benjamin S. Bloom, *Taxonomy of Educational Objectives, The Classification of Educational Goals, Handbook I: Cognitive Domain* (New York: David McKay Co., 1956).

   David R. Krathwohl et al., *Taxonomy of Educational Objectives, The Classification of Educational Goals, Handbook II: Affective Domain* (New York: David McKay Co., 1964).

   Robert F. Mager, *Preparing Instructional Objectives* (Belmont, Calif.: Fearon Publishers, 1962).

   Robert F. Mager, *Developing Attitude Toward Learning* (Palo Alto, Calif.: Fearon Publishers, 1968).

2. Krathwohl et al., pp. 49–50.

   The authors caution us, however, to regard this tabulation *as a broad generalization* — only for the purpose of offering some relative basis of comparison. A true comparative understanding of these relationships can be achieved by study of the full taxonomies.

3. Ronald C. Doll, *Curriculum Improvement: Decision-Making and Process* (Boston: Allyn and Bacon, 1964), pp. 105, 110-11.

## BIBLIOGRAPHY

Bloom, Benjamin. *Taxonomy of Educational Objectives, Handbook I: Cognitive Domain* (New York: David McKay Co., 1956).

Cremin, Lawrence A. *The American Common School: An Historical Conception* (New York: Bureau of Publications, Teachers College, Columbia University, 1961).

Cubberly, Elwood P. *Public Education in the United States,* rev. ed. (Boston: Houghton Mifflin, 1956).

Estvan, Frank. *Social Studies in a Changing World, Curriculum and Instruction* (New York: Harcourt, Brace, and World, 1968).

Merwin, William; Schneider, Donald; and Stephens, Lester. *Developing Competency in Teaching Secondary Social Studies* (Columbus, Ohio: Charles E. Merrill, 1974).

Tanner, Daniel. *Using Behavioral Objectives in the Classroom* (New York: MacMillan Company, 1972).

# 2

••••••••••••••••••••••••••••••••••••••••••••••••••••••••••••••••••••••••••••••••••

# Planning

••••••••••••••••••••••••••••••••••••••••••••••••••••••••••••••••••••••••••••••••••

## NEED FOR PLANNING

Since teaching is correctly described as a creative act rather than an exact science, it would appear that planning might stifle creativity. Yet, especially for the beginning teacher, formal written unit and lesson planning is essential if only to mobilize creative forces and apply them to a worthwhile teaching act in the classroom. In teaching, as throughout all of our purposeful existence, some planning is essential.

Although planning takes considerable time and effort, its advantages outweigh its disadvantages. Lessons go better for a number of reasons. Because the teacher has planned, the material he or she needs is ready when necessary for use. Films, pictures, clippings, and cartoons are not easy to acquire just before a lesson is to be presented. Projective devices should be checked to see that they are in working order.

When a lesson is derived from a master plan, its focus is clear to the students and to the teacher. When students sense the structure of a lesson, when they can see the direction in which their activities are leading, they are more motivated, learn better, and are more likely to remain actively involved. Moreover, when work is planned, students can help to determine objectives and procedures. The "consumers" are involved in the production; they are not presented with a take-it-or-leave-it situation.

But, in fact, the most important advantage of planning is that it demands that the teacher think about the subject and its significance for the young people being taught.

### Levels of Planning

When the teacher takes a good look at a course, three different levels become apparent. First, there is the totality, the *course* itself. Second, the course is composed of smaller blocks called *units*. Finally, these units are composed of operational parts known as *lessons*. Teachers generally plan units and lessons. If they happen to be serving on a curriculum committee, or if they have a special mandate from the chairperson, they may develop courses. This possibility is dealt with in Chapter 11, "Electives and Curriculum Considerations." However, since classroom teachers devote most of their planning time to units and lessons, it is these issues that will be considered in this chapter.

Because lessons are the *operational* parts of units and are the ultimate testing ground of all planning, there is a temptation for teachers to think that (1) they should begin planning at this level and/or that (2) most of their effort in planning should be expended here. These statements require critical analysis.

As a rule, the broader the level of planning (i. e., the unit level), the more abstract, generalized, and useful the ideas generated. A narrow level of planning (i. e., the lesson level) provides specificity, concreteness, and subordinate ideas. Unit-level ideas tend to be obscure without supportive lessons. Lesson objectives incline towards the trivial if they are not contributing to the construction of unit-level concepts.

The thoughtful reader will note in this chapter, hopefully with some aesthetic pleasure, the symmetry of unit and lesson. The lesson plans replicate, in a number of ways, the structure of the unit. The unit plan is the daily lesson "writ large"; the unit is the macrocosm, the lesson the microcosm.

## The Unit

A *unit* is an organization of learning experiences around a concept, problem, or theme. Poverty, discrimination, world order, and social deviance are concepts upon which a unit might focus. "How can we save the environment for future generations?" and "Can war be eliminated?" are problems that a unit might tackle. An historical period (e. g., the Renaissance, the Federalist era) is a legitimate unit topic if the events selected for study relate to a central idea. For example, a series of events that occurred during the administrations of John Quincy Adams, Andrew Jackson, and Martin Van Buren form a unit only if each of the events selected contributes to an understanding of a theme, such as "The Rise of the Common Man." A vital attribute of a unit is that it is selective — it excludes all material unrelated to its central theme. In this way, focus, a key element in successful instruction, is maintained.

The teaching time required to implement a unit varies from three to six weeks. It is important that its approximate length be established early in the planning period. Otherwise other units will be crowded or eliminated.

*Types of Unit Plans.*    The two most common unit plans are the *resource unit* and the *learning unit*. A resource unit is a pool of materials and ideas related to a theme or a problem, which is constructed with no particular group of students in mind. Resource units are often put together by departments, districts, and even nonschool agencies. Experienced teachers build their own as they collect and categorize materials through the years. A learning unit is a coherent plan of instruction designed for a particular class. In constructing a learning unit, the teacher selects and organizes ideas, materials, and activities for the purpose of producing daily lesson plans. Since this is the type of unit organization most immediate to instruction, it is the type that will be discussed in this chapter.

*Composition of Learning Units.* The essential elements of a learning unit are: title, objectives, materials, activities, and evaluation techniques. The title is, naturally, the first part to be decided upon. The most important part of a learning unit is its list of objectives. Without objectives, the unit would be like a tempest-tossed ship, without course or destination. Unit objectives are usually classified as understandings, skills, and attitudes. They indicate the behaviors that the *students* will engage in, not the activities that the *teacher* will perform. As we discussed in Chapter 1, a behavioral objective might be phrased, "students will be able to identify examples of status consciousness," *not* "to teach the concept of status consciousness."

The materials section of a learning unit contains either the data that will be the object of the students' attention, or references to the contents and sources of such material. Cartoons, charts, graphs, pictures, quotations, handout maps, and newspaper articles are examples of data that might actually be inserted in a unit folder. Titles, locations, and descriptions should be indicated for filmstrips, games, wall maps, audio and video tapes, books, and resource people so that they may be made available when the relevant lessons are being planned. Summaries or outlines of content are frequently included in the materials section of the unit plan.

The activities section of the learning unit includes descriptions of what the students will be doing during the unit. Activities can include class discussions, committee work, debates, role playing, psychodramas, independent study, field trips, group research, TV viewing, newspaper writing, film production, and listening to guest speakers. This section is most commonly divided into introductory, developmental, and culminating activities.

## Developing a Learning Unit

*Selecting a Topic.* The two best reasons for selecting a topic for a learning unit are that the students will benefit from it and that they will (or can) be motivated to pursue it. What students will study is determined to a large degree by various agencies, from the state Department of Education to the social studies department in the school. In most cases, if the teacher looks carefully, he or she will find flexibility in the demands of the curriculum producers. Bulletins frequently *suggest* rather than *mandate*, while offering options from which to select. Teachers should guard against the all-too-human tendency to avoid the rigors of inventive planning by regarding all suggestions by authorities as compulsory orders.

A teacher may want to consult with his or her department chairperson before teaching an unprescribed unit. If so, a general outline of objectives and materials should be submitted. The teacher may then develop a complete and coherent learning unit and submit that to the chairperson for final approval.

Unit planning provides the teacher with the opportunity to involve students in setting up their own learning. In determining a topic, students may be asked to express their preferences by choosing from a list of options. A student committee may be formed to consider the results and to help the teacher in planning. The goals of the course will, naturally, suggest appropriate unit topics. Curriculum guides from states and other localities should be studied. Colleagues, especially those with experience, should be consulted, or even recruited to coauthor the unit.

Some of the questions that the teacher should consider in deciding upon a topic for the unit are:

1. How are my students going to function better in society by having studied this topic?
2. Do my students possess the skills necessary to use the materials required by this topic?
3. Are the students intellectually sophisticated enough to profit from a study of this subject?
4. Would the activities necessary to develop this unit conform to the style of learning to which my students are accustomed? Would it be possible to teach them a new style if required?
5. Is the topic one that would be appropriate for this community at this time?
6. Are my students emotionally mature enough for this topic?
7. Are sufficient materials available to develop this topic?

After a broad unit topic (e. g., labor unions, nationalism, social deviance) has been decided upon, the teacher must determine the perimeter of the topic. Will the unit sweep from medieval guilds to today's AFL-CIO? If so, the teacher will have either a full course or a superficial unit. The teacher can limit the topic; for example, to American labor in the nineteenth century, or can state a manageable problem: have labor unions contributed to the atomization of American society? A unit dealing with concepts like nationalism or social deviance is sufficiently narrow if it is directed towards finding and refining an appropriate definition of the concept or three or four generalizations directly related to it.

## DETERMINING OBJECTIVES

Whether they deal with theme, problem, or concept, learning units are set up to achieve predetermined objectives, usually classifiable as ideas (knowledge, understandings, generalizations), skills, and attitudes (values). These must be decided upon once the unit topic is fixed.

Most teachers begin with ideas and attitudes and then determine which skills are necessary to produce them. Thus a unit on the American War for Independence might have as an idea objective to understand that belief in freedom was an important cause of American hostility toward the British government. An attitude objective could be to appreciate the sacrifices made by our founding fathers. Reading interpretation skills might be strengthened by studying colonial documents to determine what made the colonists so angry in the dozen years that preceded the battles of Lexington and Concord. Evaluation skills might be developed by asking students to rank given examples of sacrifices made by selected historical persons.

The ideas-first approach to determining objectives has considerable merit but has a major disadvantage. Ideas and attitudes offer a focus and a clear line of development. However, when they are the pivots, there is no guarantee that skills will be taken up in the sequence best suited to their development. In fact, there may be considerable repetition of some skills and omission of other important ones.

An alternative method is to base units on the sequential development of skills. (We have in mind such objectives as print reading, map reading, and interpretation of charts.) Where deficiency in skills is a major problem of students, or where skills are regarded as primary by those responsible for determining educational goals, this is the approach to be followed. The obvious disadvantage of the skills-first mode of organizing a unit is the loss of the unifying element (e. g., chronology or causality) in the development of ideas.

Unless otherwise directed, the teacher will probably begin to determine objectives by identifying the big ideas the unit should develop. The teacher should first become immersed in material relating to the topic (texts, monographs on the teacher's intellectual level, curriculum guides, old notebooks) and peruse ideas expressed by students. A good way to generate a synthesis of these ideas is to put on paper, or, even better, into a tape recorder, as many thoughts as possible on the topic. If this can be done with a colleague or two, so much the better. There should be no limit to what is recorded; editing and refining come later. The flow of ideas should not be allowed to stop.

The goal of this brainstorming is to come up with statements at high levels of generality without worrying, at the time, about their degree of probability. Some examples of big ideas that one might come up with are: (1) labor unions are more effective when they include workers from all phases of an industry, rather than from just part of it; (2) nationalism is more likely to occur when people in a region share a common language; (3) deviant behavior occurs at all levels of societies at all times.

While brainstorming is a good way to produce hypotheses, the library will provide some readymade big ideas for selected topics. One of the most useful sources is Berelson and Steiner, *Human Behavior, An Inventory of Scientific Findings.*[1] Book reviews in professional journals like the *American Historical Review* are excellent sources of hypotheses and generalizations. Teachers' guides and teachers' editions of texts should also be perused for big ideas.

The three or four big ideas produced become unit objectives once they have been edited and refined. (Attitudinal and skill objectives are considered in Chapters 5 and 6 of this book.) The teacher then begins to identify subobjectives and to place these in the proper sequence. Subobjectives may be (1) stated as understandings or concepts, contributing to the production of generalizations – which may be the terminal objectives of the unit – or they may be (2) briefly presented as the major divisions of a content outline. An example of (1) above is the following understanding: the civil disobedience of Gandhi became a model for powerless people who wanted to improve their chances in life. This statement is a subobjective of the unit objective represented by the following generalization: deviant behavior has been and can be beneficial to society. As an example of (2) above, "Ceremonial Leader" might be a division of a content outline for a unit called "The Roles of the United States President."

## MATERIALS AND ACTIVITIES

As a next step, the teacher decides what materials and activities are appropriate for achieving the subobjectives, which will henceforth be called *aims.* Whether the materials should be decided upon first and the activities shaped to fit them or vice versa is a moot point. The decision depends upon what is most conducive to achieving the stated objectives. As a rule, when ideas are the most important aims, materials are selected before activities. Where skills have priority, activities are determined first.

In considering materials, the teacher should ponder the following questions:

1. What would be particularly motivating (vivid, controversial, problematic) for this class?
2. What materials would provide for the different aptitudes and interests of these students?
3. What materials would provide the most direct route to the achievement of the unit objectives?

In seeking materials, the best place to start is the social studies office in the school. Even materials not stored there are very likely to be indexed there. The department book room should be searched for texts, supplementary books, and maps. The library is a vital source of materials, best approached through the numerous guides, indexes, and bibliographies, so important to researchers.

The audiovisual room, or the file of audiovisual materials, should be consulted as well. The architects of some modern schools have made it easier for the teacher by locating media resource libraries in a central area accessible to all teachers in the department. One important rule to be followed in seeking materials is, "Ask for help."

When a list of promising materials has been made, the teacher should consider the following:

1. Can these be readily reproduced for student use if necessary?
2. Can I arrange for any special equipment that would be needed for them?
3. Are each of the items within the capacity of some of the students?
4. What is the order in which these materials should be introduced?

In considering which of the many possible activities would be most appropriate, the teacher should ask the following questions:

1. What activities would be most useful in introducing, reviewing, and summarizing the unit work?
2. What activities would be the most motivating and most likely to maintain the interest of the students?
3. What activities should be placed early in the unit to identify and clarify objectives?
4. What activities will maximize student participation?
5. What selection will provide for the individual differences of the students?
6. What combination of activities will provide the best balance between cooperative effort and individual effort?

It should be noted that homework assignments are activities that must be given careful consideration when the unit is being planned. Assignments should be characterized by the same diversity as in-class activities. Students need more motivation to undertake assigned work at home than they do in the classroom, which provides support, encouragement, and rewards and does not have such distractions as TV and the telephone.

## EVALUATION

The procedures to be followed in evaluating students' work and the unit itself are discussed in Chapter 10; however, a few considerations are in order at this time. If a full examination were to be constructed and included in a unit prior to teaching it, the teacher would feel constrained to cover all of the items.

Teaching for exams inhibits experimentation, flexibility, and creativity. On the other hand, when teachers compose questions for the unit test near completion of a unit, they often find that they have omitted some important points or neglected some exciting relationships. The process of making up examination questions often gives the teacher a perspective on the unit that makes teaching more meaningful.

A useful plan is to make up a considerable number of tentative items. These should be at hand when the unit is being refined, but they should be put away while the unit is being taught. In this way, the questions will help to shape the unit, but they will not straitjacket the teaching of it.

## A UNIT OF PLANS

A unit plan may be considered complete when all of the necessary elements of instruction have been identified or collected and organized. However, if the teacher wishes, he or she may develop lessons before teaching the unit. If done so, the learning unit becomes the title, the objectives, and the sequential arrangement of daily lessons. Exhibit 2-1, "Social Deviance," at the end of this chapter illustrates this type of unit plan.

The obvious advantage of this arrangement is that, in theory, the teacher may now concentrate all of his or her time and energy on teaching. An alternative procedure is to make lessons each day as the unit progresses, on the theory that, since teachers are not clairvoyants, they must respond to contingencies that develop. In practice, however, unit planners should have a good idea about the shape of lessons before the unit begins and make adjustments as the unit is being taught. The construction of lessons before the unit is taught does, however, help substitute teachers if their presence is required.

## LESSON PLANNING

The lesson plan is rooted in the unit of which it is a part. However, it has an organic unity of its own. It resembles the unit in its structure and component parts, but has a dynamic quality that the unit lacks. The lesson plan is at the action end of the teaching-learning process. Whereas a unit provides for a variety of learning experiences, approaches, and methods, each lesson rests on a particular set of beliefs about the goals of instruction.

### Beginning the Plan

In planning a lesson, the teacher determines an aim to be reached by a class over a given amount of time, whether this be a forty-minute period or a longer unit of time. The aim represents the starting point in planning because, in determining it, the teacher is stimulated to ask the question, "Why am I teaching this lesson?" The goal of the lesson is suggested by the reasons found in answering this question. Every worthwhile social studies lesson should show evidence of having been planned (1) to produce student growth with regard to some helpful skill(s), (2) to inculcate some beneficial habit(s), and (3) to highlight some desirable attitude(s) by making use of pertinent subject content as a vehicle for development. The instructor's reasons for teaching a particular lesson should revolve around this axis (see Figure 2-1).

When the teacher has included certain skills, habits, attitudes, and subject matter in a plan, the next step is to provide for their successful attainment in executing the plan. The key to success here rests with the problem to be delineated and delimited, which is stated as an overall question to be answered.

Since every lesson taught should be relevant to the present lives of the youngsters, it is incumbent upon the teacher to plan accordingly by choosing a pertinent problem and by following this selection with supportive subject matter. Every teacher is assumed to know his or her pupils on an individual basis;

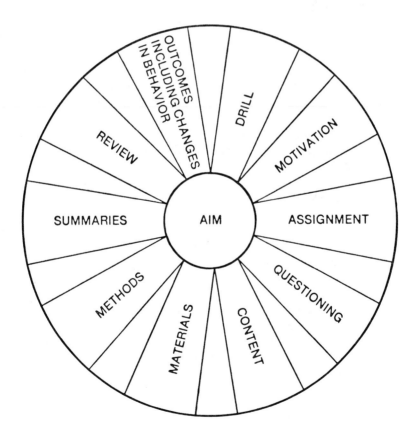

**FIGURE 2-1.** *The importance of the aim in lesson planning*

this knowledge should be helpful in linking the factual material to be worked on in the lesson with the needs of the youngsters in the class.

Once the problem aim has been selected, the teacher must choose the data that will assist the class in identifying and attaining this aim. This is a difficult task; it involves sifting through available knowledge in order to amass a judicious and appropriate body of subject matter with which to illumine the aim. If the unit plan has been diligently prepared, the work at this stage is minimized. The teacher should be aware that the content selected should emphasize pupil independence and creativity, rather than a rigid learning sequence. Precautions should be taken to exclude content unrelated to the attainment of the aim.

The next step in the planning procedure involves the choice of materials that will provide the data, facilitate pupil comprehension, involve many students actively, and help to attain the aim by the end of the time block set aside for teaching that particular social studies lesson.

## DIVERSITY OF APPROACHES

The planning procedure described thus far is appropriate for a variety of types of lessons: lectures, group work, panel discussions. They should all have major and subordinate aims, a body of information, and materials. However, as we consider the activities to be pursued by the young people, we are struck by the diversity of possibilities. Consequently, our attention will be limited in this chapter to one of the most basic approaches to instruction: the developmental lesson. Other chapters in the text will be devoted to the treatment of methods such as simulation, independent study, and valuing.

Briefly stated, the *developmental* lesson seeks to deal with one concept in a limited time frame by raising a problem (motivation), exploring possible answers to the problem (development), and finally, restating and applying the concept (summary and application) to new situations. In order to raise a problem — which may be done by presenting contradictory data or challenging value sets — developmental lessons employ the techniques of inquiry learning. In inquiry learning, the emphasis is on problem solving through reflective thinking. Students are expected to proceed through these stages: (1) identifying a problem, (2) hypothesizing a solution, (3) testing the hypothesis, (4) drawing conclusions, and (5) applying conclusions to new situations.

During inquiry learning, students often reach different conclusions than those anticipated by the teacher. This is encouraged. The purpose of this mode of teaching is not to coerce students into reaching particular generalizations. The tentative conclusions that are listed in the teacher's plan are never seen by the students. These generalizations are derived by the teacher as a guide in selecting data and activities. As far as the students are concerned, this type of planning produces a structured environment in which free thought can flourish. Without the direction provided by the tentative generalization in the teacher's plan, the lesson might well flounder.

The process of scientific inquiry is the underlying aim of inquiry learning. The type of data selected largely determines the particular skills to be exercised during a lesson—for example, reading paragraphs for the main idea; interpreting charts, graphs, and maps; or determining what songs and fables reveal about a culture. The attitudes that inquiry learning develops include curiosity, healthy skepticism, respect for evidence, tolerance of uncertainty, and willingness to consider different points of view. Each lesson will help to build one, several, or all of these and other attitudes.

## PLANNING THE DEVELOPMENTAL LESSON

In constructing a developmental lesson, the teacher assembles the problem(s), the aim (tentative generalizations), the data, and, finally, the activities appropriate to the data. Recently, a few textbooks have been published with excellently organized units and lessons that save the teacher much work in planning. In addition, many individual units of top quality have been produced. If the teacher can acquire class sets of these, so much the better. But if this is not possible, these books can at least be scrutinized to see how the materials and activities are organized.

In the first lesson in the unit on social deviance (Exhibit 2–1), students are presented with data that suggest that the Hell's Angels and Mahatma Gandhi were in some ways similar and in some ways different in their reactions to prevailing norms. The students are really being asked to identify the problem, "What is appropriate behavior in society?" and to develop some rules to deal with the problem. It should be noted, however, that the students might identify a problem different from that anticipated by the teacher or might state it somewhat differently than the teacher did.

Often, as in the case cited, the data suggest the problem(s) and provide focus for the ensuing discussion. However, the teacher must be prepared to stimulate, guide, and direct the discussion. The most common activity in which the teacher engages is questioning. An entire chapter in this text is devoted to the art of questioning, but it is important to suggest here some special attributes of developmental questioning.

The purpose of this type of questioning is to induce students to engage in high-level thinking—to analyze, synthesize, and evaluate. In some cases, these cognitive levels may be achieved immediately. Usually, however, students are asked to respond first to several lower-level questions to be sure that they understand and can interpret the data and that they are in agreement on at least the literal meaning of the data. The reader is encouraged to examine the accompanying exhibit to see how provocative data and careful questioning set the stage for high-level thinking.

Crucial to developmental teaching is the teacher's skill in keeping the lesson in focus, providing new data when appropriate, maintaining an orderly discussion, improvising questions, involving all the students, and performing the many acts that are necessary for successful teaching. Nevertheless, careful planning in providing achievable goals, stimulating data, and well-conceived questions is vital to the production of an environment in which these other skills can thrive.

Although inquiry learning is similar to other learning approaches in that it has aims, methods, and materials, the following statements underline the qualities peculiar to the inquiry mode:

1. Objectives are phrased as hypotheses to be tested rather than as facts to be learned.

2. Materials usually consist of raw data — frequently primary sources — from which students derive conclusions.

3. Activities usually require considerable student-to-student interaction and less teacher direction than do other means of instruction.

Lessons are frequently "won" or "lost" in the first five minutes of presentation. The most crucial factor is the degree of pupil attention aroused as the teacher begins the lesson. If interest is heightened initially on the part of the students, their attention will be captured and they will participate more freely. Therefore, the teacher must take special pains to plan for effective initial motivation. This may take the form of an anecdote pertaining to the aim; a newspaper item linking a current event with the aim; two quotations presenting contrasting viewpoints on the problem issue that is the aim; a striking statement with which the class may take issue; an intriguing and amusing cartoon which elicits pupil responses related to the aim; or, used most frequently, incidents related directly to the experience of the students themselves, having a bearing on, and leading up to, a solution to the problem aim. Thus, for example, any lesson relating to the movement of peoples, whether on the American frontier or coming from the Old World to the New World, can be planned to arouse initial pupil interest by getting at the reasons for their own movement and that of their families from previous locations to their present residences.

In this case, once having elicited the reasons for this move, the teacher must be prepared to relate them to the aim, providing for a smooth and natural transition into the body of the lesson. Whichever initial motivational device is used, the teacher must plan to reinforce and to sustain the initial pupil interest by means of periodic employment throughout the lesson of *interest maintainers,* similar to the initial motivation or other types previously mentioned.

With respect to planning for the actual content to be used in a lesson, the question is frequently asked, "Just how much more social studies than a teenager must a teacher know in order to put across an effective lesson?" The answer lies not in the quantity of subject matter, but in the ability of the teacher to select that content most appropriate to the efficient illustration of, or challenge to, a particular concept; that is, to use subject matter as a means to an end, rather than as an end in itself. A teacher with a great storehouse of knowledge in history and the social sciences has a greater chance to tap relevant knowledge with a direct bearing on the aim set for a lesson or a series of

*Exhibit 2-1. Unit: Social Deviance* **21**

lessons. The selection must be tailored directly to the concept to be examined. The concept, included within the aim, represents a commonly believed universal truism, for example, "in the economic sphere man's desires are limitless."

The true measure of efficient planning is the degree of learning on the part of the students. To this end provision must be made for summaries after each new point has been taught. These summaries can be either medial or final, depending upon whether the teacher wishes the youngsters to recast individual concepts in a context different from that originally presented or to tie together in a neat package all new concepts taught within the framework of the lesson. In this regard, reference should be made to Chapter 3, "The Art of Questioning," to see how teachers can plan for different types of effective summary questions to "clinch" the concepts by applying them to the current scene, to help students solve problems vital to their own interests.

A lesson plan should also have an assignment that partly reviews the previous lesson and partly anticipates the new lesson. Included within the assignment should be some factual and some thought-type questions, with options for pupil-initiated projects going beyond the mere answering of questions — for example, drawings, model constructions, mapmaking, and independent research reports. The chief purpose of such assignments is to bridge the gap from one lesson to the next, thereby facilitating the teaching-learning process.

## EXHIBIT 2-1.   Unit: Social Deviance

*Compiled by Peter De Curtis and Daniel Holly*

A. *Generalizations*

   1.   All groups have shared norms that they enforce as a community.

   2.   Deviant behavior occurs in all levels of societies at all times.

   3.   The time and location of behavior determines if it is deviant or not.

   4.   Deviant behavior has and can be beneficial to society.

   5.   Social situations created by the larger, more powerful society can create deviance.

B. *Skills*

   1.   The student should, through this study, become more skilled in analyzing his or her own problems as well as those of friends and acquaintances.

   2.   The student should start to read more widely on the subject.

   3.   The student should be able to analyze his or her conclusions and test them for reliability and authenticity.

   4.   The student should develop ability in reading charts and making correlations for them.

### Lesson 1.   Related generalizations 1, 3, 4

A.   *Data*

1.   Have students read *Hell's Angels 4.*[2]

B.   *Questions*

1.   Describe the behavior of the Hell's Angels and the Breed.
2.   Is their behavior accepted by society? Why?
3.   Are there any similarities in the lifestyle of the Hell's Angels, the Breed, and ours?
4.   Do the Hell's Angels and the Breed have common values, beliefs, and standards? What are they?
5.   It has been said that these two groups created their own society. Would you agree?
6.   Why do you think someone would want to join the Hell's Angels or the Breed?
     a.   Would you?
     b.   Why or why not?

C.   *Further Data*

1.   Have students read *Civil Disobedience* by Mahatma Gandhi.[3]

D.   *Questions*

1.   According to Gandhi, what is civil disobedience? Give examples.
2.   What is the purpose of civil disobedience?
3.   Is civil disobedience a remedy for societal ills?
4.   Is civil disobedience deviant behavior? Can it be good? Can it be bad?
5.   Compare the activities used by Gandhi to those used by the motorcycle gangs. To what extent do you think they were similar; different?
6.   When is deviance good or bad? Give examples.

### HELL'S ANGELS 4, BREED 1*

*There's truthfulness in our life. We're all tied by a bond of friendship.*
*A friend is the most important thing in life. We're wealthy and we*
*don't have a dime. Just friendship.*

That Salvation Army-style sentiment is the unlikely canon of a muscular, bearded band of "hog" riders known as Hell's Angels. A hog, of course, is a motorcycle, and the Angels have long been first among riders of the open road. Born in California in the late 1940s, the black-clad, swastikaed Angels and their roaring

*Reprinted by permission from *Time* (March 22, 1971).

*Exhibit 2-1.   Unit: Social Deviance*   **23**

bikes became the terrors of Highway 101. Guzzling beer and shaking the country-side with obscene laughter, they broke up legitimate motorcycle rallies and often sacked small coastal towns. Perversely, pop music (*Black Denim Trousers and Motorcycle Boots*) and film (*The Wild One*) romanticized such outlaw riders as tragic, misunderstood loners, giving the Angels a place that they scarcely deserve in American folklore.

As the bike culture burgeoned, the Angels' legend became as grimy as their beards, Levi's and leather vests. In 1965 they tore up an Oakland peace rally. Four years later came Altamont. Commissioned to protect Mike Jagger and the Rolling Stones at a rock concert held at the California speedway, the Angels waded into the crowd with pool cues, leaving an 18-year-old black, Meredith Hunter, dead in their wake. (The Angel who killed him was acquitted on the ground of self-defense.) It all bolstered the legend that the Angels were the toughest, meanest cyclists around.

Last week an upstart band of East Coast rivals called the Breed decided to challenge the Angels' pre-eminence. The arena they chose was a Cleveland motor-cycle show. The results, after only 60 sanguinary seconds: four members of the Breed either stabbed to death or dying, including one of two Breed castrated; one Angel, Jeffrey Coffey, 22, of Hartford, Conn., dead. A total of 21 others from both gangs were injured, and 57 were charged with first-degree murder. It was the deadliest rumble in the history of maverick motorcycle gangs.

*Charity Event.* The fight had been brewing for months. The Breed are a band of newcomers, created about two years ago and concentrated mainly along the Eastern Seaboard. They grew quickly by the simple expedient of accepting vir-tually anyone who wanted to ride with them. They are generally younger than the Angels (many of whom claim to be Viet Nam veterans) and are eager to make names for themselves. Recently they began bragging that they were tougher than the Angels. According to one biker, a local Breed member entered a sleazy Cleveland bar three months ago with a spray can and wrote: BREED—H. A. STOMPERS in 2-ft.-high letters behind the bar. At Christmas in the Golden Nugget, another Cleveland hangout, a dozen Breed members took on—and whipped—an equal number of local Angels in a fistfight. The Breed were ready for a full-scale rumble.

They selected as their battleground the Fourth Annual Motorcycle Custom and Trade Show sponsored by the Cleveland Competition Club, an organization that unlike Hell's Angels, the Breed and sundry other outfits, is chartered by the American Motorcycle Association. Staged in a three-story brick hall in the heart of Cleveland's predominantly Polish Southeast side, the annual show is designed to brighten motorcycling's image, and has never witnessed as much trouble as a fistfight. The proceeds were to go to a crippled children's fund.

*No Old Ladies.* On the afternoon of the battle some 150 Breed members assem-bled at a ramshackle barn they had rented as a "repair shop for cycles" in Brunswick, a farming community about 15 miles south of Cleveland. Next door the Rev. Robert C. Hilkert watched with understandable alarm as male members of the gang piled into their jalopies, pickup trucks and a gray hearse. He asked two of the Breed's "old ladies" why they were not going to the show. "Father," one replied, "we don't ask our men questions." Explained a local gang leader: "When you go to a hassle, you don't take your old ladies with you."

Within an hour, the Breed battalion trundled into a parking lot near the building, quietly paid their entrance fees, and checked their walking sticks and canes (no check was made for concealed weapons). Marching two by two, military fashion, they surrounded the 60-by-90-ft. walled auditorium. Among those within their ring were about a dozen Angels watching over the gaudy bikes they had brought to display. As hints of a hassle spread, the floor began to clear. Soon another dozen or so Angels barged into the auditorium. As the band played *Knock on Wood*, a member of the Competition Club heard someone cry: "It's on!"

It was — with dreadful swiftness. Most spectators hardly knew what had happened until they saw blood spilling across the hall floor. One eyewitness, Leslie Morgan, thinks he saw the spark that touched off the battle. "I saw two Hell's Angels come up to a Breed and try to take his colors [jacket and club emblem] off. The Breed started yelling for help. They got his jacket down to his elbows; then one of the Angels pulled a knife from his belt and stabbed the Breed two or three times in the stomach. He fell screaming to the floor."

Dave Corwin, head of the three-man private guard force, later admitted: "We expected trouble, but nothing like that." As soon as he heard the scuffling, Corwin dashed into the auditorium. "The only knife I saw was the one coming at me," he recalled. "I nailed the guy with my nightstick and that was the last I saw of him. Anyone who put up a fight, we'd knock against the wall, throw down the stairs and out the door. That would take the fight out of them." Added off-duty Patrolman Thomas Burton: "I tried to break it up, but I was knocked down once and once I slipped on the blood. It was all over the place."

Most witnesses felt that the Angels had drawn first blood; the tortured ethic of the hassle dictates that the man who goes for his hardware last loses face. Most present also believed that the Angels were not expecting a ruckus, or they would not have been outnumbered 6 to 1. If that is true, the Angels showed much better reactions than the cops, who had been forewarned by a federal narcotics agent. When the Breed rolled up to the hall, an off-duty patrolman immediately notified police headquarters, and two dozen wagons and cars full of police were dispatched. But the police lieutenant in charge was told inside the hall that there was no trouble, so he dispersed his men outside. When the brawl broke out, only five policemen and their private guards were inside the auditorium.

*Like Elephants.*    With ten of their band held in Cleveland without bail on charges of first-degree murder and another lying in state (in full Angel regalia with his cycle by the coffin) in a Lower East Side Manhattan funeral parlor, the Angels might have been expected to lie low for a while. Yet even as dozens of the clan gathered to pay tribute to "Groover" Coffey, some 15 to 30 Angels pushed their way into a nearby leather goods shop and began to rough up the owner. When his 17-year-old girl friend appeared, one Angel reportedly said: "We're here for a funeral, but this looks like a party." Then eight of the group allegedly dragged the girl to a loft above the shop and tortured and raped her repeatedly for six hysterical hours. The Angels were arrested and booked on charges of rape, sodomy, assault, criminal trespass and unlawful imprisonment.

There is likely to be more purposeful violence between the Breed and the Angels. Said one biker: "Angels are like elephants — they never forget." Does the prospect of another round of bloodletting worry the Angels? No, says New York Angel President Sandy Alexander: "Who has fear in the fraternity of the doomed?"

*Exhibit 2-1. Unit: Social Deviance* **25**

## CIVIL DISOBEDIENCE*

*Mahatma Gandhi*

A little reflection will show that Civil Disobedience is a necessary part of nonco-operation. You assist an administration most effectively by obeying its orders and decrees. An evil administration never deserves such allegiance. Allegiance to it means partaking of the evil. A good man will therefore resist an evil system or administration with his whole soul. Disobedience of the laws of an evil State is therefore a duty. Violent disobedience deals with men, who can be replaced. It leaves the evil itself untouched and often accentuates it. Nonviolent, or civil, disobedience is the only and most successful remedy and is obligatory upon him who would dissociate himself from evil.

There is danger in Civil Disobedience, only because it is still just a partially tried remedy and has always to be tried in an atmosphere surcharged with violence. For when tyranny is rampant, much rage is generated among the victims. It remains latent because of their weakness and bursts in all its fury on the lightest pretext. Civil Disobedience is a sovereign method of transmuting this undisciplined, life-destroying, latent energy into disciplined, life-saving energy whose use ensures absolute success. The attendant risk is nothing compared to the result promised. When the world has become familiar with its use and when it has had a series of demonstrations of its success, there will be less risk in Civil Disobedience than there is in aviation.

My error in trying to let Civil Disobedience take the people by storm appears to me to be Himalayan, because of the discovery I have made that he only is able, and attains the right, to offer Civil Disobedience who has known how to offer voluntary and deliberate obedience to the laws of the State in which he is living. It is only after one has voluntarily obeyed such laws a thousand times that an occasion comes to him civilly to disobey certain laws.

Study questions for comprehension

1. Some people think that civil disobedience is just as destructive to society as the use of violence. What is your opinion?
2. Gandhi states that you help "an administration . . . by obeying its orders . . . ." Would you agree? Do you believe that there are situations when to conform to society is wrong? Explain.

## Lesson 2.   Related generalization 2

*A. Data*

1. Distribute *Table on Distribution of Offenders by Offense and by Social Class.*[4]

*Reprinted by permission from Sarma, *The Gandhi Sutras*, Devin-Adair Co. Copyright © 1949 by D. S. Sarma, renewed 1977.

**TABLE 2-1.**  *Distribution of offenders by offense and by social class*

| Offense | Upper (16% of sample) | Middle (55% of sample) | Lower (29% of sample) |
|---|---|---|---|
| | *Violations* | *Violations* | *Violations* |
| Traffic | | | |
|   Driving without a license | 4% | 51% | 44% |
| Theft | | | |
|   Articles less than $2 | 10 | 61 | 29 |
|   Articles $2 to $50 | 5 | 69 | 26 |
|   Articles more than $50 | 8 | 59 | 33 |
|   Auto theft | 2 | 60 | 38 |
|   Forgery | 1 | 90 | 9 |
| Alcohol and narcotics | | | |
|   Buying alcohol | 5 | 37 | 58 |
|   Drinking alcohol | 8 | 59 | 33 |
|   Using narcotics | 0 | 36 | 64 |
| Property violations | | | |
|   Breaking and entering | 8 | 67 | 24 |
|   Destroying property | 8 | 70 | 22 |
|   Arson | 5 | 85 | 10 |
| Offenses against person | | | |
|   Fighting and assault | 2 | 45 | 52 |
|   Armed robbery | 0 | 88 | 12 |

Because of independent rounding of figures, percentages do not always total 100 percent.

*Reprinted by permission from *Social Forces,* Vol. 44, No. 4 (June 1966). "Hidden Delinquency and Social Status" by Lamar T. Empey and Maynard Erickson. Copyright © The University of North Carolina Press.

*Questions*

1. What does 16%, 29%, and 55% of the sample mean?
2. From the chart, which group has the highest rate of violations? How do you know? Why?
3. From the chart, does one's social class influence the type of crime committed? Give an example from each social class. Why?
4. From the chart, is deviance an act or a result of deprivation? Explain.

B.  *Further data*

1. Distribute *Table on Correlation of Theft with Social and Personal Characteristics.*[4]

*Questions*

1. What personal characteristics seem to have a relation to stealing? Why?

*Exhibit 2-1. Unit: Social Deviance* **27**

2. Is stealing associated with any specific socioeconomic group?
3. Have any of your notions concerning the causes of delinquency been altered by this chart?

**TABLE 2-2.** *Correlation of theft with social and personal characteristics*

| Social and personal characteristics | No. theft (N:529) | Some theft (N:304) | High theft (N:79) |
|---|---|---|---|
| 1. Sex: | | | |
| % Male | 37% | 61% | 67% |
| % Female | 63 | 39 | 33 |
| 2. Age: | | | |
| % 14 and over | 13 | 17 | 25 |
| % 13 | 48 | 52 | 50 |
| % 12 and under | 39 | 31 | 25 |
| 3. Grade: | | | |
| % Seventh: | 54 | 50 | 53 |
| % Eighth | 46 | 50 | 47 |
| 4. Birth order: | | | |
| % Youngest | 18 | 16 | 24 |
| % Oldest | 44 | 43 | 28 |
| % Other | 38 | 41 | 48 |
| 5. Family: | | | |
| % Broken | 6 | 5 | 11 |
| % Complete | 94 | 95 | 89 |
| 6. Mother's occupation: | | | |
| % High status | 23 | 25 | 12 |
| % Middle status | 25 | 30 | 34 |
| % Low status | 52 | 45 | 54 |
| 7. Father's education: | | | |
| % College | 28 | 27 | 34 |
| % High school graduate | 31 | 33 | 23 |
| % Less than high school graduate | 41 | 40 | 43 |
| 8. Community: | | | |
| % Suburban | 58 | 33 | 9 |
| % Urban fringe | 54 | 38 | 8 |
| % Small town | 62 | 31 | 7 |

*N* means the number of students in the group.

Percentages total 100 percent for the characteristics numbered 1 to 7, but in Number 8 they do not total 100 percent because the figures are from the localities.

*Source:* Adapted from Robert A. Dentler and Lawrence J. Monroe, "Social Correlates of Early Adolescent Theft," *American Sociological Review,* vol. 26, no. 5, Oct. 1961.

## Lesson 3.    Related generalization 2

A.    *Data*

1.    View the movie *The Invisible Child.*[5] This film is a documentary on the causes, treatment, and prevention of juvenile delinquency. It is also the story of 750,000 troubled boys and girls who pass through juvenile courts each year and the millions more who go unnoticed, unguided, and unseen.

*Questions*

1.    What are some of the causes of juvenile delinquency?
2.    Why do you think a person would participate in this type of behavior?
3.    From the movie, which actions did you regard as deviant? Which as normal? Why?
4.    If a close personal friend engaged in car theft, shoplifting, or drug taking and it were publicly known that he or she did so, would you continue to associate with this person? Why or why not?
5.    If a person you know is engaged in deviant behavior, what kinds of things (such as the nature of the act or the closeness of the friendship) would make you try to dissuade him from continuing?

## Lesson 4.    Related generalizations 3, 5

A.    *Data*

1.    Distribute mimeographed sheet *Deviation from Cultural Norms, Eight Behavior Acts Commonly Regarded as Deviant.*[6]
2.    Have class vote by filling in chart.

*Questions*

1.    Why did you vote as you did on each issue?

**LESSON 4 DATA.**    *Deviation from cultural norms* *

---

**Eight behavior acts commonly regarded as deviant**

1.    Shoplifting frequently.
2.    Smoking in the school restroom.
3.    Regularly cheating on tests or final exams.
4.    Engaging in a boycott of a store that does not hire ethnic minorities.
5.    Dating a person of another race or religion.
6.    Regularly using hallucinogenic drugs, such as LSD or mescaline.
7.    Carrying out a planned attack on another person with some kind of weapon, such as a knife or a gun.
8.    Drag racing on a public street or highway.

---

*From *Research Experiences in Sociology* by W. Laverne Thomas and James H. Norton, copyright © 1972 by Harcourt Brace Jovanovich, Inc. Reprinted by permission of the publisher.

*Exhibit 2-1.   Unit: Social Deviance*   **29**

| Class vote behavior act | Considered deviant | Considered *not* deviant | Would continue to associate | Would *not* continue to associate |
|---|---|---|---|---|
| 1 | | | | |
| 2 | | | | |
| 3 | | | | |
| 4 | | | | |
| 5 | | | | |
| 6 | | | | |
| 7 | | | | |
| 8 | | | | |

2.  What might cause you to change your vote?
3.  If the majority of the class voted that attacking a teacher with a knife was not deviant, would you condone it?

### Lesson 5.   Related generalization 5

*A.   Data*

1.  Read the play *Fortune and Men's Eyes* by John Herbert.[7]

*Questions*

1.  Is homosexuality considered deviant? Why?
2.  Is homosexuality within an institutional framework (i. e., prison) acceptable to the society outside the framework? Why or why not?
3.  Why might prisons encourage homosexuality, while most other institutions, such as schools, do not?

### Lesson 6.   Related generalizations 2, 5

*A.   Data*

1.  Have students read mimeographed sheets on *Karen* and *Eddie.*

*Questions*

1.  What factors contributed to the delinquency of Karen and Eddie?

Identify the following factors in the case studies given.

2.  What was the crucial point, if any, in the lives of Karen and Eddie that led to their getting into trouble?
3.  Did Karen's physical defect have to result in deviant behavior? Explain.
4.  What kinds of solutions could you offer for Karen's and Eddie's problems?

## LESSON 6 DATA.    *Eddie**

Eddie was the seventh child born to his parents. By the time he was four he had learned the law in his family: survival of the fittest. Eddie's father was a truck driver. He was also an alcoholic. Sometimes Eddie's father did not return home on Friday night with his paycheck and the family had to get along on what they had. Eddie's mother was a small, fragile woman who could not control the older sons. Eddie did not always get his share of food and attention.

Finally, Eddie's mother left Eddie's father. The first four children were boys who had grown to love their strapping, wild father and they decided to stay with him. The mother took the three youngest, two boys and a girl, with her.

She met a college professor who wanted to marry her but was not very enthusiastic about accepting responsibility for the children. Nevertheless, they got married and for several years had a relatively stable family life.

Eddie's brother and sister were four years older than he. They entered high school and were out of the stepfather's way. But Eddie wasn't. The stepfather wanted Eddie's mother to take short trips with him but he did not want Eddie along.

When Eddie entered the seventh grade, the stepfather found a weekend babysitting job for him. Eddie often stayed out all night Friday and Saturday nights babysitting for a couple who owned a bar and occasionally did not return until 6:00 or 7:00 in the morning.

Eddie quickly perceived the opportunities for freedom this situation gave him. Even when the couple did come back at 2:00 A.M., Eddie would stay out until 7:00 A.M., telling his parents they came home late again.

One night Eddie went joy riding with some high school students. He had not meant to get into trouble. He had just run into a group of teenagers, who, because he had the appearance of a high school student, took him along.

The police picked them all up and Eddie was turned over to his parents on probation. In front of Eddie, the stepfather told the mother that this was what he had expected, considering the type of father Eddie had.

Out of revenge Eddie began a series of wild antics — joy riding, sniffing glue, shooting out street lights. His stepfather became so angry that he sent Eddie to live with his grandparents.

Eddie and his grandparents did not get along at all. They objected to his clothes, his hair and his language. There was constant bickering. At this time Eddie was also having trouble at school.

Finally one day when Eddie was waiting in his grandmother's car for her to finish shopping, he decided to drive around the block. He was fifteen then and had no license. As he shot out of the parking lot, he collided with another car, injuring a child in the other car.

Eddie was sent to juvenile hall. His grandparents said that they would not take him back.

Eddie is now fifteen years old, sturdily built and good looking. He considers his real father a bum and does not want to live with him. His mother cannot talk the stepfather into taking Eddie back. Eddie says he is sorry for the trouble he had caused and does not know what he would do "if I had a kid like me." He says he would like to amount to something but has had so many bad breaks that he doesn't see how he can do it.

*Exhibit 2-1.  Unit: Social Deviance*  **31**

**LESSON 6 DATA.**   *Karen\**

Karen was born with a pronounced harelip. She became aware that she was different from her peers when she was about four years of age. She remembers her friends mimicking her speech at a birthday party. Her mother became very upset by this and began to keep her away from other children.

However, when the time came for Karen to go to school, her mother could no longer protect her from the cruelty of other children. Karen often came home in tears and began to miss many days of school, since she would throw a tantrum if she were made to go.

To add to Karen's physical problem during her second grade year her parents began to quarrel bitterly. Finally, when she was in the fourth grade, her mother and father got a divorce.

Meanwhile, Karen had a younger sister, Myra, who was growing into a very attractive child. The relatives were drawn to Myra, which left Karen feeling rejected. Even her mother began to favor Myra by buying her frilly dresses and setting her hair in curlers, something she had never done for Karen.

Karen then developed the habit of overeating. She would steal a dollar from her mother's purse and buy candy and other sweets to gorge on. As a result, she became overweight.

Her mother found out that Karen was stealing, but felt guilty about the way she had neglected Karen and thought that this might make up for the mistreatment. As Karen moved into the seventh grade, however, her mother decided that a girl her age should not be allowed to steal and she put a stop to Karen's petty thievery.

Karen panicked, her source of sweets cut off from her. She then began to steal from the places where she used to buy. She even bragged about her stealing around school to get attention. Soon she was associated with a group of thrill-seeking students.

In the middle of her eighth grade year she was caught breaking and entering a bakery with some tenth grade boys. She went to juvenile court, where she was released in the custody of her mother.

Her mother, terribly ashamed, punished Karen severely. She would lock her in her room after dinner every night at 7:30 to keep her off the streets.

Karen tolerated this punishment for three months. One day when her mother was out, Karen and Myra got into a fight. Karen hurt Myra badly, became frightened and ran away from home.

She managed to avoid being caught for two and one half weeks. However, during that time she was introduced to marijuana and other drugs by the young people she stayed with. When she was picked up by juvenile authorities, Karen had some narcotics in her purse.

When the judge heard the case, he decided that Karen might be better off in a juvenile home while things were worked out among Karen, her mother and sister.

Karen is now fourteen years old. She is very overweight and has severe acne on her face and neck. She is not sure that she wants to return home. She has strong fears about hurting her sister again and possibly harming her mother.

### Lesson 7.   Related generalizations 2, 3

A.   *Data*

1.   *Depression: I'll Drink To That.*[8]

*Questions*

1. Is drinking in itself a form of deviant behavior? Can it be?
2. What are the differences, if any, between a bank president with a drinking problem and someone "down on the Bowery" with the same problem?
3. Who drinks in American society?
4. Do you view alcoholics differently from drug addicts? Why?

---

**LESSON 7 DATA.**   *Depression: I'll drink to that\**

---

Jay Santbe considered himself to be nowhere. He was afraid to ask girls out, and he was always feeling depressed. He viewed his job as having no future. Rarely did he even leave his apartment except to buy food or to go to work. He had no friends to speak of, and he had nothing in life to look forward to. Life for Jay was completely introverted. Jay began to drink; alone every evening in front of the television set he would have a few to "feel good." Soon, he began drinking more to dull his inner pain. As he drank more, the ugliness inside him grew larger and larger, and his hatred and inner depression drove him to imbibe more and more.

The life of Jay Santbe was never the same. His depression and anxieties were too much for him to handle. He lost his job, and had to face the social curse of welfare. Jay began to hate himself, his life and the world. One day in June, 1972, Jay Santbe killed himself in a drunken rage by gouging himself with a letter opener 14 times.

Alcohol itself is a rather simple substance but when coupled with the human environment, has a tremendous range of effects. We, as Americans, try to lower our inhibitions and ease our lives by imbibing alcohol to reach the desired effect of being "high." We tend to drink liquor as we live, at a very fast pace, under tense and hostile conditions. But we believe that alcohol is an escape, a way of running away from our tensions, a way of suspending time.

Every person is different. Therefore, any one person's response to liquor is unpredictable. But our culture does not look down upon drinking even though it can hurt. We tend to forget that intoxication is an illness; it is a state where cerebral and motor controls are severely impaired. Yet, we will offer almost anyone a drink to "calm their nerves."

As stated above in the case of Jay Santbe, alcohol is used in our culture to relieve depression. But more commonly, liquor did not end depression; it only enhanced it. Others find that drinking does bring about what they seek — relief from depression — and are fearful of giving up drink because they fear that pain will return.

S. W. Morrison has a wife and four kids. He is a junior vice-president of a small textile company, and owns a modest house in the suburbs. Ever since he was a young child he has repressed strong homosexual drives within himself. He feels that they are wrong, and that all homosexuals are sick and a curse to society. Whenever S. W.

---

*Reprinted by permission from Hughes, *Phoenix* XV, no. 23 (March 26, 1974).

*Exhibit 2-1. Unit: Social Deviance* **33**

**LESSON 7 DATA.** *(Continued)*

becomes intoxicated, and the opportunity frequently presents itself, he has homosexual relations. When he becomes sober, he only denies his sexual relations with other men claiming that he didn't know what he was doing because he was under the influence of alcohol. What alcohol does in this situation is serve a dual function. The liquor obliterates the unfavorable feelings towards homosexual arousal, and yet allows him to indulge in homosexuality.

As we grow up, alcohol is presented to us through the advertising medium as being the magic elixir. We are taken up into the trap of big business by believing that our lives will be made better and more glamorous by imbibing. Posters, billboards and TV, radio and magazine advertisements contain either a man with a voluptuous woman that can be ours by just drinking a certain type of scotch or we are led to believe that a new whiskey will create a grand mystique within us. Every time our parents and relatives come together they have a few 'social drinks' and we constantly see people on television offering each other a drink. What are we as children to think? We cannot wait to grow up and try liquor ourselves so that we can feel the magic of the liquid. American society is surrounded on all sides by the ocean of alcohol, and we are trapped.

Jane Simmons is a young, unmarried woman, who works as the secretary to the manager of a large midtown office. Jane is a nice lady, well liked and respected by her friends for her quiet and passive attitude. She is always calm in a social or work situation and shows no hostility or dislike for her boss. Rarely does Jane drink, but on occasion she will have one or two. In the past year Jane has startled her employer twice; after she became intoxicated at office parties she insulted and defamed him. After both occurrences, she has no recollection of what went on. If it happens again Jane will lose her job; her boss says that her actions are not good for office morale.

People with similar problems are those who, although heavily under the influence of alcohol, do not appear drunk to the casual observer and are fully capable of handling complicated business. These people, upon regaining their sober selves, have absolutely no idea of what took place, where it happened or who was involved. They are burdened with a tremendous amount of repressed feelings, and are overtaken by their inner selves after becoming influenced by drink.

A second related group, are those people who consciously use alcohol to break down psychological barriers. From time to time, these people are asked to perform an undesirable action. The restrictions placed upon them are often more powerful than their will. Though they really try to perform the task, they cannot. Alcohol is used to break down many of these inhibitions, so that the person can go on as if everything were normal. A lawyer can now argue his case before the jury; an actress is now able to overcome stage fright; a young boy can now ask a young lady out for a date, a policeman can now face his job and the assemblyline worker can tolerate the mental anguish for another day.

For one segment of our population, liquor is very much like morphine to a drug addict. These imbibers seek out only one thing: oblivion. These people are continually drinking in order to achieve a happy bliss. Reality is only a terror to these people, and they just could not live without having a bottle by their sides. These people suffer the ills of liquor, they have lapses of memory, they acquire cirrhosis of the liver, esophageal varices, polyneviopathy, loss of family, loss of job, loss of self-respect and often the loss of life itself. But these people do not care; they want to live in their own little social world of oblivion that no one can crack.

**LESSON 7 DATA.**  *(Continued)*

---

We turn to drink in order to better our lives. We want to escape the problems of our highly complex and strongly paced age. But drinking is just an escape into another world. It does not envision the end of our problems, nor does it melt them away; drinking only fosters our life's bleakest moments and causes new ones to grow. Alcohol can only serve to enlarge the depression we live in because we are constantly hurting ourselves. Pouring liquid into our bodies does not change our psychological state, we are still the same and always will be unless we are willing to change in the face of reality; we cannot act by running away. Reality will always catch up to us and cause us continued grief. Alcohol is, of course, an answer to the problem of mental depression, but it is the wrong one.

---

### Evaluation (sample questions)

*A.*  *Data*

1.  Distribute letter and quotes.

Councilman,
New York City Council
City Hall
New York, N.Y. 10007

Dear Sir:

I wish to express my opposition to the *Homosexual Bill* in the New York City Council.

I am against this Bill because it is aimed at trying to legalize homosexual behavior. In addition I am opposed to the practical implications and applications of this proposed legislation. As just one example — in housing — this Bill, if passed by the Council, can expose tenants and homeowners, their families, and children, under force of law, to a form of behavior and lifestyle they have a right to avoid and reject. Other grave objections could also be cited in regard to the Bill.

Please refuse to vote for this legislation if it comes before you in committee or on the floor of the Council.

Very truly yours,

"All persons born or naturalized in the United States, and subject to the jurisdiction thereof, are citizens of the United States and of the State wherein they reside. No State shall make or enforce any law which shall abridge the privileges or immunities of citizens of the United States, nor shall any State deprive any person of life, liberty or property, without due process of law, nor deny to any person within its jurisdiction the equal protection of the laws."

— Fourteenth Amendment, United States Constitution

"We hold these truths to be self-evident, that all men are created equal, that they are endowed by their Creator with certain inalienable rights, that among these are life, liberty and the pursuit of happiness."

—Declaration of Independence

*Questions*

1. As a member of the New York City Council, how would you vote on this issue? Why?

**Culminating activity**

*A.   Data*

1. Have each student maintain a scrapbook consisting of ten articles on deviance, collected from newspapers and magazines. Five of these articles must support the value judgment that deviant behavior can be good and five of the judgment that it can be bad.

2. Each student will write a supporting paragraph on each of the articles to show whether they can differentiate between good and bad deviance.

## ENDNOTES

1. Berelson, Bernard and Gary Steiner, *Human Behavior*, New York: Harcourt, Brace and World, 1964.
2. "Hell's Angels 4, Breed 1." *Time*, March 22, 1971, pp. 18-19.
3. Gandhi, Mahatma. "Civil Disobedience." *Tradition and Dissent*. Edited by Florence Greenberg. Indianapolis, Ind.: Bobbs Merrill, 1971, pp. 228-29.
4. Hughes, Helen M. *Delinquents and Criminals*. Boston, Allyn and Bacon, 1970, pp. 40-41, 105.
5. *The Invisible Child*. Association of Sterling Films, Ridgewood, New Jersey, n.d.
6. Thomas, W. Laverne, and James H. Norton, *Research Experiences in Sociology*. New York: Harcourt Brace Jovanovich, pp. 9-10, 63-65.
7. Herbert, John. *Fortune and Men's Eyes*. New York: Grove Press, 1967.
8. Hughes, Jack. "Depression: I'll Drink To That." *Phoenix*, March 26, 1974, p. 14.

# 3

•••••••••••••••••••••••••••••••••••••••••••••••••••••••••••••••••••••••••••••••

# The Art of Questioning

•••••••••••••••••••••••••••••••••••••••••••••••••••••••••••••••••••••••••••••••

The art of questioning is one of the most fundamental skills the teacher can use to facilitate learning. Skillful questioning can be used to arouse the curiosity of the students, to motivate them to search out knowledge, to challenge their minds, to stimulate their imaginations, and to help clarify the ideas and concepts of a lesson. The nature of the questions asked by the teacher, the sequence in which they are asked, and the way student responses are handled can greatly influence the quality of discussion in the classroom and the effectiveness of a homework assignment or any other type of assignment.

## THE NATURE OF QUESTIONS

The nature of the questions asked depends upon the type of responses desired. The effectiveness of a lesson depends upon how well the teacher strikes a balance between factual and thought-provoking questions. Factual questions help students to recall data, while thought-provoking questions help students to utilize data in the formulation of ideas, analyses, relationships, and interpretations. This is why an effective lesson plan contains some well-thought-out questions. The success or failure of a lesson may depend upon the teacher's questioning skills. A few provocative questions may help to launch a lively discussion on a given topic and, therefore, might be called pivotal questions. When teachers prepare written lesson plans, they design them to revolve around three or four pivotal questions that relate to the objectives of the lesson.

It is often necessary to construct a body of factual material to be used during a given lesson or learning activity. Factual answers result from questions that ask what, when, or who. But these questions are usually dull, and nothing is gained by having students repeat memorized facts. A skilled teacher can avoid overutilization of factual questions by one or more of the following means. He or she may allow students to have the facts in front of them. The teacher can prepare tables, charts and/or diagrams on hand-out sheets or can utilize the chalkboard or an overhead transparency to supply students with this knowledge. Students might also be encouraged to consult their textbooks or notebooks to obtain factual knowledge.

Another technique is to incorporate the necessary facts in the question. For example, "Why do you think Disraeli, a conservative, supported the Act of 1867 giving city workers the right to vote?" The "when, who, and what" are included in the question. This helps to save the time that would ordinarily have been wasted in eliciting such factual material in order to ask the really important question of why. This question is much more interesting than the three factual questions and thus preserves the interest of the students. In addition, the students' interest is focused on the important idea — why Disraeli wanted to give city workers the right to vote — rather than the factual material. The teacher does less talking and provokes students into thinking and exchanging ideas. The "do you think" part of skillful questioning is to allow students the option of never being "wrong" enough to restrict future willingness to answer again. Even should a student's answer be factually inaccurate, since the answer was what the student "thought" was the correct answer, this mistake may be used to probe, with other students, from where the misinformation stemmed.

Another pitfall is the asking of questions that require students to answer with a series of facts. When a student does not answer with a complete series of facts, the teacher might ask, "What else?" The solution is the same as before: include the facts or ideas in the question. Instead of asking for a series of factual items, the teacher may take each item and ask the student to define, clarify, or apply the information. For example, instead of asking what weapons employers used against labor unions, the teacher might ask, "To what extent do you think the blacklist hindered the organization of unions?" or "Why do you think many labor leaders consider a good company town to be unsatisfactory to the worker?"

Factual questions can also be faulted in that they usually call for brief answers. Thus they encourage guessing and shouting in chorus. Some experienced teachers call this mass answering. These questions can usually be answered with yes or no and invite careless guessing.

Thought questions require reflection and sustained answers from students. Questions that require *explanations* such as, "Why do you think the United States entered the Vietnam War?" or "To what extent do you think westward expansion made slavery a burning national issue prior to the Civil War?" are good examples. Another type of thought question would be the *you* question, such as "If you were Secretary of State now, how would you handle the Middle East crisis?" "If, in 1939, you were a citizen of Nazi Germany, would you have supported the policies of Adolf Hitler?" *Paradoxical* questions are also a type of thought question: "The climate of Puerto Rico is believed by many to be much more pleasant than that of New York City. Why, then, do you think many Puerto Ricans migrated to the cities of the North in the 1940s and 1950s?" or "One of the causes of the War of 1812 was the seizure of New England ships by the British. Why, then, do you think New England voted against a declaration of war?" Another version of the thought question requires the student to follow the teacher as the latter *transposes a personality* in history to some other time period. For example, "If Hamilton were secretary of the Treasury today, what do you think would be his attitude towards our unbalanced budget?" The teacher may wish to ask a *moral question*, such as, "In your opinion, was the United States justified in declaring war against Spain in 1898?" and then request a defense of the expressed opinion. Another type of thought question asks the student to *compare and contrast*, such as, "How does the government of Great Britain differ from our government?" You will note that all of the above questions require students to do extended thinking in order to answer them. This will help to enliven the teacher's lessons and con- tribute to extended discussions among students.

*Inductive questions* call for reasoning from the specific to the general. For example, "What conclusions on the quality of life before and after the Industrial Revolution can you draw from the following facts: the Industrial Revolution caused unemployment, the use of child labor, and the growth of slums and yet reduced the cost of necessities, raised living standards, and eliminated back-breaking labor?" *Deductive questions* call for reasoning from the general to the specific. An example of the deductive question might be, "Necessity is the mother of invention. To what extent do you think this quota- tion could apply to the Industrial Revolution?" These are all examples of ques- tions that require thinking on the part of students and are good summary or medial summary-type questions.

## SCOPE OF QUESTIONS

In planning to ask thought questions rather than factual questions, there are some pitfalls to be considered. Teachers must know the ability and readiness of their students. Some teachers discuss material for which their class is not yet ready. The teacher must limit the scope of his or her questions to match both the ability level of the students and their readiness to handle the questions that the teacher plans to use. The teacher should not attempt to ask students questions that require them to deal with too wide a scope of informa- tion. A question that is large in scope may be well suited as a summary ques- tion, but in the earlier part of a lesson, it may cover too wide a scope of information for the students to handle.

## THE MECHANICS OF QUESTIONING (INTERACTIONS)

Questioning is an art that must be developed through experience. But there are some mechanical aspects of questioning technique that can easily be mastered. They may require some thought on the part of the new teacher, but, if used regularly, they will become routine procedure for the more experienced teacher.

1.  Formulate pivotal questions in advance and write them into the lesson plans. Additional questions are usually framed in terms of student responses or in terms of previous questions and discussions. But pivotal questions planned in advance give direction and thrust to a lesson and help to accomplish the lesson objectives.

2.  Ask questions simply and clearly so that every student can hear and understand them. Much of teaching is the art of communication. The teacher must be heard and understood in order to guide the learning experience of the students.

3.  After asking the question, pause to allow it to sink in and to give students time to think before calling on a student for a response.

4.  Hold the interest of the class by calling on a student after asking the question, not before.

5.  Address questions to the entire class. Ask students to respond or explain to the entire class, not to the teacher alone.

6.  Distribute questions widely among volunteers and nonvolunteers. It is generally desirable to start with volunteers and to involve the non-volunteers after the lesson has developed momentum. The non-volunteer should not be made to feel harassed but must understand that a response is expected, if not to that particular question, then perhaps to a subsequent one. When the nonvolunteer fails to respond, the teacher might move on quickly to the next pupil, with a casual reminder to the nonvolunteer that he or she will soon be called upon again. Do not fail to follow through on this promise.

7.  Call on the inattentive pupil and do not repeat the question for him or her. Call on another student or have another student repeat the question for the inattentive student.

8.  Beware of mannerisms and catch-phrases that divert pupils' attention from the question's importance. Saying perfunctorily "Okay," or "Class, what do you think?" or repeatedly tugging at the chin or nervously pacing can divert student attention from the question.

9.  Use positive reinforcement. A measured statement about the student's manner, such as "That was well expressed," encourages the student while at the same time withholds teacher evaluation of the substance of the recitation, which might unnecessarily steer the discussion in a teacher-dominated direction.

## THE MECHANICS OF QUESTIONING (WORDING)

The wording of questions is more than a matter of correct English and careful phrasing. It determines in large part the response the teacher gets from students. If students do not understand the question and what is being asked of them, then they are unable to respond, and the discussion will fall flat.

There are some characteristics of good questioning that can be helpful. The teacher may find it helpful to use these as a standard for some of the questions he or she used in the past.

1. *Clear and definite.* The meaning of a question must be clear. If it is vague or ambiguous there will be no answer at all or some answer wide of the mark set in the teacher's mind when he or she wrote the question. An example of an ambiguous question might be, "How does a freight car differ from selling shoes?" This question might draw puzzled looks or some wild guessing. On the other hand, "Which has relatively higher overhead costs, a railroad or a shoe store?" focuses attention directly on the point. One question at a time is enough for students to handle. Multiple questions confuse students by asking them to think in two directions at once.

2. *Succinct.* Many questions are spoiled by excess verbiage that wastes time and dissipates student interest. Wordy introductions are unnecessary and often confuse students. A question such as, "Why may we say that the House of Lords committed suicide when it voted for the Act of 1911?" is much better than, "What in your opinion do you think is the reason why it has been said that the House of Lords really committed political suicide when the upper house – the Lords – voted for the Parliament Act of 1911 rather than against it?"

3. *Natural language, vivid, challenging.* If the teacher can use ordinary conversation in class, the atmosphere is likely to be free and easy. Social and natural speech is a genuine outgrowth of pupil-teacher rapport. Being natural, however, does not mean speaking the way the students speak. If the speech of the students is alien to the teacher, then, certainly, the teacher should use his or her own speech pattern. Don't be condescending. A colorful phrase or dramatic touch can help get a question across effectively. Example: "Why was Korea called a dagger pointed at the heart of Japan?"

4. *Group-oriented.* When asking a question, remember that each student is part of a group considering the problem set in the question. Students should not receive any indication as to who will be called upon to respond. Asking, "What do you think . . . [pause] Mary?" is preferable to "Mary, what do you think?" In the latter case, only Mary is involved in thinking about the answer. The frequent use of "I"

reflects teacher dominance. "Give me your conclusions," implies that the student is answering the teacher's question as an individual to be graded instead of as a member of a group considering a problem. When the teacher asks questions using the term "we," there is a tacit recognition that teacher and class are united in working towards a common goal. An example might be, "Based on this information, what conclusions can we draw?"

5. *Adapted to ability of students.* The need to use simple words for the language-deficient learner is generally recognized, but many teachers assume that the comprehension of honor students is on a graduate level. The task is to enrich the vocabulary of the bright student without interrupting the logical development of an idea or the flow of a discussion.

6. *Free from mannerisms.* A mannerism is something of which we are unaware until it is called to our attention. A good way for a teacher to discover existing mannerisms is to tape record one of his or her own lessons. Upon playing back the tape, the teacher may discover some annoying mannerisms. From time to time, we acquire these mannerisms and, therefore, it is a good practice to occasionally use the tape recorder.

7. *Effective forms.*

   a. *Analytical questions.* The teacher can test the effectiveness of a question he or she has composed. Does it result in several sustained responses? Does the response provide data and opinion relevant to the objectives or topic?

   Most of the teacher's questions will meet these standards if they take the analytical form: "why," "explain," "explain the fact that," "give us the reasons," "prove," "which," "account for," "tell the meaning," "what is the importance of," "analyze," "tell why you agree or disagree that," "give illustrations," "how do you explain." For example, "Why has the Security Council been called the police arm of the UN?" and "Whatever is, is right. Explain" are analysis questions.

   b. *Evaluative or thought-provoking questions.* Evaluative or thought-provoking questions are akin to analytical questions and often start with such words or expressions as "evaluate the statement that," "clarify the statement that," and "show how." Often a quotation is provided and pupils are asked to explain, e. g. "Explain the statement, 'The pen is mightier than the sword.'" The evaluation or analysis of a statement is a most effective device, for example, "Prime Minister Nehru said, 'If we do not have co-existence, we will have no existence.' What do you think he meant?"

   c. *Contrast or comparison questions.* Contrast or comparison questions take the form of "compare," "contrast," "what is the difference," "what is the similarity." The same idea can be phrased in an analytical form: "The statement has been made that the industrial and scientific revolutions have enabled the common man today to live better than the kings of old. Do you agree? Why?"

d. *Relationship or cause-and-effect questions.* Relationship or cause-and-effect questions ask pupils to show a connection or a relationship: "show how," "account for," "what are the causes or results of." In a sense they are much like contrast or comparison questions but are pitched on a slightly higher level, for example, "To what extent do you think there is a connection between our Middle East policy and oil in Iran and Arabia?"

e. *Personalized questions.* Personalized questions involve the pupil in current, personal, analytical, or evaluative situations, such as, "Which would you rather be, a bolt tightener in an auto factory or a craftsman of the Middle Ages?" or "If you lived in 1789. . . . " A public opinion poll at the beginning and end of the period serves the same purpose; for example, "How many believe that the French Revolution was inevitable? How many do not believe this? Tell why." "Your uncle tells you that because he has no children, he should not have to pay education taxes. What would you say to him?"

f. *Descriptive questions.* Descriptive questions begin with such words and expressions as *tell, discuss, describe, state,* and *illustrate.* They serve to elicit a story or a set of facts and are usually followed by contrast, comparison, and relationship questions.

8. *Problem or anecdotal situations.* Problem or anecdotal situations challenge pupils; for example:

a. A classmate cuts his initials on his desk. He maintains that he may do so in a free country where his father pays taxes. What would you say to him?

b. DuPont salesmen solicited business from Inland Steel, but failed to get the order. Inland Steel salesmen solicited business at General Motors and were turned down with the comment, "You scratch our backs and we'll scratch yours." What does this show about the relationship between DuPont and General Motors? To what in this story would the Federal Trade Commission object? In what way does reciprocity of this type violate the Sherman Act?

c. Relate the famous anecdote told by Konrad Heiden in *Der Fuehrer.* In 1932, *All Quiet on the Western Front* was shown in German theaters. Hitler objected to the film, fearing it would go against the spirit of militarism he was trying to inculcate in the German people. He appealed to the movie houses to stop showing the film; they refused. He asked the government to prevent the showing; it declined. He ordered his Storm Troopers to picket the theaters; the tactic boomeranged. Finally, in desperation, he sent his Storm Troopers into the theaters, armed surreptitiously with boxes of white mice; and, at a signal, the lights were thrown on and the mice released. The patrons fled in panic. Outside stood hundreds of Storm Troopers, arms raised, shouting, "Sieg Heil." After four days of pandemonium, the government banned the film.

*Questions:*    Why did the Nazis want to stop showing the film? How do you account for the fact that the government banned the film rather than the Nazis? How should a democratic government deal with private armies that violate the liberties of others? Why was Hitler called a man who used "gangster methods"? As a citizen in a democracy, how would your method of trying to effect changes differ from that of the Nazis?

## KEY WORDS

A number of key words can be identified in teachers' questions that give students clues to the cognitive level expected in the reply.

1. *Knowledge-Level Questions* (Remembering):

| | | |
|---|---|---|
| define | list | show |
| describe | name | state |
| distinguish | recall | tell |
| identify | recognize | write |

2. *Comprehension-Level Questions* (Understanding):

| | | |
|---|---|---|
| compare | estimate | predict |
| conclude | explain | relate |
| contrast | extend | rephrase |
| demonstrate | illustrate | tell in your own words |
| differentiate | infer | explain the meaning of |
| distinguish | interpret | give an example of |

3. *Application Questions* (Solving):

| | | |
|---|---|---|
| apply | develop | solve |
| demonstrate | plan | |

4. *Analytical Questions* (Analyzing):

| | | |
|---|---|---|
| analyze | compare | distinguish |
| categorize | contrast | recognize |
| classify | discriminate | |

5. *Synthesis Questions* (Creating):

| | | |
|---|---|---|
| create | formulate | propose |
| develop | make up | |

6. *Evaluation Questions* (Judging):

| | | |
|---|---|---|
| choose | decide | select |
| evaluate | judge | what do you consider |

## PITFALLS IN QUESTIONING

It is relatively easy to avoid pitfalls in questioning. Some common pit-falls are familiar to us all.

1. *Multiple questions.* The most common pitfall in questioning happens when, before a student can start to formulate a reply to the first question, the second is shot out. The student surrenders in confusion. For example, "Give the reasons for the Senate's opposition to the Treaty of Versailles. If you were a senator, would you have voted for the treaty?" "Why did the Industrial Revolution start in England? What conditions made England the home of the Industrial Revolution?" The teacher must formulate a single question carefully. He or she must ask it and add nothing until, and unless, poor responses or failure to reply require reformulation in simpler terms.

2. *One-word fact answers or yes-no answers.* Questions using "Who?" "Where?" "When?" "What?" fail to elicit a meaningful, sustained response and often result in chorus answers. Avoid asking, in a discussion of the evolution of political democracy in England, "What advance occurred next? Who was responsible for it? What did it provide?" Instead, provide the facts and ask for explanation: "To what extent do you think World War I led to the granting of suffrage to women in England?" The former questions result in a series of one-word answers that are time-consuming, encourage guessing, and prevent discussion. The latter question promotes discussion and stimulates thought.

3. *Whiplash questions.* Questions that start with the declarative and end with the interrogative are whiplash questions; for example, "Napoleon's armies were defeated and Napoleon was exiled where?" or "Manifest Destiny was the term used to describe what?" In the declarative phase of the question, pupils are preparing to receive information when suddenly they are whipped with a question for which they are generally unprepared. Start questions with the interrogative.

4. *Fill-in questions.* Fill-in questions omit a word that a pupil must fill in; for example, "The New Deal occurred during the presidency of _____." This type of question has the same faults as the whiplash question.

5. *Leading questions.* An example of a leading question is, "Don't you *really* think there was nothing else for the United States to do?" Such

questions control and dominate thinking and frequently shut off discussion designed to explore a question more fully. Questions should be worded as objectively as possible in order to encourage independent conclusions. At times the slanting takes an unwitting form, particularly where opinion is nearly unanimous. "Why was Napoleon a great man?" "Why is the International Court of Justice a failure?" These take for granted "greatness" and "failure." Greatness and failure are matters of opinion based on values. More objective formulations that lead to genuine discussion are: "Was Napoleon great?" "Should we write down the International Court of Justice as a failure?" Few historical issues are so clear as to not be open for reevaluation.

6. *Vague or ambiguous questions.* "What happened in 1973?" "What about dollar diplomacy and the Monroe Doctrine?" Instead of a vague or ambiguous question a teacher should ask, "Explain how the application of the Roosevelt Corollary helped American business interests in Latin America." One teacher started a lesson in a class with this question: "What were the guiding principles of our foreign policy in the Caribbean?" He should have asked instead, "How did our interests in the Panama Canal affect our policy in the Caribbean area?"

7. *Guessing questions.* Guessing questions can also be ambiguous and vague. Inexperienced teachers, who seem to feel it necessary to elicit every detail of information, often resort to this question form. It is far more important to have pupils explain the material and understand the relationship than to elicit detail. Thus, if the class misses a point, it is wiser to give it to the students than to tug. Avoid "And by what other means has the common man attempted to build a better life?" Ask instead, "Explain the statement that the free public school was an important agency for helping the common man improve his lot." For a more sophisticated group, ask, "Explain the statement that free schools promote economic and social democracy."

8. *Overlaid or verbose questions.* Pupils tend to get lost in questions that are not clear and simple. "In the light of the development of colonialism throughout the world and the colonial experience on the American continent, how did the Northwest Ordinance prevent colonialism and imperialism and safeguard equality on our continent?"

9. *Tugging questions.* "Think. What else?" and similar exhortations tug at a pupil's patience and do not stimulate thought.

10. *Crossexamination.* In the course of a developmental lesson, it may be necessary to assist a pupil who is trying to make a contribution. The pupil so assisted is grateful for the help and still can enjoy a feel-

ing of success. However, help in this fashion must be distinguished from crossexamination, which embarrasses the pupil and tends to neglect the rest of the class. Several questions directed specifically to a single pupil rather than to the class would fall into this pitfall category.

11. *Questions answered by the teacher.* A question that the teacher answers deprives pupils of the opportunity to participate.

12. *Repetition.* Teachers should avoid the pitfall of repetition. Pupils tend not to listen the second time.

13. *Rapid rephrasing.* Rephrasing a question has the same confusing effect upon pupils as the multiple question, if the rephrased question follows the initial question in rapid succession. Only rephrase a question after students have had ample opportunity to reflect on the original question.

14. *Asking many questions.* When a teacher must ask many questions in order to have pupils give a desired response, it is indicative that none of these questions is pivotal. A pivotal question tends to elicit several responses, and, accordingly, few pivotal questions are needed in a discussion.

## QUESTIONS FOR INQUIRY AND DISCOVERY

### Statement of Philosophy

Learning how to learn is the essence of the inquiry process. As knowledge increases in a geometric progression, social studies teachers become increasingly aware that we cannot "cover all the material." Indeed, we cannot cover all the data that the social sciences encompass. Hence, we have turned to *process* as our salvation. We *can* teach a process of testing hypotheses and transferring useful principles to alternative situations. Building one's own structure by examining alternatives is what Bruner defines as *discovery*.[1] As questions for inquiry and discovery must be developed within this framework, we must strive to *select, organize,* and *present* subject matter with the greatest transfer value.

### Facts, Concepts, and Generalizations

Think of any current issue or theme and write a fact, concept, or generalization concerning the issue. Ask yourself the following questions: why should my students learn that fact? What will they be able to do with that bit of information? The *fact* should be the focal point in understanding some larger idea and not merely memorized for its own sake. Courses of study (subject matter) should be organized into conceptual themes providing generalizations that are both substantive and universal.

The "larger idea" or *generalization* should be a broad, inclusive statement in complete-sentence form that serves as a principle or rule for social studies. It should be characterized by:

1. Derivation from social studies content but *not* content itself.

2. Universal application with no major exceptions.

3. No specific reference to a particular case, person, place, or time.

4. Inclusion of those principles that constitute the underlying structure of each social studies discipline.

5. Derivation from inductive (experimental) reasoning, if possible.

6. Abstractions that can be broken down into gradations of complexity, so that they can be understood by students at different grade levels.

### Questions, Hypotheses, and Transfer

Questions concerned with inquiry-discovery learning should (1) contain at least two concepts, (2) call for alternatives, and (3) involve decision making on the part of students. Questioning within this framework should encourage students to *identify* issues, *state* hypotheses, and then *clarify, probe,* and *resolve* conflicting ideas and positions. Asking questions within this framework should enable the teacher to group students to represent varied alternatives or points of view. For example, consider this question: "*Rich* nation or *poor* nation, which *suffers* more in an *energy* crisis?" Groups might include those nations rich in GNP, such as the United States; those nations rich in resources, such as Saudi Arabia; nations relatively poor in GNP, such as India; and nations relatively poor in resources, such as Ghana. By structuring a consideration of the energy crisis in this way, social studies students must consider (1) what constitutes "rich" and "poor" nations, (2) what constitutes an "energy crisis," and (3) what constitutes "suffering."[2] The emphasis is clearly on how one "measures" these significant concepts and the initial question becomes the key to this discovery process.

Discovery questions must serve to open doors. Consider the question, "What form of violence is most serious today?" Students must determine (1) what is violence, (2) what are some examples of violence, and (3) how one determines degrees of violence.[3] The door is opened to identifying the problem, the underlying assumptions of the problem, alternative solutions, and perhaps new questions and solutions. Consider the following questions. How could they be used in planning lessons, and how could students be grouped most effectively to answer them?

1. Who is most responsible for a corrupt government?
2. Are we more, or less, civilized than our ancestors of 1000 years ago?
3. Federal or local government: which should provide most directly for citizens?
4. To what extent should law and order be a goal of society?
5. Do news media manipulate or merely screen the news?
6. How does technological progress affect the poor?
7. Does improved communication increase or diminish the chance of world war?
8. Creditor or debtor: who suffers more in a period of inflation?
9. "History is a lie." To what extent do our history books refute or support this idea?

**Inquiry Sequence**

The instructor who is committed to inquiry must be particularly conscious of the direction that classroom discussion takes and must be prepared to intervene at propitious points. Consider this simplified sequence of questioning, broken down into four steps:

1. The teacher asks questions that encourage the students to give their opinions, hypotheses, or positions relative to the problem at hand.
2. The students respond to the teacher's open-ended questions by offering their own opinions.

At this point, the students might spontaneously support their positions and challenge fellow students to do likewise. If they do, they have arrived at point 4, which is defined as an inquiry sequence because students are probing their positions. It is, however, unlikely that this will occur with consistency. At this juncture, the teacher may choose to intervene and use his influence to get students to ground or *clarify* their positions—point 3.

3. Teacher requests probing and clarification. The teacher may ask questions that encourage definition of terms or reasons for positions. Teacher questions often include, "Why do you think that . . . ?" "What do you mean by . . . ?" "Is there any evidence that . . . ?" "What are your reasons for . . . ?"
4. Students probe and test out hypotheses and positions.

It is more desirable for students to probe other students' positions than to have the teacher intervene and request probing. When students begin to ask one another for justifications, they have internalized a key aspect of the inquiry process. Teachers should note this as a measure of the success of utilizing the inquiry approach. It should also be noted, however, that if the teacher does not intervene in the absence of student probing, student interaction will fall short of those higher cognitive levels of participation required by inquiry-discovery lessons.

### Inquiry-Discovery Question Checklist

Consider this checklist in evaluating the validity of inquiry-discovery questions:

1. Do the questions lead to problem formulation?
2. Do they aim toward *student* explanation of the problem?
3. Are students called upon to *analyze* their explanations and test their hypotheses?
4. Are the questions open-ended?

In the next few decades, technical progress is likely to bring about a deeper understanding of many phenomena that are now known but not fully understood. As teachers, then, we should be more inclined to search out the deeper, underlying ideas than to present the technical surface that is so likely to change. As automatic devices are increasingly summoned on behalf of our problem-solving and routine activities, we will increasingly turn our talents towards research and development in the sense of problem identification.

As we enter this new era, it becomes increasingly necessary to provide students with confidence in the belief that they have the skills needed to look critically at their environment and, to a large measure, control their own destiny and influence the decisions affecting them. Teachers who develop the art of questioning within the inquiry-discovery framework may go a long way towards providing students with this confidence.

### THE SOCIAL SITUATION

The problem is twofold: to get every student in the class to take part in the class discussion and to give each student a challenge that he or she is able to meet.

If we leave classwork to volunteers, the aggressive student will take over the discussion, and the retiring one will get lost in the background. If volunteering is taboo, the atmosphere is artificial and strained. The skilled teacher calls on both volunteers and nonvolunteers, as recommended earlier in this chapter. The teacher does not allow any one student or a handful of them to dominate the lesson. When a normally shy boy raises his hand unexpectedly, the teacher is quick to call on him to give encouragement. The teacher directs the easier questions to the slower students. When difficult thinking is involved, the teacher lets the brighter ones take the lead and then checks with the slower ones as to their understanding. In this way, everyone takes part.

The problem of participation is a crucial one in socialized procedures. A class can learn to give the student who seldom speaks a chance, but that still leaves the issue of the student who will never say anything unless prodded. Some teachers follow a procedure of occasionally calling on a student who has not taken part in the discussion. Others rely on private talks out of class to find the reasons for the situation in an attempt to remedy it.

Some teachers confuse socialized discussions, being discussed here, with the recently popularized *rap sessions*, which may be useful for guidance and therapeutic purposes. The social studies teacher views the socialized discussion as a vehicle for developing learning concepts. Learning takes place as students share and build on each other's ideas in a discussion that has direction and leadership.

To achieve these ends, several recommendations will prove helpful:

1. The questions should be logically subordinate to a lesson objective and arranged sequentially so that the discussion follows an orderly pattern. Stated conversely, the theme is developed through a series of sequentially arranged questions. (The sequence of the questions should be compatible with the chosen teaching-learning strategy.)

2. Allow several pupils to answer each question. When fact questions are asked, the answer can be stated briefly and the discussion terminated. Thought-provoking questions, however, tend to yield many responses.

3. Interaction can be cultivated by encouraging pupils to face one another, speak audibly, and evaluate and challenge one another's responses. To help promote interaction and socialization, the teacher might ask: "Who can add to . . . ?" "Who can improve upon . . . ?" "Do you agree or disagree with . . . ?" "Who can explain why so-and-so said . . . ?" Since modern mass media often result in uniformity of opinion, the teacher should urge the probing of original or hypothetical ideas and situations to stimulate classroom interaction.

4. Pupil questions should be turned back to the class where the questions are germane to the discussion and where they are on the pupil level.

5. Interaction and socialization are more easily achieved when instruction includes a variety of teaching strategies. (Unpredictability heightens pupil response.)

Recently, research findings indicate that teachers tend to afford fewer response opportunities to those pupils arbitrarily designated as low-ranking students. The "lows" were less frequently encouraged to participate in class discussion or to interact with the teacher. If such research proves accurate, teachers must make determined efforts to identify and modify those attitudes that might contribute to the fulfillment of these negative expectations.

You can measure whether you are creating a socializing experience by the nature of the exchange of views, the nature of the arrow of recitation (T-P-P-P-P rather than T-P-T-P-T), the number of pupils who respond to a single question, and the interest and excitement engendered. Videotaped self-evaluation can be most useful to the teacher seeking to improve classroom socialization.

## HANDLING OF STUDENT RESPONSES

It is not enough to ask a good question. The teacher must know how to handle the response, whether it be thoughtful or half-baked, pertinent or irrelevant, conventional or unexpected.

Consider the problems presented by these difficult types of responses and some suggestions for meeting them.

### Obtaining Effective Responses

Whereas factual questions merely beg a right or wrong answer, thought questions require further inquiry. No matter how excellent the answer, the teacher must be sure that the student knows what he or she is talking about and that the rest of the class understands it. The only way to find out is to question further.

Students, especially those who are more articulate, sometimes arrive at the right combination of words without grasping fully their implications. Skillful crossquestioning tends to probe and clarify ideas for the class. For example, "What did you mean by calling Ghana a 'backward country'?" or "Why did you mention her lack of resources?"

Teachers should not ask for repetition of answers to thought questions, except to insure audibility. To insure mastery, a teacher should ask for the same idea from a different viewpoint. For example, a student has given an analysis of the power of committees in Congress. The teacher might ask the class, "Do you agree or disagree that the committee system makes Congress just a rubber stamp? Why?"

Finally, avoid the pitfall of repeating answers. Generally, a question that elicits a sustained answer offers less temptation to repeat, but even this area of response requires that the teacher be alert.

## Inaccuracies

Accuracy builds respect for truth. Carelessness in the use of facts should be checked on the spot. The method and strength of correction, however, should be consistent with the importance of the particular fact to the matter at hand. Error in the use of facts which are only incidental to the matter at hand should be corrected as unobtrusively as possible without disturbing the flow of thought. Usually, a quiet parenthetical correction will suffice. For example, if in the course of an answer, the statement is made that Congress authorized an immediate *ten* billion dollars in Lend-Lease, it is sufficient to interject parenthetically "seven billion." It is another story, however, if the statement is made that Franklin Roosevelt gave Lend-Lease without consulting Congress. This error in fact could result in a distortion of history with respect to the part played by Roosevelt in World War II and his role in a democratic government. Errors such as this one, which may lead to distortion of main themes, should be corrected. Other students may be asked to correct the error, or the entire class can check the statement against facts or ideas given in texts or printed notes. A question that will elicit the significance of the fact or idea will help to emphasize the importance of accuracy and to justify time spent in corrections.

In many instances, omission of facts may distort main ideas. In this case, the teacher should crossquestion students in order to elicit the importance of the omission. An effective alternative is to assign a student or a group of students to research omissions and to report back to the class their significance to classroom themes.

In each instance, the teacher must judge whether the error warrants a casual correction or an extended treatment, depending upon its importance to the theme at hand and the amount of time at his or her disposal. It should be noted that, in making corrections, going from one student to another in search of the correct statement of fact is stifling, of little educational value, and slows down the pace of a lesson. Instead, the teacher may make the correction or have the class consult textbooks or notes. In cases where the fact in question is pivotal to the theme of the lesson, a critical-thinking question should accompany or elicit the correction, since the analysis of the fact in question is far more important than the fact itself.

## Inadequate Answers and Muddled Thinking

An effective teacher must meet the challenge of a student whose thinking is confused. If a student does not understand the point of a question, the teacher might (1) personalize the situation ("Suppose you were . . . "), or (2) put the situation in the negative ("Suppose the United States had *not* intervened . . . "). These variations may open the student's eyes. If an answer is confused, the source of the trouble must be identified first. In a case of muddled thinking, the step-by-step Socratic method is the usual treatment.

### Unexpected Responses Relevant to the Topic

An effective teacher should not insist upon a particular phraseology or pattern of thinking unless accuracy or precision of thought is involved. All responses pertinent to the discussion, however unforeseen, should be accepted. If necessary, the teacher may rearrange the sequence of questioning. Very often unexpected but relevant responses lead to higher interest and greater classroom interaction.

### Digressions

Regardless of interest or absolute value, digressions are ill-advised. In some instances, it is worthwhile to have students explain why a particular issue is not relevant to the topic at hand both as an exercise in logic and as a method of clarifying the focus of the lesson. It should be noted, however, that discussions of current event problems may, from time to time, be deemed significant enough to substitute for preplanned lessons. This determination should be made by the instructor on the basis of the educational needs of the students.

### Checklist for Self-evaluation

The following checklist may be useful to teachers in appraising and improving their questioning technique.

1. Do I ask a few broad, pivotal, thought-provoking questions rather than many inconsequential ones?
   a. Is there an openness in the questions that *guides* the students without *controlling* their thinking and leading them to a set answer?
2. On what level are my questions?
   a. Are my questions within the comprehension of and adapted to the individual abilities of my students?
   b. Are my questions personalized and do they draw on the life experiences of my students?
   c. Are my questions relevant to contemporary issues?
   d. Are my questions consistent with my teaching strategy?
3. How do I ask my questions?
   a. Do I ask the entire class before I invite one student to answer?
   b. Do I distribute my questions among the entire class and do I ask them of volunteers and nonvolunteers?
   c. Do I avoid repeating questions or answers?
   d. Are my questions succinct, simple, and clear?

*Exhibit 3-1. Western Studies* **55**

    e. Do I vary the phrasing of my questions?

    f. Do I avoid "whiplash" and leading questions?

    g. Do I avoid chorus and tugging questions?

4. How do I treat answers?

    a. Do I follow up incorrect answers and take advantage of them?

    b. Do I refer pupils' questions or answers to other pupils to promote socialization?

    c. Do I encourage pupils?

    d. Do I use correct answers as steppingstones to the next question?

5. What are the outcomes of my questions?

    a. Do my questions stimulate thought and reasoning?

    b. Do my questions elicit concepts and generalizations as well as facts?

    c. Do my questions stimulate creative thinking?

    d. Are they interesting enough to sustain attention?

    e. Do they arouse crossdiscussion?

    f. Do they stimulate further questions?

    g. Do they help achieve the aim(s) of the lesson?

........................................................................................................

# EXHIBIT 3-1. Western Studies*

........................................................................................................

1. "Just as no event stands alone in history, so no nation and no man stands alone." Explain.

2. To what extent can we say about the United States what Pericles said about Athens in *The Funeral Oration?*

3. If it were possible for modern America and ancient Athens to exchange lessons in democracy, what could each learn from the other?

4. Would you, a boy or girl of the 1980s, be dissatisfied with the type of education of ancient Sparta?

5. If you have ever had a Pyrrhic victory, tell about it.

6. The Renaissance has been called a revolution. Using two examples to support your opinion, do you agree with this statement?

7. Which would you rather have been, a serf during the Middle Ages or a slave before the Civil War? Why? (A lord during the Middle Ages or yourself today? Why?)

*These questions are offered as examples of pivotal questions which might be used by the classroom teacher. They are organized according to curriculum topics.

8. "He who holds the purse strings rules the household." To what extent do you think the development of Parliament supports this statement?

9. When the Nazis conquered France in 1940, one of their first orders was to ban celebration of Bastille Day. Do you think this was a wise move on their part? Explain.

10. Franklin Delano Roosevelt described a reactionary as a sleepwalker walking backward; a conservative as a man with two feet firmly on the ground but not moving; a liberal as a man walking ahead looking where he is going; a radical as a man with two feet in the air. Explain this statement by using two examples from the French Revolution.

11. "Power corrupts; absolute power corrupts absolutely." Explain this statement by citing examples from seventeenth- and eighteenth-century French government (or any government).

12. Napoleon considered himself "a son of the revolution." Do you agree or disagree with Napoleon? Why?

13. The leaders of the Metternich system should have seen the handwriting on the wall in the revolutions of the 1820s and 1830s. What is your opinion of this statement?

14. In voting for a president in 1848, the French people voted for the name, not the man. Explain.

15. "A kind of marriage existed between nationalism and democracy in the nineteenth century." Do you agree or disagree with this statement? Why?

16. There is a saying that the first law of nature is self-defense. How would you apply this statement to the rise of trade unions during the early part of the Industrial Revolution?

17. Perhaps a better name for the Industrial Revolution would be the Industrial Evolution. Give two reasons to explain why you agree or disagree with this statement.

18. Suppose you were a socialist (capitalist) in a debate. What arguments might you give to support your views? As a member of the audience what questions might you ask?

19. Suppose you are a Russian peasant of the nineteenth century. Compare your daily life with the life of an American today.

20. What is your opinion of Hitler's techniques to make people forget their economic grievances?

21. Two of Mussolini's statements explaining the philosophy of fascism are: "The child as soon as he is old enough to learn belongs to the state." "Nothing for the individual, all for Italy." Explain how these statements illustrate the nature of fascism.

*Exhibit 3–2.  American Studies*     **57**

22. Explain whether or not you consider the term "the Cold War" an appropriate one.

## EXHIBIT 3–2.  American Studies

### History

1. "The Crusades was the opening chapter in the story of the discovery of America." Explain this statement.
2. If you were a European of the sixteenth- and seventeenth-century period, would you be willing to leave your home to come to a strange New World? Explain.
3. In which of the early English or Spanish colonies would you have wanted to settle? Why?
4. To what extent do you think geography influenced the lives of the people of the English colonies? Spanish colonies?
5. As a colonist, how do you think natural resources and climate would have affected your home and methods of transportation?
6. You are an indentured servant who has finished your contract. What plans will you make for the future?
7. To what extent was an American Indian woman of the seventeenth century more independent than the colonial white woman? (twentieth-century white woman?)
8. If you were a slave on a plantation in Virginia between the seventeenth and eighteenth centuries, how would you have felt as your family was broken up?
9. You are living in a Spanish colony in Latin America. You have read the Declaration of Independence. What would your reaction be?
10. Were the Articles of Confederation a fulfillment of revolutionary goals?
11. The Articles of Confederation commanded respect neither at home nor abroad. Tell why you agree or disagree with this statement.
12. "Even though the time in which the United States was under the Articles was called the 'Critical Period,' there were many things accomplished." Explain this statement.
13. If you were a farmer (or a merchant) in New England, how would you have voted on the question of the ratification of the Constitution in 1789?

14. The Constitution of the United States has been called "a bundle of compromises." Explain this statement.

15. Political parties do not always respond to the people's demands. Tell why you agree or disagree.

16. Many western congressmen voted for war against England in 1812. Congressmen from the Northeast voted heavily against going to war. How would you account for this?

17. You are the leader of a newly independent nation of Latin America. How would you feel about the issuance of the Monroe Doctrine?

18. Describe two ways in which present-day communes are like (and unlike) utopian communities.

19. Jefferson said it would take 1000 years to settle the Louisiana Territory yet it took only 75 years. How do you account for the rapid settlement of the West?

20. "Manifest Destiny was a form of imperialism." Explain why you agree or disagree with this statement.

21. An historian stated, "geography determined which states would secede from the union." What did he mean?

22. Anne Hutchinson has been called a forerunner of the women's rights movement. Do you agree with this characterization?

23. If you lived in the 1850s, would you have considered John Brown a hero or a murderer? Why?

24. It has been said that you don't have to be female to be a feminist. Would you agree?

25. Some historians believe that the Civil War could have been avoided; others feel it was "irrepressible." With which view do you agree? Why?

26. If you were an American farmer, would you prefer life today or in the early 1800s? Why?

27. "The Civil War was a victory of the political and economic ideas of Hamilton over those of Jefferson." Do you agree with this statement? Why?

28. You are the chief of the Sioux Indians in 1876 at a great meeting of all Indian tribes. Many members of the tribe wish to go to war with the Americans. What would you tell them as their chief? How would you have felt as the wife of the chief?

29. As a cowboy (miner or farmer or wife) living in the West in the 1880s, how would you describe your life?

30. A. Phillip Randolph became less radical in the course of his career. What changes in the lives of black workers may have contributed to this change?

*Exhibit 3-2. American Studies* **59**

31. It has been said that the art and literature of a period of American history give us a picture of life during that period. Give at least two specific examples that will prove or disprove this statement.

32. It has been said that the Supreme Court decision in *Brown* vs. *Board of Education* set a social revolution into motion. Would you agree with this statement?

33. If you were a "muckraker" of the 1980s, what evils would you attack? Why?

34. The Watergate scandal was only important because President Nixon resigned the presidency. Do you agree with the statement? Why?

35. You are an urban planner. What problems must you solve to create cities in which people can live good lives?

36. You are a civil rights leader and you are asked, "How has the civil rights movement changed between 1960 and 1980?" How would you answer this question?

37. Discuss two ways in which the women's movement has helped or hindered the search for equal rights for women.

38. "Inflation is a cruel tax on all Americans." Give two reasons why you agree or disagree with this statement.

39. Why do you think President Kennedy called his program the "New Frontier"?

40. Why do you think the Seneca Falls Declaration of Sentiments paraphrased sections of the Declaration of Independence?

### Foreign policy

1. In view of the aim of the American Revolution, why do you think countries like France and Spain were willing to cooperate with the colonies?

2. What lessons can be learned from our difficulties with Britain and France over the role of neutrals and over trading with nations at war?

3. How might John Adams have used the war fever in the United States to insure reelection in 1800? How do you account for the fact that presidents are usually reelected when the country is at war?

4. Jefferson once said that if the French held on to New Orleans, "we must marry ourselves to the British fleet and nation." What did he mean?

5. Since violations of sea rights were the stated cause of the War of 1812, why do you think the section of our country most dependent on trade most opposed the war?

6. "The undeveloped West was, in a sense, an American colony." To what extent do you think this is an accurate statement?

7. "The Spanish American War of 1898 marked a turning point in American history." Explain.

8. The Maximillian Affair has been called the first major test of the Monroe Doctrine. Explain.

9. Theodore Roosevelt once said, "I took Panama and left Congress to debate about it." What do you think he meant?

10. Wilson's Fourteen Points have been called an expression of American idealism. Explain.

11. According to Wilson's war message, what were the reasons for American entrance into World War I?

12. If you had been alive in 1920, would you have favored or opposed United States entrance into the League of Nations? Why?

13. If you were Secretary of State in 1933, what advice would you have given President Roosevelt on the subject of recognizing the Soviet Union?

14. The United States has been called the arsenal of democracy in the 1940s. Explain.

15. "The United Nations is not a world government." Explain.

16. It has been said that the Gulf of Tonkin episode was a turning point for American policy in Vietnam. Explain.

17. In 1973, President Nixon declared that the United States had achieved "peace with honor" in Vietnam. What is your view of this statement?

18. "The Truman Doctrine was the opposite of the Monroe Doctrine." Give reasons why you agree or disagree.

### Pluralistic society/ethnic studies

1. What do you think is meant by the statement, "Chemically, all men are created equal"?

2. Do you think the film *The Godfather* gave an accurate portrayal of life in an Italian-American family?

3. How did the experience of the Chinese in America modify their cultural institutions?

4. Why do you think labor unions oppose the free immigration of Chinese and Japanese into the United States?

5. The United States presents an example more of a "salad bowl" than a "melting pot." Do you agree or disagree? Why?

*Exhibit 3-2. American Studies* **61**

6. Why do you think blacks like W. E. B. DuBois were hostile to Marcus Garvey?

7. Organizations like Aspira have tried to aid Puerto Ricans to adapt to American life. Explain.

8. The limited amount of arable land in Puerto Rico has affected the island's economic development. Explain.

9. The nationalist group agitating for the independence of Puerto Rico has not attracted a very large following. How might you explain this?

10. Why do you think most Americans believed it was the Indians who were at fault in most of the Indian wars?

11. Some people have said that the Indians were in the way of progress. How did this idea seem to excuse the way the Indians were treated?

12. How do you think movies and television have shown relations between Indians and white settlers?

13. Why would you oppose or favor the ending of the use of the terms Chicano and Anglo to describe Mexican-Americans and non-Indian Americans of the Southwest?

14. To what extent do you think the problems of Mexican-Americans are similar to, or different from, those of Black Americans and Indians?

15. There are some people who demand that the land once lived on by American Indians be returned to them. How do you feel about this demand? Why?

16. If you were a Japanese living in California in 1942, how might you have felt if you had been placed in a concentration camp?

17. To what extent do you think the history of the Jews in Europe helps to explain why middle-class Jews did so much to help new Jewish immigrants?

### Government

1. How would you explain that despite the different circumstances under which they were founded, the thirteen British colonies had developed similar governments by 1750?

2. It has been said that the exposure of the Watergate conspiracy and its results prove that the American constitutional system works. Explain why you agree or disagree with this point of view.

3. How do you think the work of Bernstein and Woodward of the *Washington Post* affected the Watergate scandal?

4. It has been said that the ideas of Jefferson and Hamilton were necessary to the survival of American democracy. What do you think? Give at least two reasons to support your opinion.

5. Jefferson felt that the power of judicial review allows the Supreme Court to act as dictator over the other branches. What arguments would you use to support or reject this view?

6. "The art of statesmanship is to foresee the inevitable and to expedite its occurrence" (Talleyrand). Explain.

7. What do you think the colonists meant by "no taxation without representation"? How does the Constitution try to insure taxation with representation?

8. If you had lived in the days of Hamilton and Jefferson, to which political party would you have belonged? Why?

9. Why do you think nullification was a threat to the American constitutional system?

10. "The basic institutions of American government and the prevailing political philosophies of today were shaped in large measure during the colonial period" (Nettles). Cite two pieces of evidence to support or refute this statement.

11. Explain the statement, "Individual rights are not absolute."

12. It is argued that capital punishment is "cruel" and, therefore, unconstitutional. Do you agree with this argument? Why?

13. Do you feel it is reasonable to assume that anyone who claims the protection of the Fifth Amendment is guilty? Why?

14. "Juvenile offenders should not be tried in separate courts; they should stand trial in regular courts and have all the protection given to adult defendants." Do you agree or disagree with this statement? Why?

15. H. L. Mencken said, "Judges are law students who grade their own papers." What do you think he meant?

## Culture

1. We often hear people speak longingly of "the good old days." Would you have preferred to live in "the good old days" of the colonies (1840s, Reconstruction, Gay Nineties, Roaring Twenties) than to live today? Why?

2. It has been said that the frontiersman and pioneer farmer had an outlook on colonial life quite different from that of the planter and merchant. How might you explain this?

*Exhibit 3–2.  American Studies*   **63**

3. How do you think conditions in the colonies changed the educational ideas the colonists had brought from the Old World?

4. How do you think the closing of the frontier affected American values and institutions?

5. Why do you think Frederick Jackson Turner believed the frontier was a central factor in the development of American life?

6. Why do you think Western life has been so popular as a subject for American songs, stories, television plays, and motion pictures?

7. If you were writing an article on free universal education, how would you describe its role in the development of American life?

8. "Americans get too much of their recreation from 'spectator' amusements." Do you agree or disagree with this view?

9. Compare the effects of *Porter* vs. *Hall* and *Harrison* vs. *Laveen* on the rights of the American Indians.

10. "Spanish should be the primary language of education in the public school for Puerto Rican and other Spanish-speaking students." Do you agree or disagree with this statement?

11. "All Americans should have the right to guaranteed protection against poverty." Do you agree or disagree with this statement?

12. Why do you agree or disagree with this statement: "No country can ever end poverty, for there are always people who work harder and get rich and others who do little work and remain poor."

13. How have the efforts of Cesar Chavez helped or hindered the efforts of Mexican-Americans to improve their lives?

Urbanology

1. How would you make use of maps (charts, graphs) in studying urban areas?

2. What factors would you consider in describing what a city is like?

3. How is the geography of your community different from and similar to that of the communities near you?

4. If you came to New York City in 1850, would you want to live there?

5. Using a map of the United States, explain the reasons why St. Louis, New Orleans, and Minneapolis were founded where they are. What similarities of site are shared by these cities?

6. It has been said that the United States is a nation of cities. Explain.

7. Why do you think cities attract such a variety of people?

8. As a city develops, its problems increase. Explain this statement.

9. "Cities have always served as trade and communications centers for rural and city people alike. But because they are centers of crime, strikes and riots, they often do more harm than good." Do you agree or disagree with this statement? Why?

10. Explain whether or not you agree that being poor in America means more than simply not having money.

11. If Jacob Riis were writing today, which neighborhoods in New York City do you think he might be describing? Why?

12. Why do you think Martin Luther King, Jr. was opposed to rioting in the cities as a means of achieving racial justice?

13. Should the federal government be concerned with urban problems? Explain.

14. "Bad housing is like a disease." Explain this statement.

15. "Addicts are lawbreakers and should be treated as lawbreakers." Do you agree or disagree with this statement? Why?

16. "Eliminate poverty and you will eliminate crime." Do you agree or disagree with the statement?

17. "Museums and concert halls should charge high admission prices to support themselves financially." Do you agree or disagree?

## EXHIBIT 3-3.   Culture Studies

1. The Soviet Union is a prisoner of its geography. Do you agree or disagree with this statement?

2. Russian history provides us with many examples of cultural diffusion. What evidence can be found to support this statement?

3. Historians have used such words as "brilliant" and "magnificent" to describe Moslem civilization from 700 to 1200 A.D. Do you think these words are appropriate descriptions?

4. If the Nile River had dried up, how do you think Egypt's history would have been affected?

5. "The Middle East today is a crossroads of history and culture." Explain this statement.

6. "The Middle East today is the powderkeg of World War III." Tell why you agree or disagree with this statement.

7. Why do you think oil has been called "king" in the Middle East?

8. "A careful study of African history shows that Africa has been isolated from the rest of the world." Give evidence to prove or disprove this statement.

9. "The African people are more diverse than the Europeans." Explain this statement.

10. To what extent do you think African art influenced the postimpressionists?

11. "The Chinese language and writing system have served both to unite and separate the Chinese people." Explain this statement.

12. How do you think the monsoons have affected the lives of the people of India?

13. "Religion in India has served to unite and to drive the people apart." Explain this statement with examples.

14. The North Indian Plain has been called the "breadbasket of India." Explain.

15. Why was Gandhi called Mahatma, "The Great Soul"? Do you think he deserved the name? Why?

16. How has the fact that Japan is made up of many islands affected the lives of the Japanese people?

17. How do these three words describe Japan's response to Western influence: adopt, adapt, adept?

## ENDNOTES

1. Jerome Bruner, *The Relevance of Education* (New York: W. W. Norton, 1971), p. 71.
2. Barbara Olmo, "Designing Inquiry Lessons," *Social Science Record* (Autumn 1974) p. 37.
3. Ibid.

# 4

••••••••••••••••••••••••••••••••••••••••••••••••••••••••••••••••••••••••••••••

# Independent Study

••••••••••••••••••••••••••••••••••••••••••••••••••••••••••••••••••••••••••••••

## WHAT IS INDEPENDENT STUDY?

Let us place ourselves in the middle of an independent study center. What is happening? One student is sitting at a table. The student is referring to a mimeographed packet. It contains specific tasks. A book is opened to a page assignment from one of the tasks. At the other end of the table is another student with the same packet. But this student is viewing a filmstrip. In another part of the room, a group of students are discussing their common experiences based on an out-of-school activity from which they have recently returned. A teacher is negotiating a learning contract with a student who is presenting an outline of a proposal to be undertaken. Another student is filling in completion questions in a workbook, while the student next to him is working his way through a commercially produced programmed-instruction task. We also notice a student browsing through an encyclopedia to survey preliminary material for a research project. All of these students are taking part in this school's independent study program in that they are learning primarily on their own, outside of the traditional classroom setting. This chapter will deal with all of these forms of independent study and how to establish an independent study program that embodies all of these forms.

We engaged the independent study teacher-coordinator in a conversation that revealed some details on the physical setting of the room and on student logistics. We found out that although this room was well equipped with electrified individual learning booths, other schools are operating completely satisfying independent study programs without special equipment. The teacher also pointed out that many of the students were not present in the room but were in the school library, media center, and typing center, as well as in various community institutions.

## WHAT IS THE RATIONALE FOR INDEPENDENT STUDY?

A trend that is gaining momentum in education is to allow students more opportunities for self-realization. J. Lloyd Trump described the school of the future as a place where much more emphasis is on the development of individual student responsibility for learning and growth, and where individual differences among students will be recognized as never before. Students in that visionary school would spend much more time in independent study outside of classrooms.

This chapter seeks to move towards making that school of the future a reality today. As teachers, our main concern is the learning process. Where and when learning takes place is of minor importance as long as it does take place. The classroom is merely one location where a teacher can function and students can learn. This chapter presents basic plans for independent study that serves as an alternative to learning in the classroom and as an enrichment of the standard social studies program and gives specific procedures for establishing a social studies independent studies program based on learning kits. It is hoped that the model presented will be modified and adapted for use in a wide variety of school settings. This chapter also presents alternative plans for independent study.

An independent study program is a viable option for almost any high school. For decades, independent study programs have shown their worth in colleges. The widespread acceptance of informal educational schemes—such as open classrooms on the elementary level, alternative schools, and "schools without walls"—further attest to the validity of the concept of independent study. More directly, experience all over the country has shown that independent study works on the high school level.

Independent study means that the student learns *outside* the formal classroom. The student utilizes the facilities of the school, follows a curriculum, engages in a variety of learning experiences, and has his or her progress monitored and evaluated. The student has individual contact with a teacher-coordinator who assists, instructs, and evaluates the progress of the student.

The independent study program takes into account variations in rates of learning and variations in student strengths and weaknesses. By permitting flexibility in the allocation of student time for completion of the course of study, the independent study program tends to promote the efficient use of time. The faster student need spend only the amount of time necessary to master a course and can then move on to other interests. Those with skill difficulties can extend the course and have greater contact with the coordinator, since different students learn best in different ways. There are many forms of independent study. Students, with teacher guidance, can choose the most appropriate form.

Independent study, when chosen by the student, emphasizes student responsibility. The student is placed in a position where he or she must allocate time and set short-term goals, since progress in some forms of independent study may not be monitored on a daily basis. Success in independent study is made sweeter by the student's knowledge that he or she has ventured into a new realm of personal responsibility and performed well. Further, the student has gone beyond the confines of the formal classroom curriculum and should find the experience individually satisfying.

Independent study has curricular implications which can add variety, interest, and scope to a person's education. Interdisciplinary studies, often difficult to carry out in a classroom setting, can be facilitated in independent study form. Teachers of different departments need not have the same schedule in order to collaborate on an independent study program. Finally, independent study can permit the individual to explore areas not touched upon by the school's established curriculum through the use of the student-initiated minicourse described in this chapter.

## HOW DO WE EVALUATE WHAT IS HAPPENING?

Since the mode of learning is tailored to the individual, so must the form of evaluation. Independent study provides an opportunity to evaluate a student in a comprehensive manner. This does not preclude formal testing. Where a formal learning packet is used, formal testing can be a useful evaluative tool. A written test is designed, based on the objectives of the packet. Other techniques of evaluation are utilized in direct relation to the amount of teacher-student contact and the nature of the activity.

There are examples of less formal techniques of evaluation available to the independent study teacher-coordinator. In one school (see Exhibit 4-2), formal testing is not used. Here, teachers rely exclusively on on-the-spot interviews and examinations of written work and other student creations, e. g., models, exhibits, and displays. The teacher-coordinator should keep written records of all interviews and on-the-spot evaluations. Progress charts can be hung in a conspicuous place as an incentive device for students. When we discuss in this chapter the contract method and out-of-school activity programs of independent study, self-evaluation of one's own goals will appear as a basic element of independent study. In the last analysis, independent study should afford the student an opportunity to weigh his or her own achievements.

## PREPARING THE INDEPENDENT STUDY KIT

Independent study kits can be structured using various formats. (The term kit is interchangeable with the terms *packet* and *LAP* — Learning Activity Packet.) Commercially prepared programs are available, but school- or district-designed kits are more commonly used. A kit designed by teachers has many benefits. Construction of the kit requires no special knowledge of the technique of programmed instruction. The kit is likely to provide variety for the student, it utilizes varied resources, and it can easily be geared to the curricular needs of students.

These are the steps followed in constructing independent study kits:

*Step 1.*   Acquire or create a course of study. A lesson-by-lesson course of study serves as a good basis for an independent study kit. It should include an aim, behavioral objectives, and content for each lesson.

*Step 2.*   Gather all materials in one place, which will be readily available to students doing the learning activities. Include such items as textbooks, periodical reprints, teacher-prepared materials, filmstrips, records, and any other materials customarily used in your school. Then, match each resource with the lessons in which it might be used. Be sure to include specific page numbers, dates of articles, frames of filmstrips, etc., in your notes for future reference. Now you are ready to begin the process of writing.

*Step 3.*   You will be writing a series of lessons for the individual student. Each lesson, or set of learning activities, should contain all of the components of a good lesson and any outside activities that might ordinarily enrich the classroom experience. (See Chapter 2 for more details on this.) Also, each lesson should, where possible, provide more than one learning activity aimed at teaching the same objectives. (Samples are available in the appendix.) Each lesson should be constructed so that the average student will spend about an hour on it. We have found that anything taking more time leads to frustration. For the less academically oriented student, a greater number of lessons of shorter duration are desirable. This provides the satisfaction of completion on a regular basis and thereby encourages progress in the course.

Specific learning activities run the entire gamut of social studies skills and might involve activities such as:

1. Reading from a text and responding in writing to a series of pivotal questions.
2. Constructing "pro" and "con" arguments on a controversial question.
3. Translational skills, such as map, chart, graph, picture interpretation.
4. Short-essay writing.
5. Brief opinion surveys with analysis and interpretation.
6. Viewing and interpreting a filmstrip.
7. Listening and reacting to a recording.

In short, lessons should include any achievable, interesting task that will help the student to reach the objectives of the lesson.

*Step 4.* Once the basic set of lessons has been constructed and put in order, it is useful to survey the whole packet to see where any special instructions or reviews might be necessary. After lesson 5, for example, the teacher might put in a reminder to begin thinking about a project and to see the coordinator for assistance and approval. Sometimes where a cluster of new concepts has been introduced, an optional review lesson might be desirable.

*Step 5.* In the kit, individualization of instruction has to some extent been achieved by offering the students a variety of ways to complete each lesson and by permitting progress at an individual rate. To further individualize the course, require an individual project from each student. The introduction to an independent study kit should contain general reference to such a project. The requirement should be clearly spelled out, and an appendix listing possible projects might be useful. Of course, the objectives, standards, deadlines, and procedures concerning the project should be carefully worked out in conference by the student and the independent study coordinator.

*Step 6.* Standard routines and clear instructions were found to minimize student confusion and to clarify objectives. They also permit the coordinator to use time efficiently in dealing with individual learning problems, as opposed to repeatedly explaining requirements. Construction of a clear introduction, suitable for any kit in the program, is a worthwhile investment of time and effort. The instructions can:

1. Explain the nature of the kit that the student will be using.
2. Advise the student of study habits that will lead to success.
3. Explain general requirements for passing the course.
4. Explain the nature of the evaluative techniques to be used in granting credit.

It is also useful to make available a style book and research manual for student use in preparing written projects.

The above procedure should be a good springboard for development of your own school's independent study kits in social studies. Although the tone of the instructions is prescriptive, they are not meant to comprise a faultless model for the construction of independent study kits. The nature of your kits will be based on curriculum needs, student characteristics and interests, available resources, space, and teacher involvement.

## INDEPENDENT STUDY—FOR WHOM?

What type of student benefits from independent study? Can any student benefit from at least one experience in independent study? These two questions are best answered through an explanation of the variety of ways in which students learn. Not all students learn best in the same environment. While classroom interaction for social studies learning is suitable for a majority of students, every teacher has encountered some students who would do better in an alternate situation. Some very bright students are held back in a heterogeneous class and would find directed reading assignments combined with challenging research an enriching experience. Some slow students find keeping up with the rest of the class a frustrating experience and could pace themselves better with a learning kit. Then, there are the students who find it difficult to remain in a structured situation for a full classroom period and would do better in an informal resource center than in a formal classroom.

The adolescent learner is sometimes characterized as introspective and desirous of doing his or her "own thing." Sometime during his or her learning career, the student ought to be given the opportunity to learn by way of direct confrontation with personal feelings and thoughts. While we think of independent study for the exceptional student, we ought not to ignore the need that exists in all students to display their self-starting and self-sustaining learning ability.

## VARIETIES AND SETTING OF INDEPENDENT STUDY

While a majority of independent study programs are based on some form of directed experience — such as kits or programmed instruction — and take place in a library, resource center, or study hall, others place little or no restriction on the student as to the resources to be utilized or the physical setting in which the learning is to take place. Some independent study programs begin with an inventory of student interests and require the student to expand his or her interests. The student is charged with obtaining his or her own resource material. This is more in the nature of original research.

An independent learning experience can also be in the form of an *action learning* project by which students involve themselves in a community problem. This out-of-school learning activity places students in direct contact with government and private agencies; they learn about social change by becoming part of the process. Other students undertake independent study by volunteering their services in a social agency, such as a preschool center or a nursing home. These students carry out the broadest goals of social studies in the area of human relations. They are usually required to keep a log of their experiences and report back to their teacher, sponsor, or community service "seminar."

## STUDENT-INITIATED PROJECTS

Frequently, a student displays an interest in some aspect of social studies that is not covered in the curriculum. At other times, a student wants to reach a greater depth of understanding of some aspect of the curriculum. The student-initiated project affords the student the opportunity to pursue his or her interest.

The student-initiated project seeks to exploit the momentum of a student's interest by permitting the student to state his or her own educational goals and to develop a method of helping the student to evaluate the achievement of these goals. The student has the satisfaction of knowing that he or she is undertaking a unique activity and is participating in the evaluation of his or her own progress.

This is carried out through the use of a contract system. At one or more meetings with the coordinator, the student develops a contract that includes a statement of objectives for the experience, descriptions of materials and procedures to be used in achieving the objectives, and a clear listing of the evaluative techniques. A sample contract is included in Exhibit 4-2.

In some instances, a student may need assistance in discovering a relationship between personal interests and an appropriate social studies topic. A preliminary interview to help the student apply a self-inventory to this problem is helpful. Prior to this interview, a student may be given a Planning Guide Form. It may be completed with the assistance of the teacher. Some teachers prepare a list of possible topics from which a student can select a topic or can formulate ideas on how to develop his or her own topic.

Using the contract technique, students have produced original material in specific categories. One category is the historical survey—such as "What were the motives of the delegates to the 1787 Constitutional Convention?"—in which students synthesize the findings of professional historians. Another specific category is local history projects—such as a gathering of information from cemeteries, obituaries, maps, and legal documents—by which students act as historians themselves. Still another category is a current community survey—such as an impact study on the need for a railroad connection to their community—where the student plays the part of political scientist, sociologist, economist, or community planner. In each of these categories, the teacher has helped to direct the creative energies of a student to a very personal and worthwhile educational end.

## OUT-OF-SCHOOL LEARNING ACTIVITIES

### Rationale

The four walls of a school need not be the limits of learning in social studies. Social studies are both reflected by and applied to society. The community can serve as a worthwhile adjunct to a school's social studies program when students participate in out-of-school learning activity.

In such a program, a portion of the student's time is spent in an institution of the community assisting in and learning about a specific agency or profession.

Although the activity can provide some career insights to the student, it also has many other implications for social studies. The student views the real world from the perspective of social studies and applies social studies concepts to the experience. For example, a student who was engaged in a beautification campaign in a local park was in contact with the local park department, the labor union for park workers, the mayor, and the city council. The simple project of painting park benches required a change in the labor union's contract and in city ordinances about the utilization of nonunion workers. In the process of negotiations, the student acquired the knowledge and skills inherent in creating change and thereby developed a sense of efficacy.

### Planning

The traditional role of lesson planning is converted to organizational work when a teacher undertakes to coordinate out-of-school learning activity. The coordinator assumes the role of salesperson of the concept of external learning in order to compile a list of cooperating community individuals and agencies who would be willing to work with young people. Planning how to approach nonpedagogic people in the community is essential. Those people must be convinced that they have knowledge and skills that may be transmitted to young people. They must be shown that allowing a student to intern or apprentice with them need not take special time away from their normal course of business: simply explaining to students what they are doing and why they are doing it is often sufficient and not excessively time-consuming. It may also be pointed out to people in the community that a well-trained apprentice may actually save them time in the long run, provide a pool of potential future employees, and help in the running of their department (e. g., a political office).

Opportunities to engage in out-of-school activity are advertised in the school. Bulletin boards and school newspapers are utilized. Student applicants are interviewed and are placed by mutual agreement. In some schools, an entire class of "community service" students is formed. After a certain number of days in the "field," students return to the class to share experiences and possibly to listen to an expert. In this way, a student who is working in a day-care center can listen to an expert on child development recruited from a local college, or a student working in a home of senior citizens can hear a social-security specialist describe information on recent legislation that would affect senior citizens and that should be imparted to them.

Both the school and the outside agency should cooperate for the purpose of enhancing the student's development. The student will also be able to consult the teacher-coordinator when problems arise.

### Evaluation

Record keeping in out-of-school activity is as essential as in any other learning process. Students should keep a log of their daily activity and submit it to the teacher periodically. Students should also include a daily verified attendance voucher. However, important as these evidences are, they cannot take the place of direct monitoring by the coordinator. On the most basic level, this monitoring may take the form of periodic phone contact to verify student attendance and progress. Ideally, though, monitoring may consist of on-site visitations by the coordinator. Unlike the situation in the traditional classroom, where students may be observed at work daily, students at a community placement are somewhat on their own. On-site visitations not only provide a first-hand view of what is occurring between the student and the community person but also give both parties a concrete sense of their connection to the school. Problems and concerns may be addressed immediately, and corrective action instituted as necessary.

At the end of their community placements, students may be asked to submit written reports and projects. These plus an interview could be the basis for granting course credit. It is also possible that students could be required to give an oral account of their experiences before a class or meeting of students. However, if academic credit is to be awarded, more stringent requirements are advisable. Students working at community sites may often learn concepts similar to those identified in traditional courses, but they will be learning them by actually becoming immersed in the real world's daily functioning. For example, consider the potential for students in an American government course to learn by working in a politician's office. In practice, they would confront such questions as: How do politicians perform their legislative duties? What are the legal responsibilities of a legislator? How do legislators learn the needs of their constituents? and How do politicians handle their constituents' problems? To confirm that, indeed, the students are learning these things will be more difficult since the teacher will not be observing the students on a day-to-day basis. The teacher will have to set up a series of social studies questions beforehand — in cooperation with the community person — which the students will be required to explore while at the site. This step will insure that the community person will provide an academically equivalent learning situation as well as that the students receive guidance in their field experience. In order to answer the questions for themselves on the basis of their experience, the students will be provided with suggested behavioral activities that will show not only their understanding and knowledge by the production of concrete projects but also will aid the agency to function. Thus, to answer the question of how politicians deal with their constituents' problems, the suggested activities might include listening to, and later, answering, the politicians' incoming calls. At the end of each week, students may note how many calls were dealt with and what type of problems they were. They might note which problems were referred elsewhere and which ones were accepted. They then might be given an actual case to work on, during which time they would describe the nature of the problem and the way they aided in its resolution. This is not a test in the traditional form that schools have administered them, but it is a measurable task that can be used for evaluation purposes.

## Types of Out-of-School Activity

The opportunities for out-of-school activity are manifold. Students interested in field work in the behavioral sciences should be sent into schools, hospitals, senior citizen facilities, and day-care centers. Those mainly interested in the political sciences should be placed in contact with elected representatives and government agencies. Law-minded students should be steered towards judges, law offices, and police headquarters, while history buffs should be exposed to local historical societies and museums. Whichever the direction may be, the student will return to the school an enriched person and, possibly, will be able to enrich the learning of other students with whom ideas will be exchanged.

••••••••••••••••••••••••••••••••••••••••••••••••••••••••••••••••••••••••••••••••••••••••••••••••••••••••

## EXHIBIT 4-1.   Independent Study Kit on Problems of the American Economy

••••••••••••••••••••••••••••••••••••••••••••••••••••••••••••••••••••••••••••••••••••••••••••••••••••••••

This course attempts to deal with the basic problems of the American economy, the issue of government responsibility for stabilizing the economy through various levels of action, the effects of various economic interest groups, and the future of the United States economy.

---

**Reading key**

The following abbreviations refer to books that are to be used several times in this independent study course outline:

A:    Antell, *Economics—Institutions and Analysis*, New York: AMSCO School Publications, Inc., 1976

Am:   Ammer, *Readings and Cases in Economics*, Boston: Ginn and Company, 1966

---

**Lesson 1.   Can our economic system satisfy the needs and wants of our people?**

Objectives

- To define *scarcity, wants, needs,* and *allocation*
- To describe how economic decisions are made in our economy
- To describe the theory of the market economy

Learning activity

Read A, pp. 1-8.

1. Why is the economic problem of scarcity considered to be the major problem of economics?
2. How does our society decide who shall receive the goods and services produced by our economic system?
3. Define the terms *scarcity, wants,* and *allocation of resources.*

**Lesson 2.   Is our society emphasizing the right economic goals?**

Objectives

- To list and evaluate the economic goals of our society
- To describe ways of measuring achievement of economic goals
- To define *production, goods, services, employment,* and *constant dollars*

Learning activity

Read Am, pp. 4-7.

1. Define the following economic goals: *freedom, efficiency, growth, stability,* and *security.*
2. Would you add any other goals? What are they? Why? Why not?
3. Sometimes economic goals conflict with each other. Explain how this might happen in each of these cases:
   a. A large factory in a region plans to automate its operations. As a result, 30 percent of the workers in the factory will be fired. (Hint: efficiency vs. security)
   b. The government places controls on wages and prices.
   c. The federal government, through the Federal Reserve System, takes steps to make money easier and cheaper to borrow. In this way, the government states, buying and business investment will be stimulated.

Now read Am, pp. 15-17.

4. What problem is examined in the article?
5. To what extent are the economic goals adequate to deal with the problem of dwindling resources?
6. How might we change our goals?

• • •

## Lesson 5.   Can economic stability be achieved by controlling the money supply?

**Objectives**

- To explain how banks create money
- To evaluate the role of the Federal Reserve System in controlling money and credit
- To explain how the following influence money and credit supplies: *commercial banking, rediscount rate, reserve requirements, open market operations,* and *stock market margin requirements*
- To evaluate the true effectiveness of the above in view of the continuing inflation
- To define *credit, monetary policy, currency, money*

**Learning activity**

View the filmstrip "Money" in the library.

1. Define each of the following terms and explain its role in controlling the nation's money supply: *commercial banking, rediscount rate, reserve requirements, open market operations,* and *margin requirements.*
2. How does a commercial bank create money?
3. Why is the Federal Reserve system considered to be the major instrument for regulating the nation's supply of money?
4. Can economic stability be achieved through the use of the powers of the Federal Reserve system? Give reasons for your answers.

---

- HAVING ANY DIFFICULTIES?
- DON'T FORGET. TEACHERS ARE AVAILABLE
  ALL DAY IN THE RESOURCE CENTER.
- THEY ARE THERE FOR *YOU.*
- DON'T BE AFRAID TO ASK FOR HELP.

---

Notice that at strategic parts of the course, students are encouraged to clarify any questions or problems they may be encountering as a result of working on their own.

*Exhibit 4–2.   Student Contract for an Individualized Project*     **79**

A few lessons later, observe how students are encouraged to use other means to obtain information.

### Lesson 17.   Can America have both a healthy environment and a healthy economy?

**Objectives**

- To describe the extent of environmental damage done by the process of industrialization
- To evaluate attempts already made to maintain a clean environment
- To analyze losses to business and labor resulting from stricter controls on environmental pollution
- To analyze effects on the economy of the costs of "cleaning up"

**Learning activity**

Go to the library and view the filmstrip "Economy versus Ecology."

1. If you had voted in the Colorado referendum about the Winter Olympics, how would you have voted? Explain.
2. What do Ehrlich and Commoner think of the future of the world? What is your opinion about their ideas? Explain fully.
3. Explain the opposing viewpoints on the SST. Why has this dispute been called a classic case of economy vs. ecology? Should the United States government finance the building of an SST? Why?
4. Why do we need a national policy on energy? List some provisions that you think should be included in that policy.

•••••••••••••••••••••••••••••••••••••••••••••••••••••••••••••••••••••••••••••••••••

## EXHIBIT 4–2.   Student Contract for an Individualized Project

•••••••••••••••••••••••••••••••••••••••••••••••••••••••••••••••••••••••••••••••••••

Name:  _____

Project Advisor:  _____

1. *Title or focus of project:* (Please see that the project is narrowed down or limited in scope to measurable proportions)

_____

_____

2. *Form of project:* (e. g., paper, sculpture, musical composition)

_____

_____

_____

_____

3. *Objectives:* (State in behavioral terms what you expect to learn and what skills you expect to acquire as a result of completing the project)

_____

_____

_____

4. *Materials or books to be used:*

_____

_____

_____

5. *Methodology:* (How are you going to complete the project? What steps do you expect to follow?)

_____

_____

_____

6. *Evaluation techniques:* (What methods shall be used in judging the successful completion of this contract? Will there be an oral defense before a panel made up of the chairman, your mentor, and another member of the department, will there be a written test, or will other techniques be employed?)

_____

_____

_____

*Signature:* _____

*Exhibit 4-3.  Writing Curriculum for Community Placement Sites*     **81**

## EXHIBIT 4-3.  Writing Curriculum for Community Placement Sites[1]

1. The curriculum is mainly concerned with subject area content.

2. Time should be allotted (approximately 20 percent) at the community resource site to do the actual writing or perform the indicated tasks. The better part of the remaining time is to be spent acquiring the skills and knowledge necessary to do the tasks.

3. Reading activities related to the community site must be included in every curriculum package. These readings optimally should be drawn from the community site's own literature (pamphlets about skills used by the people in the field and articles about how the organization functions and how it relates to other organizations) and should provide the students with information that will help them obtain the ability to work effectively in their particular placement site.

4. The curriculum must be created in a collaborative effort with the community site people. The higher the degree of involvement on the site person's part in the creation of the curriculum, the greater likelihood that the site person will adopt its goals as his or her own and thereby provide the students with a meaningful experience.

5. Evaluation of student work and progress must be shared by the coordinator and the site person. Realistic appraisal of the site's capabilities and limitations (time and space available and number of students acceptable) should determine methodology. In certain learning settings, the unique expertise needed to evaluate performance may rest solely with the site person. In many cases, however, the coordinator may be expected to have a greater involvement in the evaluation.

6. Instructions should be specific. If a student is expected to write, say so. If a student is to explain orally, then instructions should be specific with respect to this. The material in the curriculum must be as self-explanatory as possible. This is extremely important since the opportunity for immediate clarification of vague or confusing terms, such as would be available in a traditional classroom, may be limited.

7. A wide range of evaluatory techniques should be used. Photographic essays, tape-recorded interviews, demonstration of skills acquired, and tours of site facilities are but a few of the possible evaluative tools.

8. Optional activities should be provided in the curriculum in two ways:
   a. Student choice among predetermined activities, or
   b. Opportunity to design new activities with the coordinator and the site person's approval.

## ENDNOTE

1. Based upon guidelines created by City-As-School Alternative High School, New York City. This unique high school conducts 95 percent of its courses at external learning sites.

## BIBLIOGRAPHY

Hilgard, Ernest R., ed. *Individualized Instruction,* 1964 Yearbook of the National Society for the Study of Education, Chicago.

Hillson, Maurie and Ronald, Hyman T., eds. *Change and Innovation In Elementary and Secondary Organization,* New York: Holt, Rinehart and Winston, 1971.

Howes, Virgil M. *Individualization of Instruction: A Teaching Strategy,* New York: MacMillan Co., 1970.

Howes, Virgil M. *Individualizing Instruction in Reading and Social Studies: Selected Readings on Programs and Practices,* New York: MacMillan Company, 1970.

# 5

•••••••••••••••••••••••••••••••••••••••••••••••••••••••••••••••••••••••••••••••••

# Dealing with Values

•••••••••••••••••••••••••••••••••••••••••••••••••••••••••••••••••••••••••••••••••

Schools have always dealt with values. Classroom procedures and behavior and democratic ideals and processes are examples of values taught without question through the years. Yet today there is a great deal of controversy and renewed interest concerning values education. The substance of this chapter is to examine the new role of values education in the social studies classroom and to suggest strategies that teachers can utilize to promote values education in their own classrooms.

The first tasks are to understand the meaning of the term value as it is being used here and to discuss the distinction between teaching values and teaching about values. A value is a belief or conviction a person holds, affirms, and defends. Essentially, in this sense, value is synonymous with value judgment. Teaching values implies teaching students specific, predetermined values. For example, teaching students to respect the rights of others in class discussions is teaching the value that everyone has the right to be heard. Teaching students to engage in scientific inquiry is teaching another value.[1] Teaching about values is teaching students what values are, the process by which they are arrived at, and the role they play in the students' personal lives and in society at large.

In addition to democratic values, schools have traditionally taught many social values. Values that have the force of law, for example, have been and continue to be accepted as part of school curricula. For example, humanistic values, the dignity and worth of the individual, are also generally accepted as proper aspects of school programs.[2] The problem in teaching specific values, however, lies in the question of how to distinguish between values to teach and those not to teach. Today many previously accepted values are being questioned and re-examined. To cite one case: taking another person's life is illegal and is considered wrong according to most humanistic sets of values. Euthanasia, however, is now an urgent social concern. Questions of euthanasia are becoming more pressing as medical science redefines the threshold between life and death. The value and definition of human life, in this context, takes on a new meaning, and the outright value judgment "taking life is wrong" has become, for many persons, a matter for re-evaluation and qualification.

While there will always be a core of social values passed on by the schools as well as by other agents of socialization, the size of that core is steadily shrinking. The need for students to be able to make their own value judgments, to arrive rationally at their own values, takes on increasing importance. To allow students to determine their own values in controversial matters, such as euthanasia, and in less controversial but nevertheless important areas, such as employment preferences, is one of the goals of teaching about values.

A great deal has been written in recent years about the stages of moral reasoning, values clarification, and the best method with which to teach students about values. The names of Piaget, Kohlberg, and Simon have become familiar to educators involved with values education. It is not the purpose of this chapter to evaluate extensively the theoretical basis of values education nor to judge the viability or worth of the various theories.[3] Rather, this chapter deals with specific teaching strategies that teachers may use in their classrooms. It is hoped that these suggestions will provide teachers with a practical basis upon which to construct strategies and techniques suitable for their own classrooms.

These strategies are derived from values-oriented courses that have been taught in various high schools, but the procedures they involve can be adapted to earlier grades. They are suitable for students achieving on all ability levels. The strategies draw upon various teaching methods, but emphasis is on the inquiry approach. Learning materials include readings from many sources and multimedia materials, prepared both commercially and by the teachers involved in the courses. The courses include units on controversial topics – such as abortion – and on death, a subject now becoming part of the social studies curriculum in many places.[4]

Values-oriented courses generally differ somewhat from more traditional social studies courses. While values-oriented courses include concepts from history, economics, and political science, they emphasize concepts from the behavioral sciences – anthropology, sociology, and psychology. While they provide students with training in basic social studies skills, such as the interpretation of statistical data and participation in group discussions, they also encourage the skill of values clarification. The latter is accomplished by presenting students with selected moral exercises, some of which will be described in this chapter. One such exercise, called moral dilemmas, allows students to analyze conflicting values and encourages them to formulate value judgments. The resulting value judgments are then tested and further evaluated.[5]

Although the strategies are taken from courses devoted entirely to values, they can be utilized within more traditional social studies courses. A course in American history provides many opportunities to introduce moral reasoning and values clarification; for example, in an evaluation of the treatment of the American Indians. Life for many Indians is fraught with conflicts that may act as springboards to the moral dilemma technique. Examples are life on vs. life off the reservation, where traditions are preserved; passive resistance vs. militancy to achieve social gains; and preservation of Indian identity vs. integration with the general population.

Since so much emphasis is placed on discussion in values education, there should be an open, free atmosphere in the classroom. Students should be encouraged to speak their minds and to feel secure enough to express themselves freely. The teacher should maintain a neutral position, as much as possible, on controversial issues, or take the position of devil's advocate, if necessary, to encourage debate. It is especially important that the teacher not judge students' opinions. The aim of teaching about values is, generally, to help students analyze and clarify their own values, not to inculcate certain values. On an examination, for example, if students are asked to give their opinions on specific matters, it is advisable to grade them on how well they support their opinions, not on the opinions themselves.

Values education may be approached in various ways. A values curriculum may include values strategies, such as those suggested by Sidney Simon, moral dilemmas that incorporate the theories of Lawrence Kohlberg, or contemporary problems facing America today. These problems may include women's rights, drug abuse, abortion, attitudes toward death, problems of the aging, methods of childrearing, treatment of juvenile offenders, and marriage customs. Current news stories may also supply course material. For example, during a period of economic decline, workers in the public and private sectors may be faced with the alternatives of accepting voluntary wage reductions or seeing massive layoffs of colleagues with less seniority.

In a values-oriented course, the issue may be presented as a debate topic — Resolved: All workers should make small sacrifices to prevent some workers from losing their jobs. Four to six students may participate in the formal debate in two teams on either side of the question. They should be given several days in which to research and prepare their arguments. The rest of the class, serving as the audience, is then required to participate actively in the debate. Each student should prepare at least three questions to ask the debaters after the formal presentation. Before the debate, a vote can be taken to ascertain class sentiment on the question. After the formal presentation, another vote can be taken to ascertain what, if any, change has taken place. Following the formal debate period, the question may be thrown open for general discussion. After the debate, a class project can be the keeping of a file on newspaper articles concerning the issue(s) raised in the debate. These articles can be mounted on the class bulletin board. If a student thinks that an article is especially interesting, it can be brought to the attention of the class.

Values issues may arise within the school itself. For example, if the administration of a school makes a controversial decision, a class may take up the issue. In one high school, students debated the practicality of shortening the school day for an extracurricular program that was attended by a small number of students. The class was divided into committees to survey students, faculty members, and parents on the issue of continuing this program. The survey attempted to determine attitudes on the importance of this extracurricular activity vis-à-vis formal classroom instruction. Each committee made a report of its findings, which was considered by the class and then synthesized into a single report presented to the school administration.

## APPLYING STANDARD STRATEGIES
## TO VALUES LEARNING

Many learning strategies can be used in values education, such as developmental and inquiry lessons, multimedia presentations, sociodramas, role-playing, debates, and informal discussions. For example, the abortion issue can be examined by means of a series of inquiry lessons. Students can be provided with readings that include the texts of relevant legislation and the 1973 Supreme Court decision on abortion, newspaper articles on the issue, literature provided by pro- and anti-abortion groups, and letters-to-the-editor written to local newspapers. Guest speakers on both sides of the issue can appear before the class. Students can analyze the materials, raise questions, further investigate specific issues, such as when does life begin, and discuss the various points of view. The unit may include a roundtable discussion involving the entire class on the topic, "Abortion, yes or no?" Each student may prepare a one-minute oral statement expressing his or her opinion on the question, giving reasons for that opinion. After every class member has read his or her statement, the students can question each other and react to the various opinions. A culminating activity for the unit may be for each class member to write a letter to the editor about abortion. The letters may be sent to local newspapers and national news magazines. The aim of values clarification is especially noticeable in such a unit.

A role-playing situation may be used to examine and evaluate the treatment of juvenile offenders in the criminal justice system. A newspaper account of a juvenile crime can provide the basis for a mock hearing. Students assume the roles of judge, defendants, attorneys, arresting officers, social workers, victims, and parents and friends. The hearing is held for a number of class sessions. It should follow as closely as possible the actual procedures of juvenile court. The role-playing experience causes students to think about both the hearing procedures and the treatment of juvenile offenders. Lessons such as these bring out many value conflicts and moral dilemmas. For example, the students playing the roles of the defendants' parents may see their children as victims of their environment, who deserve help and mercy from the court. The students playing the victims of the crime, on the other hand, may see the defendants as dangerous criminals who should be severely punished for their violent actions. As is often the case in values education, the class may be left with many unanswered questions and a heightened awareness of the conflicting social issues involved in the treatment of juvenile offenders.

The role-playing technique can also provide a vehicle for exploring values, for example, the issues of teenage sex, abortion, and teenage marriage. The class can be given a description of the following situation. Two young people, the girl a senior in high school and the boy a freshman in college, have been dating for three years. While they have talked of marriage, they have not made any definite plans. The girl has now become pregnant, and the couple is faced with the problem of what to do about the expected baby: should they marry, should the girl have an abortion, or should she give the baby up for adoption? Students in the class are given the roles of the boy and the girl and their parents. They meet together to try to come to a decision about what the girl should do. The first half of the period may be devoted to the role-playing, which can lead to lively, exciting class discussions.

A sociodrama technique that involves the whole class and can provide a means to examine students' values may be devised in regard to the women's liberation movement, with all its conflicts and challenges to traditional relationships. The class is given a brief outline of a hypothetical situation: Two married women attempt to bring about changes in their lives by introducing to their husbands the tenets of women's liberation, such as the equal sharing of domestic chores and of child rearing responsibilities. Given only this information, the students must dramatize the situation, using their imaginations to supply the details. Some students are chosen to take part in a skit to be presented to the class. Other students are delegated to research the ideas of women's liberation and act as resource persons. The students involved in the dramatization can utilize class time to prepare their presentation. While they write a script and rehearse, the other members of the class can meet in small groups to discuss their attitudes on women's liberation. The dramatization itself may take place in one or more class sessions. The students may bring in props that lend an air of authenticity. A three-part skit could follow this scenario:

> The first part shows a typical breakfast scene, with wives, husbands, and children beginning their day. The women then attend a meeting of a women's group and there become convinced of the need to bring about changes in their relationships with their husbands and children. In the closing scene, the husbands return home and are shocked to find the normal routine altered drastically. For example, the husbands are asked to share in preparing dinner, washing the dishes, and getting the children ready for bed. Although at first the men resist, they gradually come to accept these responsibilities.

As a result of the experience, students of both sexes may gain new insight into the demands and responsibilities of marital roles. Such skits often prove to be both entertaining and enlightening. After the dramatization, informal discussions devoted to the skit and the issues it raised may be held.

### THE MORAL DILEMMA STRATEGY

The moral dilemma is another means by which to teach about values. A dilemma may arise from many different situations. An example of a moral dilemma on drug abuse is the following:

#### Ron's dilemma

Ron Weber is the president of the student organization in a large, urban high school. Ron is very popular with his fellow students and with the school's faculty. He takes his responsibilities as student organization president very seriously, and he has earned a reputation as one of the best officers the student organization has ever had.

Ron has worked very hard to set up a senior class trip to a resort area near the city. The school's principal at first refused to allow the trip because he feared students would bring drugs. Ron convinced him that it would be a worthwhile trip, and Ron promised to do everything he could to make sure there would be no drugs on the trip.

It is now two days before the trip; everything is going very well. The trip has been sold out, and it appears it will be a great success. Then, Ron's two closest friends tell him confidentially that they plan to bring marijuana on the trip.

Ron knows that if the principal discovers students using drugs on the trip, he will prohibit such trips in the future. Ron had hoped the trip would become a school tradition. Ron also remembers his promise to the principal to do all he can to keep students from bringing drugs on the trip.

Ron does not want to violate his friends' confidence and tell the principal of their plans. But he knows that if his friends do bring drugs, they will be hurting themselves and their fellow students as well. He has tried to talk them out of bringing the marijuana, but they refuse to change their plans. Should Ron tell the principal of his friends' plans?

Each student receives a description of Ron's dilemma. After the class has read the description, the teacher asks a series of questions to determine the students' understanding of the issues of the dilemma. With a show of hands, the students indicate how they think Ron should act. The class is then divided into small groups of three or four students, with each student in each group holding the same opinion. The groups are told to formulate the best reasons for their opinion and to write one question they would ask a student who held the opposite opinion. The small group discussions last about ten to twelve minutes. Then the entire class participates in a discussion of how Ron should act. The teacher may pose variations to the dilemma during the discussion, such as "Should Ron tell the principal of his friends' plans if the principal asks him specifically if he knows of any such plans?" or "If the students are caught with the marijuana on the trip, should Ron admit that he knew of their plans?" The students may also bring up variations to the dilemma during their discussion.

The possibilities for analysis are great and could be developed by the students and the teacher.

*How Can a Teacher Write an Original Moral Dilemma?* This is not difficult, as there are certain common elements found in all of them. They are as follows:

Conflict Situation

Central Character

Scenario

Need for Resolution

The idea for the dilemma can frequently be found in an historical situation or a current news item. The *conflict situation* usually arises when social norms are to be defined on the basis of tradition vs. change, or when two basic values, such as property rights and civil rights, are at variance. Personal conscience vs. obedience to authority may be used. A *central character* is needed for focus. The students should be able to identify with the quandary faced by the central character. The *scenario* establishes the setting and the complication — both of which limit the options available to the decision makers — while the *need for resolution* provides the urgency of the situation. Without the need for resolution, the students could seek to postpone the decision-making process.

A moral dilemma may also be part of a series of different types of lessons that may be used to study problems from history, such as the Nuremberg war-crimes trials following World War II. The unit can begin with a series of traditional developmental lessons about the causes and events of World War II. Then, the students can see a film about the Holocaust, such as *Night and Fog,* which depicts conditions in Nazi death camps. Films such as this one can move a class and evoke a wide range of responses from students. In addition to a discussion of the death camps themselves, the film may also provoke a discussion of the use of teaching materials of this type in the classroom.

After seeing and discussing the film, the students can read selections from writings about the war-crimes trials and actual testimony from the trials. The attitudes of the various participants in the trials can be clarified in a series of inquiry lessons. Students would then be able to compare the attitudes of the participants with their own attitudes. They may be especially interested in the conclusions of the trials concerning a person's moral responsibilities and obligations. They can then read a description of the My Lai incident during the Vietnam conflict and compare and contrast the issues in Lieutenant Calley's trial with those in the Nuremberg trials. They may discern both similarities and differences between the Vietnam situation and World War II. The culminating activity of the unit can be a discussion of the following moral dilemma, which is constructed to pose the question of following authority vs. following personal conscience.

### The security guard's dilemma

Ray Ogden is a security guard in a large supermarket. One morning, he noticed an elderly man shoplifting a piece of meat by putting it inside his coat pocket. Since the man was a regular customer in the store, Ray had had occasion to speak with him in the past. He knew the man was living on a meager pension and had barely enough money to buy food and pay for the other necessities of life. Ray felt very sympathetic towards the man and realized he was probably shoplifting only because he did not have enough money to buy the food. Yet Ray was hired by the store to prevent shoplifting. It was also the store's policy to prosecute shoplifters to the fullest extent of the law.

Ray was faced with this dilemma: Should he do his job and apprehend the man as he left the store, or should he pretend he did not see the shoplifting and allow the man to leave the store with the meat in his coat? Ray knew he would be fired if he ignored the man and his supervisor found out about it. What should Ray do?

## Needed: A Values Rationale

The moral dilemma is the main strategy of an important learning system devised by Professor Lawrence Kohlberg. Through more than twenty years of research and experimentation in various school systems in the United States and abroad, Professor Kohlberg has provided teachers with a rationale called cognitive moral development. While his theories remain controversial, they are effective at providing social studies teachers with an essential argument they can use in defending values education against those who ask, "What is happening in the classroom when traditional content gives way to values learning?"

The theory of cognitive moral development is based on a hierarchial structure of moral development. According to developmental psychologists, individuals as they grow older move through a sequence of stages — the hierarchial structure — from very basic self-involved reasoning about moral issues to high-level reasoning involving universally accepted principles. All people move through these stages in a structured pattern, although an individual may stop at a particular stage. According to the theory, educators have the ability to accelerate the upward movement of students through these stages and to insure that each individual is capable of achieving his or her highest level of moral development. Society benefits from this achievement because complicated social problems can be solved only when people reason on the highest levels.

The levels are clearly labeled, and each level contains two stages: (1) the preconventional level based on fear of punishment and reciprocity, (2) the conventional level based on peer acceptance and respect for law and order, and (3) the principled level based on the social contract and universally held ethical principles.

Teaching strategies, such as socialized and group discussions based on moral dilemmas, are supposed to place individual students in contact with other students who are reasoning on the next higher level. All individuals, according to the theory, are able to understand arguments that are one stage higher than their own. Exposure to other students' reasoning is not enough, however. Teachers should ask questions that stimulate reasoning at one stage higher and should focus on arguments at different stages.

Cognitive moral development can be achieved in individual social studies classes. It has also formed the philosophical rationale for structuring minischools. In an attempt to counter the "hidden curriculum" of schools that stress competition and punishment, minischools have been organized around the *just community* concept. In these schools, a high priority is attached to use of the democratic process in deciding on school procedures. Students are trained to conduct meetings at which high-level moral decisions can be made, in arriving at school governances through a system of student involvement. In schools such as these, democracy is not a hit-or-miss proposition, but the basic concept around which the school is organized.

## TEACHING CULTURAL VALUES

A unit consisting of a variety of lessons may be devised on a topic such as the institution of marriage. In a series of inquiry lessons, students may be introduced to marriage customs in societies other than our own, for example, in Swazi tribal society and in traditional Indian society. The students may then react to these different customs during informal discussions, when they are presented with questions such as "Does the tradition of arranged marriages lessen the strain on young people of constantly trying to impress the opposite sex and prove themselves worthy of marriage?" and "Do arranged marriages increase the chance of a happy marriage, since the couple have no choice but to learn to live together?" The students may then be asked to bring to class materials relating to marriage in our own society, such as wedding cards and invitations, family photographs, wedding cake knives, bridal veils, or copies of wedding ceremonies from various religions. The students may then research wedding customs to discover the symbolic meanings of the articles used in weddings, and may discuss their own attitudes towards marriage as it exists in our society. Mock marriage ceremonies can be conducted in class. The ceremonies should reflect various cultures and religions, so that the students can compare and contrast the different customs in informal discussions following each ceremony. They may see a film such as *Future Shock*, which includes segments on experimental forms of marriage, such as group marriage and communal living. Discussions following the film can focus on many opinions and attitudes about marriage.

As we have mentioned, films can be used in a number of units dealing with values. Multimedia techniques can also be used to explore students' values regarding the environment. A unit may open with an audiovisual presentation about ecology. While class time is being devoted to discussions of different attitudes concerning the use and importance of the environment, students can work on outside assignments to express visually their attitudes towards the environment. They may produce drawings, paintings, slides, photographs, posters, ceramics, and other artistic creations to illustrate their feelings. The works will probably reflect a wide range of attitudes and values, from an unqualified endorsement of economic development regardless of its environmental cost to a yearning for a return to a simpler, more natural way of life.

The audiovisual technique may also be used to introduce a unit on attitudes towards death. Teachers may use one of a number of audiovisual materials dealing with death, such as the Sunburst filmstrip *Living with Dying*. The students may then discuss their reactions to the film. If students express an interest in further pursuing the issue, they may be assigned topics to research, such as funeral customs around the world, attitudes towards death and afterlife in different religions, the treatment of the elderly and dying in our society and in other societies, and the treatment of death in art, music, and literature. These students may prepare oral reports on their topics and present them to the class.

## THE TEACHER'S ROLE IN VALUES EDUCATION

A supervisor noted the following after observing a teacher's lesson:

Your class underwent a most valuable, thought-provoking session. The classroom adaptation of the feature film *Five Easy Pieces* was replete with learning material. Because the film was shortened to a half-hour presentation, ample time was provided for class discussion.[6] You focused on the main theme, *identity crisis*, by asking your class, "Why do young people use graffiti?" When one of your students explained that a new name or image can be announced by graffiti, the class was placed in the midst of a vital topic.

The supervisor's observation highlights the role of the teacher whether a moral dilemma or, as in this case, a values-laden motion picture, is being discussed. In the lesson on *Five Easy Pieces*, the teacher was involving a social studies class in American studies in an examination of social values. In order to help the students undergo an evaluative decision-making process, the teacher planned the lesson around these pivotal points:[7]

1. Identification and clarification of a value question—Is it necessary for every individual to have a societal function in order to be happy in our society?

2. The assembling of purported facts—What skills did the main character have?

3. The assessing of the validity of purported facts – Did the main character think that he had valuable skills?

4. Clarification of the relevant facts – Why do people drop out of society?

5. A tentative value decision – Would the main character have remained with his family if less pressure were put on him?

6. The testing of the value principle implied in the decision – Would graffiti artists desecrate public property if they felt accepted by our society?

Value analysis, in this format, is a reflective process. By using these questions before the document (film) is presented, and then discussing each question in turn, the students in the class are given the opportunity to evaluate the causes of the identity crisis that they themselves might feel.

The teacher is helped in devising value-analysis procedures if he can master the design of learning strategies that allow students to decide for themselves the acceptability of a value principle. The following tests are offered:[8]

1. *The Subsumption Test.* After formulating a value principle (or judgment), facts are assembled to determine whether or not this value principle can be accepted as part of a larger, more general value principle that the evaluator has already accepted.

2. *The Role Exchange Test.* An imaginative exchange takes place so that the evaluator can weigh the application of a value principle from a personal vantage point.

3. *The Universal Consequences Test.* The evaluator judges a principle in the context of its acceptance by everyone in similar circumstances.

These tests are seen in classroom application as follows:

### Subsumption test

T. You think, then, that any commercial venture that is hazardous to sea life is undesirable? (T. formulates principle implicit in S.'s evaluation.)

S. Yes. (S. affirms principle as formulated by T.)

T. Why? (T. probes for general principle.)

S. Because it is a bad thing to endanger resources needed for sustaining human life. (S. gives more general value principle.)

T. What has that to do with commercial ventures that are dangerous to sea life being undesirable? (T. tries to elicit facts to complete the subsuming argument.)

**S.** Sea life produces food and much of the oxygen that is needed to support human life.

### Role exchange test

**S.** It's not right to make restaurants serve blacks if they don't want to serve them.

**T.** Would you still say that if you were black?

### Universal consequences test

**S.** I don't see anything wrong with refusing to pay my income tax when the government is going to use it for something I don't approve of.

**T.** Have you considered what would happen to the government and the country if everyone refused to pay their income tax because they didn't approve of how it was going to be spent?

Teachers are making individual curriculum decisions on topics that have previously been avoided. Topics such as "Perspectives on Death" are being introduced in order to give students an opportunity to express value judgments, in the quiet of a classroom, on vital issues that face everyone. In DeKalb, Illinois, a minicourse on death was introduced. Guest speakers were invited, including the school psychologist, an artist, a musician, a lawyer, an insurance broker, a doctor, a representative of three major religious faiths, and a soldier, who spoke on facing death on the battlefield.[9] This course allowed value judgments to emerge on war, abortion, euthanasia, growing teenage suicide rates, the entire ecological question, violence in the media, and the mounting drug problem. The essentiality of these topics cannot be disputed.

The minicourse on death is an example of a curriculum approach that does not attempt to include learning material that leads to "right answers." There is no right answer when a student is asked to write his own obituary. There is, however, a great deal of focus on the quality of one's life. This approach is referred to as values clarification. The goal of values clarification is to help students utilize a rationale of valuing. A rationale process implies a step-by-step procedure.[10] The book *Values Clarification* (Simon, Howe, and Kirschenbaum [New York: Hart Publishing Co., 1972]) lists 89 strategies for accomplishing this, among them the strategy of "Obituary."

Another of the strategies is called *value voting*, whereby students must commit themselves to an assertion and then defend their position. Value voting takes place when a teacher's question begins, "How many of you . . . ?" Students then vote on questions such as:

How many of you have ever felt lonely even in a crowd of people? Have had someone from another race to your house for dinner or to play? Think that women should stay home and be primarily wives and mothers?

In the "fallout-shelter problem," students in groups of six or seven decide which four out of ten people will be eliminated from a shelter in order that the others might survive. The list of ten includes a 31-year-old bookkeeper, his wife (six months pregnant), a Black militant (a second-year medical student), a famous historian (42 years old), a Hollywood starlet, a biochemist, a 54-year-old rabbi, an Olympic athlete, a college coed, and a policeman with a gun. There are variations on this strategy, and the teacher is urged to use any of the strategies creatively, not slavishly. The important point is that students are confronted with a decision-making crisis. For some it might be the first time that a life philosophy will begin to emerge. There are many who believe that this is what education is all about.

## FUTURISM AND VALUES EDUCATION

A frequent criticism of education is that it prepares students for life as it is now and not how it will be. While it is difficult to predict with exactitude the problems our students will face in the future, increased mechanization and automation should within a very short period of time render many present manpower skills totally obsolete. Just as in our recent past history we passed from a predominantly rural nation to a predominantly urban nation, and from an agricultural economy to an industrial economy, our students are witnessing a shift in manpower needs — from production to service. A premium, therefore, is placed on "cope-ability" rather than capability. Alvin Toffler, who uses the word cope-ability to explain the mental skill of adjusting to rapid change, challenges the schools to prepare students who can discern the pattern of future events and plan their personal lives accordingly.[11] Some schools have already answered the call. The Corvallis High School in Oregon, in its Rachael Carson Program, has established an interdisciplinary environmental curriculum in which the social studies component is responsible for introducing materials on futurism, a subject area which deals with the ways and means that human adjustments can be made to meet the challenge of change.[12]

If futurism in education catches on, the social studies educator will find a changed curriculum which is strikingly different from any in current use. Toffler eschews learning centered on fixed disciplines such as English, economics, mathematics, and biology. "Why not," he proposes, "organize the curriculum around stages of the human life cycle?" This would include a course on birth, childhood, adolescence, marriage, career, retirement, and death. He also suggests an alternate curriculum based on contemporary social problems or on significant technologies of the past and future.[13] In this call for an "education which shifts into the future tense," Toffler may be suggesting the very same rapid rate of change that has already placed our society in a state of shock. In other words his educational cure might be another form of the disease. The schools are not known for their rapid rate of change. It is more than likely that the individual teacher will have to look towards classroom strategies for introducing students to the future rather than sweeping curriculum innovations.

Social studies content abounds with opportunities for studying change and its impact on society. Materials excerpted from Colin Turnbull's *The Mountain People* easily convey the concept of how human interrelationships undergo upheaval when change is instituted too quickly.[14] The Ik people described in this book exchanged social amenities for cutthroat cruelty within a generation when they were forced to settle down and give up their nomadic existence. Whenever the themes of change and tradition are studied in juxtaposition in any society, students are offered an opportunity to reflect on these very same themes in our own society.

Games have been designed to evaluate future possibilities and probabilities. One such game is *Future*, distributed by Kaiser Aluminum and Chemical Corporation. It introduces players to various future technologies and social alternatives and forces them to choose among them. Toffler suggests games such as *Future* and also encourages the study of science fiction in the schools. In December 1971, an issue of *Social Education* contained an article by a famous science fiction author, Ray Bradbury. "Sound of Thunder" described a hunting safari that reached its destination by way of a time machine. The members of the safari were hunting dinosaurs! The discussion questions that accompanied the article guided the students in grasping the conceptual interrelationship between the very remote past and the present. Apparently the use of science fiction in social studies caught on. In February 1973, the feature article in *Social Education* presented an anthology of science fiction stories to be utilized by world history teachers.[15] Another Bradbury story, "The Smile," contained in this anthology, tells of a post-nuclear-war existence in which the smile has been outlawed. Another story, "Survival Ship" by Judith Merril, takes place on board a space vehicle whose mission is to insure the procreation of the human race. The readers are confronted with the possibility that in this situation women will play a dominant role. A series of introductory questions has the students exploring their own attitudes towards the role played by men and women in our society. The drama of science fiction seems to place our lives in the modern age in clearer perspective in providing a futuristic setting which is imaginative and yet uncluttered. Our true character stands out. This enables students to analyze our present society and to predict its destiny.

## A PERSPECTIVE ON VALUES EDUCATION

We have shown some examples of the many different strategies and techniques that may be utilized effectively in values education. There are, of course, many more. No matter which one you may use, there is agreement among those who espouse values education on these points: you cannot "teach" values. Values change, values are in conflict, and, therefore, educators must stress the valuing process.

Educators have become interested in the valuing process with the hope that they can assist students in rationally arriving at their own values. There has been hope also that students can be guided into arriving at values on a higher level of altruism through classroom procedures that expose them to levels of thinking higher than their own. If this proves to be so, the schools will have become the conscience of society, and within the schools, the social studies program will have become the conscience of the school. Will the social studies teacher accept this responsibility?

## ENDNOTES

1. For a fuller discussion of various types of values, see Edwin Fenton, "Teaching About Values in the Public Schools," *Teaching the New Social Studies in Secondary Schools: An Inductive Approach* (New York: Holt, Rinehart and Winston, 1966), pp. 41–45.

2. For examples of traditional values considered part of the social studies curriculum, see any of the older textbooks, such as Dorothy McClure Fraser and Edith West, *Social Studies in Secondary Schools: Curriculum and Methods* (New York: The Ronald Press, 1961), pp. 49–51, 62–64.

3. See, for example, Ronald E. Galbraith and Thomas M. Jones, "Teaching Strategies for Moral Dilemmas: An Application of Kohlberg's Theory of Moral Development to the Social Studies Classroom," *Social Education* 39 (January 1975), pp. 16–22; Lawrence E. Metcalf, ed., "Values Education: Rationale, Strategies, and Procedures," *41st Yearbook of the National Council for the Social Studies* (1971); Sidney B. Simon, Leland W. Howe, and Howard Kirschenbaum, *Values Clarification, A Handbook of Practical Strategies for Teachers and Students* (New York: Hart Publishing Co., 1972).

4. David W. Berg and George G. Daugherty, "Teaching About Death," *Today's Education* (March 1973), pp. 46–47.

5. For a fuller discussion of this technique, see Galbraith and Jones, pp. 16–22.

6. The classroom version is called "Living and Loving" and is distributed by the Learning Corporation of America.

7. Adapted from Jerrold Coombs and Milton Meux, "Teaching Strategies for Value Analysis," *NCSS Yearbook* (1971).

8. These tests and the ensuing "From the Rear of the Room" have been adapted from Coombs and Meux, pp. 54–62.

9. Berg and Daugherty, pp. 46–47.

10. These are Raths' seven subprocesses: (1) prizing and cherishing, (2) publicly affirming, (3) choosing from alternatives, (4) choosing after consideration of consequences, (5) choosing freely, (6) acting, (7) acting with a pattern, consistency and repetition [Louis Raths, Merrill Harmin, and Sidney Simon, *Values and Teaching* (Columbus, Ohio: Charles E. Merrill, 1966), as quoted in Sidney Simon, Leland Howe, and Howard Kirschenbaum, *Values Clarification* (New York: Hart Publishing Co., 1972)].

11. Alvin Toffler, *Future Shock* (New York: Bantam Books, 1970), p. 403.

12. The other subjects (social studies) are the history of conservation, the natural history of Oregon, and outdoor education.

13. Toffler, p. 410.

14. Colin Turnbull, *The Mountain People* (New York: Simon and Schuster, 1972).
15. Daniel Roselle, "Teaching About World History Through Science Fiction" (an anthology), *Social Education* (February 1973), pp. 96–150.

## BIBLIOGRAPHY

### Audiovisual Materials

There are numerous audiovisual materials available that are suitable for values education. The materials listed below constitute merely a sampling of the wide variety of audiovisual materials available.

### Filmstrips

*And Ain't I a Woman*, Schloat Productions, 150 White Plains Road, Tarrytown, New York 10591.

*Families Around the World*, Schloat Productions.

*High on Life*, Guidance Associates, 757 3rd Avenue, New York, New York 10017.

*I Had No Choice But to Obey: The Question of Personal Responsibility*, Denoyer-Geppert Audio-Visuals, 5235 Ravenswood Avenue, Chicago, Illinois 60640.

*Life Style 2000: Inquiry Into the Future*, Denoyer-Geppert Audio-Visuals.

*Life Style 2000: What Will We Take Into the Future*, Denoyer-Geppert Audio-Visuals.

*Living With Dying*, Sunburst Productions, Westchester Avenue, Pound Ridge, New York 10576.

*Masculinity*, Schloat Productions.

*Parenthood: Myths and Realities*, Guidance Associates.

*Personality: Roles You Play*, Sunburst Productions.

*Perspective on Death, A Thematic Teaching Unit*, P.O. Box 213, DeKalb, Illinois 60115.

*Science and Society*, Schloat Productions.

*The Indians vs. The Giant Utilities: Whose Values Prevail at Black Mesa?* Denoyer-Geppert Audio-Visuals.

*2000 A.D.*, Newsweek Education Division, 444 Madison Avenue, New York, New York 10022.

*Values for Dating*, Sunburst Productions.

*What About Marriage?*, Sunburst Productions.

*Women's Work*, Schloat Productions.

# 6

## Reading Skills

Reading is an essential learning skill in social studies. If the student is to be able to use textbooks, encyclopedias, atlases, dictionaries, newspapers, magazines, biographies, and other print resources, the teacher is faced with helping the student to overcome the barriers imposed by vocabulary and comprehension deficiencies.

### CLASSROOM DIAGNOSIS

If students are to function at their best in social studies classes, it is important for teachers to assess the students' ability in reading at the beginning of each school session. Diagnoses should continue throughout the term, with constant re-evaluation and identification of specific problems and of special interests.

At the beginning of the term, the teacher can survey the students' language skills informally by doing as many of the following as can be accomplished within the first several days: (1) For general assessment of verbal ability, the teacher can listen for fluency in vocabulary and self-expression by initiating a discussion on an important current events topic. (2) Depending upon the main objectives of the course, the teacher can assign a brief (five-minute) writing activity on topics such as "Inflation is . . ." or "Chances for peace are . . .". (3) The teacher might also distribute one or two duplicated paragraphs from available texts and ask students to read these orally and silently. (4) The teacher might follow the preceding activity by asking questions on the main concepts of the paragraphs.

The major part of this chapter is an adaptation of *A Reading Manual and Taxonomy for the Social Studies Classroom*, which was planned and designed under the direction of Muriel Mandell, coordinator of the New York City Right to Read Impact Project, with the cooperation of Anita Dore, acting director of the Bureau of English, and Florence Jackson, director of the Center for Humanities and the Arts. Vivian Grano was the social studies specialist in this project.

Teachers will also want to make sure that the text material that is selected for the class is on a level that will insure a successful learning experience for as many of the students as possible. If it is discovered that some students require easier or more challenging material, the teacher can also provide for their needs once these needs are established. There are two systems offered here for evaluating the reading level of published material. One is called the Cloze system (Exhibit 6–1) and the other is based on the Fry graph (Exhibit 6–2); both are shown in the exhibits at the end of the chapter.

To apply the Cloze system, the teacher duplicates a passage from a text. After the title and introductory sentence, every fifth word is replaced with a blank. The teacher asks students to fill in the blanks. This breakdown will guide you in evaluating the text chosen:

1. Students who can supply 57 percent or more of the missing words can handle the book independently.

2. Students who can supply 44 to 57 percent of the missing words can use the book with some support or assistance.

3. Students who can supply less than 44 percent of the words require easier material or considerable support (vocabulary development, preteaching, carefully devised questions, study guides).

An analysis of the types of errors will give clues to general verbal ability as well as indicate students' background in the particular subject matter.

If students are not available when a textbook is being evaluated, the Fry graph is useful. The teacher uses the graph by averaging the number of sentences and syllables in three hundred-word passages in the text material and plotting the convergence of this information on the graph shown in Exhibit 6–2. By using any one of these two systems, the teacher avoids student frustration with difficult reading material, which could inhibit social studies learning.


## VOCABULARY

Vocabulary development must be an important component of *all* social studies teaching. The problem exists at both extremes, from the student whose vocabulary is so limited that he or she gropes for a means of expression on issues that affect him or her personally to the glib student who uses imprecise polysyllabic terms without a true understanding of their meaning. Both of these students encounter difficulty in understanding the true meaning of reading material.

The development of vocabulary is closely related to a person's ability to conceptualize – to develop a mental image of an action or a thing and to make generalizations concerning it.

### STEPS IN VOCABULARY DEVELOPMENT

The following procedure is recommended for teachers who wish to help students develop an improved vocabulary.

### Preview

Look over material to be used to determine which words are essential to the meaning of the passage that you think will cause trouble. Look for:

1. Technical vocabulary that may be totally unfamiliar (*apartheid*).
2. Multimeaning words that can confuse (*party*).
3. Polysyllabic terms that may cause decoding or meaning problems (*extraterritorial*).
4. Figurative language with literary or historical references or allusions that are unfamiliar (*thrown in legislative hopper*).
5. Idioms (*run for office*).
6. Abstractions for which students may have imprecise concepts (*democracy*).
7. Pronoun referents (*it, which, they*).
8. Connotative words (*communist, liberal*).

### Pretest (Formal or Informal)

Check your hunches to avoid assuming either ignorance or knowledge on the part of the particular students with whom you are dealing:

1. Prepare a list of basic words to be used in the course. Start with easy words or terms and work towards more difficult ones. Ask students to check off those that they know.
2. Use matching tests (with definitions) on words, roots, prefixes, and suffixes. Use them in a sentence context where possible.
3. Have students write out the definition(s) of a word. (Use sparingly; it is easy to overdo this approach.)
4. Have students classify words under given topics:
   *physical features:*   desert, river, mountains, oasis
   *political features:*   nation, province, state, town, city
5. Have students derive the meaning of a word from context clues within a sentence or paragraph. Have them infer the meaning of an

italicized word from its relationship to other words in the sentence:

They developed pellagra, scurvy, kwashiorkor, and other diseases caused by poor nutrition.

6.  Have students derive the meaning of a word from prefix clues within the word itself. Have them infer the meaning of the word from the meaning of its component parts: in-, un-, pre-, post-, etc.

    Antisocial means_____.

    Then reverse the procedure.

    A word meaning against the society is _____.

7.  Have students complete comparisons or analogies:

    Employer is to employee as management is to (labor).

8.  Have students write:

    *synonyms for words:*   political (governmental)
    *antonyms for words:*   freedom (slavery)

9.  Before and after they study a chapter in one of their texts, check students' understanding of key words by multiple choice tests. (Students may be asked to help prepare these tests.)

10.  Give definitions of words and ask students to supply the word defined: Machines doing the work of men (automation). Clues may be added: au_____n. A list from which to choose may be supplied.


Test-like material can be used for instruction when appropriate feedback is applied. It is important, for instance, to go into the reasons why an answer is incorrect.

Teach a few words at a time *in context* — as vividly and personally as possible. Choose those that carry the concept load of the lesson.

Studying a limited number of words in depth is more productive than superficial acquaintance with long lists. Choose those that students will need at their level. There is little point in teaching "judiciary" before the student knows "judge" and "court."

1.  Build on the student's background — relate the unfamiliar to the familiar, the past to the present, the distant to the near, the impersonal to the personal, the abstract to the concrete.

2.  Provide necessary experience, real or vicarious (trips, role-playing, pictures, filmstrips)

3.  Make vocabulary development an intrinsic and pleasurable part of the social studies lesson by inviting role-playing, encouraging educated guesses, and supplying the history of a word.

4.  Help students to formulate a definition of the word by:

    a.  Giving synonyms and antonyms

    b. Classifying

    c. Enumerating other words to which the word relates

    d. Exhibiting a sample

    e. Defining the word operationally — telling what to do in order to experience or recognize the thing to which it refers

5. Supply a glossary for those words that are merely new labels for familiar concepts.

*Train* students for vocabulary independence:

1. Teach students to make educated guesses on the basis of context and context clues: synonyms, antonyms, figures of speech, definitions or explanations, descriptions, summaries, punctuation.

2. Encourage students to try to sound out a word syllable by syllable, changing vowel sounds, syllable division, or accents if the word is not recognizable at first.

3. Draw attention to word parts and their meanings (in, ex, auto, demos).

4. Involve students in word and phrase derivations (to boycott, sit-in).

5. To aid recall, assist students in inventing mnemonic devices.

6. Teach students effective use of the glossary and the dictionary, particularly selection of the meaning that is applicable in the particular context.

*Reinforce* students by supplying opportunities for application. Retention and precision come only from repeated encounters with the same words:

1. Repeated oral and written use of new words by the teacher and student will motivate students for remembering them.

2. Provide game-like opportunities for drill such as crossword puzzles, word lotto, Password, Twenty Questions, categories, charades, pantomime, riddles, jokes, and puns.

## COMPREHENSION SKILLS

Nine of the many comprehension subskills can be identified as basic to the acquisition and understanding of social studies content:

1. Getting details.

2. Finding the main idea.

3. Drawing conclusions.

4. Identifying cause and effect.

5. Categorizing.

6. Detecting a sequential pattern.

7. Making comparisons and contrasts.

8. Distinguishing fact from opinion.

9. Applying concepts.

These skills cover three levels of reading comprehension: literal, interpretive, and applied. Though they can be defined separately, many of the nine skills overlap in meaning and in use. Identification of cause and effect may lead to the main idea of a passage. Determination of a sequence may be helpful in establishing cause and effect. Separation of fact from opinion may be necessary in establishing valid comparisons. Before they begin the actual reading, students should be instructed in the purposes for which they are reading a given selection.

Effective use of such graphic aids as maps, charts, diagrams, pictures, and cartoons — which are so necessary in enhancing knowledge and understanding of social studies content — also requires considerable skill for a student to transfer content from the visual to the verbal. Visual aids can sometimes serve as a bridge in teaching the thinking skill on which reading comprehension depends. Photographs and cartoons often use details to lay the foundation for inferences, comparisons, and categories, as well as cause-and-effect relationships and sequences. Similarly, time lines, graphs, and charts give specific details or suggest inferences, cause-effect relationships, and sequences.

*Skill 1. Getting details*, at the literal level of comprehension, involves locating and reproducing the facts as presented by the author. Command of detail is the foundation of the building blocks that enable students to develop and use other skills. It includes getting answers to the questions who? what? when? where? how? from the sentence or paragraph.

This is the easiest of the skills listed, but in order to retrieve information accurately, students must be aided in understanding vocabulary, punctuation clues, pronoun referents, and other aspects of grammatical structure that help denote meaning. Many do not understand, for instance, that a pair of commas or parentheses may introduce a synonym, an explanatory phrase, or a series of examples. Even a better reader may not realize how semicolons and colons link ideas. Students need practice in converting large numerals into words and words into numerals. Many overlook qualifying words of quantity such as *few, many, seldom,* and *possible.*

For the reader for whom the material presents too great a challenge, guidance should be given by directing the student to the specific sentence in which the answer can be found. Later, this should be broadened to the specific paragraph, then the page, and later the chapter. Initially, questions for the poorer reader should repeat the vocabulary of the passage exactly. Later, questions can be rephrased.

*Skill 2.    Finding the main idea* involves determining the relationship between what is central and what is supportive so that students can establish an order of importance within a sentence, a paragraph, a group of paragraphs, or even within a longer selection. When the main idea is expressed in a simple sentence, students can be asked to find this topic sentence in the selection. Sometimes students can look for typographical clues – heavy type, italics, underscoring. Most of the time, it is a matter of deciding which idea was developed and how the sentences in the paragraph are related to and support the main idea – by repetition, by example or explanation, by development of steps in a logical order or time sequence, by comparison or contrast. Note that it is important that your detail questions lead the student to the central theme.

*Skill 3.    Drawing conclusions* requires students to analyze data, stated or implied, and draw inferences. Students must be made aware that inferences can sometimes be drawn from the inclusion of certain details and the omission of others, the use of a particular vocabulary, or the tone established by a passage. They can also be made sensitive to key words and phrases sometimes used to indicate the author's own conclusions, such as: *in conclusion, we can see that, it seems that, it would seem that, and therefore.*

*Skill 4.    Identifying cause and effect* is a reading skill requiring students to determine why an event took place or why a condition exists. *Students must be aware of the concept of cause-effect relationships before being asked to look for them in the material.* Students can be taught to look for possible cause-and-effect clues: *because, one reason why, in order to.* Recognizing this pattern can further help students to recognize and understand a main idea. Determining cause-and-effect relationships is related to the skill of detecting a sequence (Skill 6 below).

*Skill 5.    Categorizing* is a skill that requires students to group and organize specific data according to some rational principle. Students learn to sift material, separate major from minor details, and structure information in a new form. The teaching of this skill can be logically developed from the ranking of main idea and supporting details. In teaching this skill, teachers should help students establish categories for information. Frequently, this is done by the author; sometimes it can be done by the teacher in preparing students for the reading. Once the idea has caught on, students should be encouraged to establish their own categories.

*Skill 6.    Detecting a sequential pattern* in a selection entails reading to learn the chronological order of a series of events. This involves a knowledge of tense and of certain signal words: *first, then, next, before, after, last, meanwhile, in retrospect, previously.* (Other signals are categorized in Table 6-1.)

**TABLE 6-1.** *Signals*

I. Signals indicating additional ideas

   A. Signals pointing to coordinating ideas

| And | Furthermore | Besides | Not only, but also |
|---|---|---|---|
| Also | Plus | Too | Likewise |
| Another | Otherwise | After that | Similarly |
| In addition | Moreover | | |

   B. Signals pointing to final or concluding ideas

| Consequently | In conclusion | Then | For this reason |
|---|---|---|---|
| Thus | In summation | To sum up | As you can see |
| Hence | At last | In brief | In short |
| Therefore | Finally | In the end | |

II. Signals indicating a change in ideas

| In contrast | On the other hand | Although | To the contrary |
|---|---|---|---|
| On the contrary | Nevertheless | For all that | However |
| Opposed to | But | Yet | Except |
| Conversely | In spite of | Still | |

III. Signals pointing to relationships

A. Time Relationships

| | | | |
|---|---|---|---|
| In the first place | To begin with | At the same time | Hereafter |
| (Second, etc.) | Next | Following | Immediately |
| Thereafter | Last | Since (since then) | At length |
| Finally | Later | Soon | At last |
| In retrospect | Before (before that) | Formerly | Meanwhile |
| Now | After (after that) | Previously | Finally |
| Then | | | |

B. Space Relationships

| | | | |
|---|---|---|---|
| Here | Far | Everywhere | To the East |
| There | Near | Further on | Westward |
| Yonder | By | Above | Under |
| Close | Away | Beneath | Across |

C. Related in degree

| | | | |
|---|---|---|---|
| Mere | Little | Almost | Fewest |
| Only | Less | Best | Greater |
| Many | Least | Worst | Greatest |
| More | Some | Fewer | Above all |
| Most | All | | |

D. Pointing Signals

| | | | |
|---|---|---|---|
| This | That | One | Some |
| These | Those | Several | Few |

Flashbacks and presentation of material out of order pose special problems. Note that a paragraph that was used in developing cause and effect can be used to develop questions for detecting sequential patterns; however, students should be alerted to the *post hoc, ergo propter hoc* fallacy regarding sequence and cause and effect.

*Skill 7.    Making comparisons and contrasts* involves patterning factual material to highlight similarities and differences. Key phrases students should recognize are: *similarly, likewise, on the other hand, in contrast, but, conversely.* Again punctuation and grammar clues are important; parallel structure, for instance, indicates relationship.

*Skill 8.    Distinguishing fact from opinion.* As with establishing cause-and-effect relationships and drawing inferences, distinguishing fact from opinion requires substantial preteaching before students can be asked to deal with it in a reading situation. The distinction is frequently difficult and often requires considerable sophistication and critical ability. Students must learn to identify verbal clues (*some people think. . .* , *it is believed that. . .*), develop sensitivity to connotations and "loaded terms," detect bias, and learn to deal with verifiable facts as well as false or inaccurate statements that pass for fact. After determining what an author is saying, students must learn to ask appropriate questions: Is it so? How can we tell?

*Skill 9.    Applying concepts* involves the use of information in a new situation. The effectiveness of the reading can be judged best by the extent to which it influences action and attitudes. Students should be trained to relate the material to other information in order to solve problems, predict outcomes, clarify values, and establish new hypotheses. It is the most complicated skill dealt with here, encompassing all of the others. It is essential to a student's true understanding of the reading material.

## STRATEGIES FOR INTEGRATING
## READING SKILL AND SOCIAL STUDIES

Among the techniques that can be used to facilitate social studies learning by using print material are the grouping of students, the preparation of study guides, and the rewriting of materials. These techniques can support or supplement a teacher's regular mode of instruction, or they can be used for a series of separate or independent activities. In either case, some form of diagnosis of student ability is essential. Equally important is a supportive classroom attitude.

Obviously, the teacher cannot institute every suggestion in this manual simultaneously. All suggestions must be tempered to the physical and human resources at hand — time, energy, materials — as well as to an assessment of student needs.

## Grouping

To deal with skill-oriented material, a number of students can be differentiated from the class at large and set to work with separate materials or at separate tasks. Grouping has many advantages:

1. It eliminates many of the problems of heterogeneity in the classroom.
2. It provides appropriate challenges for students on different levels.
3. It permits students to pace their own progress, freeing them from the stigma of being too slow or from the boredom that results from work that is too easy.
4. It gives the teacher an opportunity to work with students as individuals.
5. It bolsters confidence and facilitates academic success.
6. It provides students with sufficient mastery of material to contribute to class discussions.
7. It promotes socialization.

While grouping generally works best in rooms with movable furniture, particularly when socialization is desired, it is also effective in fixed-furniture situations. The basic concept is that students need not all do the same thing at the same time but can work at appropriate projects geared to their own interests and abilities.

Where possible, it is important to have a classroom library including alternate texts, bibliographies, pertinent fiction, and current pamphlets and periodicals. The wider the variety of materials, the greater the likelihood of a student's finding something of interest and of value and at a level at which he or she can succeed. This also increases the availability of illustrative material at the student's disposal. Of course, a dictionary should be accessible.

Obviously, support personnel make grouping easier, but if paraprofessionals, volunteers, or student teachers are not available, the students themselves function well as group leaders, and peer teaching can be extremely fruitful for both "teacher" and student.

### Grouping by reading level

The following offer opportunities for logical grouping:

1. *Homework*
   a. Give differentiated homework assignments from the same text. Having students answer questions at their own level enables each student to make a contribution to a class discussion. The primary task is to develop appropriate questions at different ability levels. Students whose skills are limited to reading for information should be given detail questions to answer; students who can manage

more sophisticated skills should be asked more demanding questions. This type of assignment can provide the basis for greater participation of all students.

b. Give students differentiated  materials for homework so that each student can work with materials at his or her level. All students can be asked to answer the same questions based on the materials they have read.

c. Give students differentiated materials and have them answer different questions based upon the materials they have read.

2. *In-class activities*

a. Designate two to four groups based on reading level. Establish a basic assignment in a particular book. All students who can handle the material should be required to do the assignment; students who cannot handle the material should be assigned a more appropriate equivalent. Students who cannot manage the second assignment should be given even more basic material with which to work. Students who can manage independent reading should be encouraged to do it.

b. It is possible to assign a task to a group of students working together or to assign the same task to each individual in the group to do on his own. Obviously, this must depend on the teacher's purposes or goals. Students frequently profit from each other's assistance.

c. Assignments should be complete enough and specific enough to allow students to work in groups or on their own without teacher support (see the following section on study guides). While the students are working, the teacher can single out one group for attention and can proceed to teach. Or the teacher may use this time to move about the classroom, stopping to help students with individual problems, explaining necessary terms, interpreting questions or instructions, supplying additional guidance, redirecting activities, and encouraging those students who are fulfilling their assignments. Small-group instruction and individual attention are important benefits of this mode of operation.

### Other bases for grouping

1. *According to Interest.* Students choose their own groups on the basis of interest in a field of inquiry. Groups might be established to investigate several current problems, with each student selecting the problem of greatest concern to him or her. Try to keep these groups reasonably equal in size.

2. *According to Skill.* Students may be assigned to work at different sources of material in order to develop different skills.

3. *According to Point of View.* Particularly in examining some controversial issue, students might be assigned to defend their position or to defend the opposing argument instead.

4. *Arbitrary.* For example, grouping may be alphabetical, by location in the room, at random.

## Study Guides

Because of the changing curricula and the quickened pace of current events, there is usually a time lag before textbook publishers produce text material on up-to-date topics. Therefore, a teacher who finds that there is little or no available reading material on a topic may wish to prepare a study guide. This "homegrown" learning device affords the teacher the opportunity to insure that the learning material is exactly on the topic and on the learning level of the students.

A series of questions and activities keyed to written material can direct students in their reading and serve a number of purposes:

1. Set objectives for reading.
2. Enable students to handle material that might otherwise be too difficult by breaking it into manageable units.
3. Clarify or create a structure for material.
4. Reinforce vocabulary.
5. Give practice in a particular reading skill.
6. Give guidance in scanning material for specific information.
7. Serve to teach students to get an overview of a book, chapter, or shorter selection by calling attention to typographical and graphic aids (titles, subheads, introductory and summary paragraphs, and illustration, maps and graphs).
8. Lead the student to related readings and activities.
9. Help prepare students for participation in class discussions and thus foster a sense of achievement.
10. Help the teacher to diagnose student weaknesses, strengths, and interests.

### Steps in the preparation of study guides

When you are ready to write a study guide, these suggestions will help you:

1. Determine the purpose for which the reading is to be done or the assignment made; decide both the basic content (or concepts) and the skills to be developed.

2. Select a passage in keeping with your established purpose(s). Keep the length of the reading appropriate to the time available to students and their abilities.

3. Anticipate major reading problems (difficult vocabulary; confused organization; complex, compound, and awkward sentence structures; lengthy blocks of material). Key your exercises to these particular areas. Make sure that students can perform the skills required; if the required skills have not already been taught, make a note to teach them before you distribute the guide. The inclusion of one or two answers may serve as models and bolster a sense of security or ability to perform the assigned tasks.

4. Specify each step to be performed in completing the project. Make certain that all directions are clearly expressed and within students' capabilities. If this is done well, it should not be necessary to review the instructions when the guide is distributed.

5. *(Optional)* Provide exercises at various levels of instruction to accommodate all students. This can be done by including enrichment or extra-credit activities for more advanced students, as well as very easy exercises for less able ones.

6. *Caution:* Do not try to include every skill in every study guide, but do include vocabulary reinforcement in every study guide.

### Utilization of study guides

1. Study guides may be used to direct in-class activity or as homework assignments. This outline will help the teacher utilize study guides in several possible formats:

   #### System I: For one class period
   a. Motivate lesson.
   b. Students work on study guide. Teacher assists as required.
   c. Full class discussion (based on material in study guide).

   #### System II: For two or more class periods
   a. *First day:* Motivate lesson.
   b. *First day:* Students begin work on study guides with the teacher assisting.
   c. *Second day or longer:* Students continue working on study guides as the teacher continues to assist or to give small-group instruction.
   d. *Last day:* Culminating activities or lessons (based on material in study guide).

   #### System III: As homework assignment
   a. Teach lesson.
   b. Motivate students to do assignment.

c. Distribute study guide.

d. (Next day) Class lesson (based on material in study guide).

2. The use of different study guides by different students at the same time lends itself to the accommodation of individual interests and abilities (see the foregoing section, on grouping).

3. If new skills are required by the guide, develop them before distributing it. The only time it should be necessary to teach a skill while students are using the guide is when a student did not receive or did not understand the original teaching.

4. Motivate students for learning the material. *Remember that the guide is a means towards an end, not an end in itself.*

5. Distribute the guide(s). Students should begin work immediately if the exercise is to be done in class. If the guide is to be used for homework, go over it with students first to make sure they understand the assignment.

## Simplification of Material

It is frequently desirable that a given passage be revised or rewritten in order to make it more readable for some students. The guidelines that follow can also be used in the creation of original material.

### General considerations

1. Assess the level(s) of students' abilities.

2. Try to locate material on the students' levels. If none can be found, it is possible to rewrite material to make it easier to read. At the end of this section, there is a passage of textual material with three progressively easier revisions (Exhibits 6-3, 6-4, and 6-5).

3. Revision is not the same as "watering down." Retain as much of the pertinent material as possible.

4. Be sure that revised material has simple, straightforward organization, and is grammatically accurate. Avoid slang.

5. For students who can barely read and who have minimal social studies background, change expository writing to anecdotal presentation.

### Revising paragraphs

1. Shorten paragraphs. A block of print that is too solid can easily lose a slow reader. Avoid paragraphs with multiple ideas, too much supportive material, or too many examples.

2. For readers who are having a lot of difficulty, give each paragraph a heading or a number. This will help a student to locate material when answering questions.

3. Avoid changing focus from one sentence to the next.

### Revising sentences

1. Simplify sentence structure. Reduce or eliminate modifying clauses and phrases; they tend to confuse rather than to assist the reader.

2. Shorten sentence length. A long, involved sentence can frequently be broken into several shorter, more direct sentences.

3. Vary sentence length. A dulling, deadening effect is created by a string of sentences of the same length and style.

4. Reduce the number of pronouns. Repeat the antecedent in order to avoid confusion.

### Vocabulary considerations

1. Difficult words and terms that are essential to a given subject should be retained in the rewritten material. But these should be kept to a minimum. Clues in the sentence, in the form of explanations, examples, or synonyms should be added, and a glossary should be supplied. Furthermore, it is essential to provide for preteaching vocabulary, in context, before the student ever sees the written material.

2. Multisyllabic words may be difficult for students to understand and pronounce. Breaking them into their component syllables sometimes helps. Technical terms, necessary idioms, figurative language, and words used in a special sense can be supported by synonyms or brief equivalents in parentheses.

3. Underlining new words will focus students' attention on them.

4. Abstract terms can confuse and discourage readers. Unless they are one of the essential new words that must be included, make them as concrete as possible either by substitution or by including a short, clear example.

### Aids that enhance students' ability to handle written material

1. Include words and phrases that are organizational or conceptual crutches: *first, second, one reason that, for example, such as.*

2. Include short review and reinforcement phrases to help keep the main

idea and the organization of the material in mind: *the most important thing is, in conclusion, as a result.*

3. Physical presentation of material is important. Use visual appearance to focus attention on the material: doublespace, indent paragraphs strongly, use wide margins, avoid large blocks of print.

4. Proofread your copy carefully to avoid misspellings and illegibility.

## THINKING SKILLS

### Critical Judgment

Reading is not an end in itself. Teachers encourage students to read well so that they can think effectively. The pervasive influence of the mass media today raises concern for developing in students the skill of exercising critical judgment. Stated as a social studies skill, the exercise of critical judgment involves the interpretation and evaluation of a program or of material for the purpose of determining its frame of reference, point of view, reliability, and authenticity. Critical judgment can be considered an aspect of the larger technique of propaganda analysis.

The skill of critical judgment goes far beyond the identification of related ideas. Although youngsters may understand the views expressed in a magazine article, they may be unable to defend themselves against distortions or biases therein and will, therefore, accept these views as truths. Students can learn to evaluate information contained in the mass media by recognizing and learning to employ the following yardsticks:

1. Is the account slanted?
2. Is important information treated accurately?
3. Are controversial topics discussed rationally?
4. Is there clear distinction between fact and opinion?
5. Do the headlines, captions, and opening statements accurately present the news?
6. Are editorials and commentaries clearly designated?
7. To what extent is the medium "free"?

An important aspect of the skill of critical judgment is the ability to recognize the economic and political positions of the sponsors or authors of the material. In addition to the usual bibliography that should be included in the student's report of reading done, a sensitive teacher will call for background information about the author, publisher, or sponsor. Without creating a generation of cynics, the teacher must guide pupils toward healthy skepticism of the self-proclaimed "objectivity" of much mass-media material. When back issues of a periodical are available, a useful committee report would be a survey of the number of articles on a particular topic: Medicare, for instance, and an assessing of the overall bias, pro or con. A useful project is a comparative survey of newspaper headlines and lead stories on a controversial event. A variation of this would be to subscribe for one week to a number of out-of-town newspapers for a comparison not only of headlines and lead stories but also a survey of the makeup of the front pages as a clue to the attitude of the paper toward the important events of the day.

## Discriminate Choice

Beyond the intellectual skills of reading, listening, and the use of critical judgment is the concern for the ability of young people to choose their fare with some degree of discrimination. Because the teaching of this skill has, in general, been neglected, there is a dearth of practical, time-tested techniques. Nevertheless, several can be discussed here. For example, students can be made aware of the social influence of television by studying the racial and national identities of the "good guys" and the "bad guys" in video dramas. A social studies class can play the role of a board of review to establish criteria for what is suitable for public viewing. Similarly, the "board of review" technique can be used to examine the role of the public censor in relation to freedom of speech and press in the community. For the study of propaganda techniques in film making, students can analyze such masterpieces as *The Twisted Cross*, a composite of Nazi propaganda films.

Students can be helped in their choice of mass media by the alert teacher who establishes a student committee for the review and recommendation of selected movies and television programs. Reports and discussions based upon recommended viewing must be part of the ongoing classroom business. Many social studies departments prepare weekly bulletins on coming programs in the mass media to alert teachers to those that are of particular interest.

To develop sensitivity to the social and artistic values expressed in the mass media, the teacher would do well to consult with colleagues who teach the language arts. In prose, the search for social and artistic values has been part of the educational process for generations. In articles and films of interest to the social studies, the teacher can help students to distinguish between the real and the false, the honest and the dishonest. The elements of literary dishonesty can be sought whenever words are printed or spoken — for example, the stereotyped characterization, the "either-or" moral dilemma, the all-black or all-white situation, the oversimplification, the excessive appeal to sentiment, the contrived or trite conclusion. A knowledgeable teacher will not hesitate to analyze with students the technical and artistic values and techniques of film watching and newspaper reading.

To develop a feeling of responsibility on the part of students for improving the general quality of the mass media requires that the student take the role of an active citizen. Young people can be encouraged, as citizens, to write letters of criticism and commendation to the local editor, radio station, television channel, and movie theater proprietor. Many schools sponsor motion picture and television discussion clubs. Social studies classes can be expected to review film documentaries in the same way as magazine and newspaper articles. Outside the classroom, teacher and students can work with parents and civic groups to encourage the community to offer a rich variety of recreational and educational choices in the mass media.

## RESEARCH SKILLS

In our attempts to widen the horizons of our pupils and to encourage them to question the written and spoken word, the social studies teacher must provide students with opportunities for independent study, the use of reference resources and materials, and the reporting, both oral and written, of findings. These processes involve various skills: using the library, note taking and keeping a notebook, and reporting, both oral and written.

### Using the Library

For the student in social studies, intelligent use of the library means training in the use of (1) the card catalog, (2) standard reference works, (3) current periodicals, and (4) the classification system of books.

The use of the card catalog and the classification of books are usually taught elsewhere in the curriculum. No matter what provision is made for library instruction in other subject areas, pupils need specific instruction in the use of social studies reference books and current materials. Library lessons should be built around specific assignments. Whether in the classroom or in the library, the social studies teacher acts as an assistant to the librarian. The librarian, when teaching your class, should plan the lesson with you in terms of topic assigned, materials needed, and procedures to be followed. A mimeographed worksheet listing various types of reference materials to be consulted by the student in relation to the topic has proven to be of great value. Formal library lessons should be planned for each course in the social studies sequence so that the student will have become familiar with these standard reference works by the end of the sequence: dictionaries, encyclopedias, *Readers' Guide*, almanacs, atlases, *Current Biography*, *Who's Who*, and *Dictionary of American Biography*.

No occasion for the use of the library should be allowed to slip by. A student can be sent from the classroom to the library whenever a factual question arises to which the answer can be found in a reference book. In addition to the answer, students should be trained to submit a complete bibliography of references consulted. All reports on assigned subjects should include comprehensive bibliographies. A proper statement of bibliography reflects proper use of the library by the student.

## Note Taking

Taking clear, useful notes from readings, discussions, and lectures is a valuable skill. Although some teachers regard note taking as a hindrance to participation and discussion, for college-bound students, note taking is an essential tool. For every citizen, the ability to take notes increases the ability to participate effectively in civic affairs. Note taking enables the listener to follow more closely the arguments presented.

Note taking in the classroom proceeds with the teacher's systematic outline on the chalkboard of the salient points in the lesson. Students can be trained to take notes during the course of a normal socialized recitation. Oral reports by students should also require note taking on the part of the audience. Assigned viewing of television programs or the hearing of radio presentations should require systematic note taking.

Most pupils fail to understand the value of a notebook because it is not systematically used as an instructional tool by teachers. Notebooks can serve as bases for review and recapitulation of subject matter. To encourage creativity and initiative, the notebook could include special reports, homemade cartoons, annotated news articles, and vocabulary lists in addition to the class notes and homework assignments. Perhaps it is time to stress once again, through the careful keeping of a notebook, the traditional virtues of orderliness, neatness, and thoroughness.

## Reporting

Reports, oral or written, effectively serve to widen the horizons of pupils by supplementing the textbook and the work of the classroom. Students who prepare reports become experts and are brought into discussions as "resource persons." Frequent report opportunities should be provided and, to encourage general participation in the activity, not all reports need be lengthy in pages or time. Extra-credit reports can be included in each day's assignment of homework. These reports can serve as individual enrichment; the class need not share all information in every report.

Oral reports are best when incorporated into the regular class work. Often too many oral reports are scheduled for one class period. A lesson composed entirely of individual reports does not provide for essential activities: discussion, evaluation, summarization. The time for individual reports should be allocated in the daily lesson plan. Students should be encouraged to present their information extemporaneously. Here is another opportunity for the training of students to use notes or an outline.

The term paper, as a research study, is usually patterned after the college-level paper. A certain emphasis is placed on form and style, correctly cited footnotes are expected, and an extensive bibliography correctly listed is customary. Various guides to the writing of term papers are available from publishers.

If the assignment of papers is made early in the term, a sequenced schedule of due dates can be followed. In this way, topics may range widely, students do not overburden the library, and excerpts from the papers can be presented orally at appropriate points to the class. If term papers must be scheduled for one due date toward the end of the semester, provision must be made for accurate appraisal by the teacher and prompt return to the students. All written work should be returned; a student is entitled to know the grade and the reasons for it.

The topic for a research paper should be selected by the student. However, the teacher may provide a master list of topics. Term papers should reflect investigation in depth of a narrow segment rather than superficial treatment of a broad area. A term paper on "The French Revolution" is likely to be valueless as a research project for secondary school pupils. On the other hand, a paper on the "The Causes of the French Revolution" or "The National Assembly of the French Revolution: Its Accomplishments" is narrow enough to channel the investigation and broad enough for material to be available.

## MAP AND GLOBE SKILLS

Skills involving the use of maps and globes should be taught as part of the daily activities of the social studies classroom. The major purpose is to develop the student's awareness of the geographical backgrounds of historical and contemporary events.

The teacher in the secondary school has two important tasks to perform with regard to map and globe skills. First, the teacher must review and, if necessary, reteach the basic skills involved in using these materials. Second, it is important to integrate fully the use of maps and globes in the daily instructional process. Although this section emphasizes the methodology involved in integrating these skills into the total social studies program, a review of the skills is included since the teacher may soon realize that some students have not mastered them in their progress through the grades.

In order to interpret maps and globes adequately and to relate such interpretations to historical and current studies, a student in the secondary school should possess the following skills.

1. Orienting him- or herself to the directions on the map and the place the map illustrates.

2. Recognizing the scale of a map and computing distances.

3. Locating places on maps and globes by means of grid systems.

4. Recognizing and expressing relative locations.

5. Reading symbols and recognizing the realities for which the symbols stand.

Every social studies lesson might include some map work. With the possible exception of an economics class, a case could easily be made for the use of maps or globes in just about every lesson in the social studies sequence.

When should a teacher use a map? The answer depends upon the purpose of the lesson and of a particular skill activity. In daily practice, map-skills activities may be used for any of the following reasons:

1. To stimulate and maintain student interest and participation,

2. To provide specific information about people, places, and events,

3. To orient the student in time and place,

4. To illustrate the effects of great events, trends, and movements.

There are many types of "do-it-yourself" map exercises that can be prepared with a minimum of difficulty. For example, students enjoy the challenge of filling in information on mimeographed outline maps. All schools are equipped with duplicating machines, and there are a number of commercial sources for precut map stencils. Recently, map workbooks have been published that include blank maps and exercises relating map study to a particular topic in the social studies.

In addition to such exercises, pupils can participate in map studies at various times during classroom discussions. The teacher should not indicate a location on a map without first giving students the opportunity to perform this task. Pupils should indicate map locations in such a way that classmates may readily see the area under discussion. A pointer is invaluable for this purpose.

The appropriate map, prominently displayed, affords many opportunities for expression of individual differences in skill and understanding. The pupil who cannot grasp the similarities and differences between the present Northwest and the old Northwest at the time of the Ordinance of 1787 will more readily perceive the difference if a map of the United States at the end of the Revolution is used concurrently with a map of the United States today.

Whenever a point is raised that can be illustrated by reference to a map and the appropriate map is not available, it is better to make a quick sketch, however primitive, than to verbalize without giving the class a chance to visualize. In simplest visual terms, the United States looks like a side of beef, Italy, a boot, England, an hour glass, Mexico, a funnel. Incidentally, pupils may benefit as much as the teacher from the development of map-sketching skills.

Maps, of course, are made to provide information and are most often used directly for that purpose. The teacher today is blessed with a great variety of richly illustrated maps. In addition to the more traditional historical, political, and physical maps of nations and continents, a social studies classroom today may contain maps showing demographic developments, agricultural products, industrial trends, climatic conditions, and so on. Maps are also available in a variety of interesting projections. Three-dimensional plastic relief maps for classroom use can be ordered.

The teacher must consciously and deliberately take advantage of these riches. Students must be exposed from day to day to the new polar projections as often as to the old mercators. Statistical studies and geographic surveys have made available large numbers of maps for enrichment and background information. How much more exciting it is to teach the economy of the USSR employing a map indicating industrial centers, minerals, and agricultural products! Textbooks, too, are now profusely illustrated with maps, gazetteers, and plastic overlays to brighten class work and homework assignments. Frequently, major maps in the textbook parallel larger wall maps; students at their desks can follow better map studies using their books as supplements.

In order to illustrate great events, trends, and movements, it is necessary for students to employ one or more of the basic map skills. An obvious example is the use of maps in the study of the American westward movement. If a class is restricted to one wall map, as is often the case, what procedures can be used effectively? The map must be read accurately for distance, directions, physical features, and topography. As in every lesson, the teacher should stimulate the young person's imagination through a pattern of questions: "If you were the wagonmaster of a train to Oregon, would you start from St. Joseph or Independence, Missouri? Why?" "What time of year would you start? Why?" "Show the class where you think you would be at the end of the first week." "Trace the route you would take; point out the physical barriers you would expect to meet; using the scale of miles on the map, how long would it take your wagon train to reach Portland?"

Systematic map consultation in the classroom is an integral part of the study of such historical developments as wars, revolutions, and migrations. Maps and globes are indispensable in the study of the spread of religions and ideologies, the extent of conquests, the diffusion of cultures, and the spread of economic practices. Extensive use of the map and the globe by the teenager turned "warrior," "revolutionary," or "merchant prince" stimulates interest and imagination, thereby helping the teacher of the social studies reach his or her goal more readily.

## GRAPHIC SKILLS

The use and interpretation of such graphic aids to learning as pictures, photographs, charts, graphs, tables, cartoons, and diagrams provide additional opportunities to enrich teaching in the social studies. As with maps and globes, these materials may be employed to motivate, develop, or summarize learning; they provide information and ideas in concrete and colorful fashion; and they are adaptable to the various levels of pupil abilities in the classroom. Although the various graphic forms may be used in all areas of the social studies, graphs, tables, and charts are especially useful in the teaching of economics.

In presenting graphic materials for study, the teacher must recognize that their successful use often depends upon students' reading abilities as well as their proficiency in critical thinking. Captions and headings may contain difficult vocabulary or concepts requiring a degree of maturity above that of the class. The skillful teacher will adapt such material, and will devote a few minutes of instructional time to minimizing the difficulties students may encounter in the use and interpretation of the aids. Examples of study sheets based on simple graphic material may be found in Exhibits 6-6 and 6-7 in this chapter.

In selecting graphic aids for study, the teacher should consider the following criteria:

1. Is the picture, photo, or other graphic presentation relevant to the topic under discussion?
2. Does it present significant and truthful information?
3. Is it challenging?
4. May it be used to study important relationships?
5. Does it fit the level of the class in terms of the students' maturity and abilities?

In using graphics, students must understand the purpose of such studies. For example, they may study a chart or a cartoon for information. They may examine a statistical table to form a general impression of an economic or demographic trend. On a more difficult level, they may wish to use a graphic device for interpreting and applying the information it contains. In all cases, the objective for which a particular graphic is being used must be clearly set forth by the teacher and understood by the students.

Secondary school teachers tend to minimize the use of still photographs and pictures, generally preferring to substitute films and filmstrips. This is unfortunate for it creates a dependence upon the editorial skills of film producers and minimizes the degree of selectivity a teacher may exercise. A picture file containing mounted graphic materials selected by the teacher from national weekly magazines and other sources should be stored conveniently in the department office and made accessible to the entire staff. Teachers should not ignore the photographs and other graphic materials currently being incorporated into textbooks, which provide many opportunities for interpretive exercises in homework assignments as well as in class. Unless the teacher can secure a set of books for classroom use, there should be little hesitancy in requiring students to bring textbooks to class whenever a specific graphic study is planned. Also important for instruction in social studies are the many picture books being published for adult use in which the major part of historical or scientific information is conveyed through the use of photos, charts, and reproductions of original source materials. These should be made available for student reference in the school library and for teacher use in the classroom.

Graphic materials can enrich instruction on all levels of ability. Students who are deficient in verbal skills can be provided with much information needed to study a given topic through the study of simplified graphic presentations. For example, Table 6–2 may be used to develop important concepts with regard to Athenian democracy. From this table even the slower learners will perceive the limited nature of Athenian citizenship, the inferior position accorded to women, the dependence upon slave labor, and the restrictions placed upon those not born in Athens.

In planning activities, the teacher should provide opportunities for students to prepare their own graphic materials. They may be incorporated into bulletin-board displays, notebook work, homework assignments, special reports, and the like. Through such activities, students are more likely to perceive the processes involved in creating such materials and will develop a greater respect for the results of the work of others.

## A SUMMARY STATEMENT ON SOCIAL STUDIES TEACHERS AND STUDENT LITERACY

While reading, as a learning skill, does not have the monopoly it once had before the advent of the media revolution in education, it remains essential. Nothing yet invented contains the teaching capability of a textbook or a paperback book. The magic of reading provides the student with vital insights that are not readily available from other learning tools in the same compact form. Reading material, in addition, can be mastered at the learner's individual rate, and, therefore, a reading assignment lends itself to individualization. For this reason, teachers will continue to assign reading passages in text material and in teacher-designed study sheets.

As a skill, reading is essential for the enlightened citizen. In order to make civic judgments, a citizen must read background literature, such as newspapers and pamphlets. There is no conflict between teaching reading and teaching social studies. They are permanently linked to each other.

**TABLE 6–2.**  *Athens, 450 B.C.*

| | |
|---|---|
| Adult male citizens with power to vote | 40,000 |
| Citizens without political power (women, children, some men) | 80,000 |
| Foreign-born residents of Athens | 80,000 |
| Slaves | 250,000 |
| Total population | 450,000 |

•••••••••••••••••••••••••••••••••••••••••••••••••••••••••••••••••••••••••••••••••••••••••••

# EXHIBIT 6–1.    Sample of a Cloze Test

•••••••••••••••••••••••••••••••••••••••••••••••••••••••••••••••••••••••••••••••••••••••••••

### How does a bill become a law*

Lawmaking and the Constitution. Lawmaking is one of the most important jobs of government. For laws are the (1)_____ by which a government (2)_____ the activities of its (3)_____. By telling them what (4)_____ may or may not (5)_____, the government makes it (6)_____ for large numbers of (7)_____ to live together in (8)_____. Laws also deal with (9)_____ important matters, such as (10)_____ taxes people pay and (11)_____ services they receive in (12)_____ for taxes. These services (13)_____ keeping order, helping people (14)_____ need, and protecting the (15)_____ from its enemies.

  In (16)_____ absolute monarchy or dictatorship, (17)_____ are made by one (18)_____. This is probably the (19)_____ and simplest way to (20)_____ them. In a modern (21)_____, on the other hand, (22)_____ is neither fast nor (23)_____. The people elect hundreds (24)_____ representatives. These men come (25)_____ different parts of the (26)_____. They belong to different (27)_____ parties and represent people (28)_____ all sorts of interests. (29)_____ do these representatives agree (30)_____ what laws to make (31)_____ our nation?

| | | |
|---|---|---|
| 1. _____ | 12. _____ | 22. _____ |
| 2. _____ | 13. _____ | 23. _____ |
| 3. _____ | 14. _____ | 24. _____ |
| 4. _____ | 15. _____ | 25. _____ |
| 5. _____ | 16. _____ | 26. _____ |
| 6. _____ | 17. _____ | 27. _____ |
| 7. _____ | 18. _____ | 28. _____ |
| 8. _____ | 19. _____ | 29. _____ |
| 9. _____ | 20. _____ | 30. _____ |
| 10. _____ | 21. _____ | 31. _____ |
| 11. _____ | | |

*Reprinted by permission from Schwartz and O'Connor, *Exploring Our Nation's History*, Globe Book Company, Inc.

*Exhibit 6-1.  Sample of a Cloze Test*     **125**

## Cloze test answer sheet

Students must supply the *exact* word for the purpose of estimating percentages. However, a student who can provide a suitable synonym obviously comprehends the material, and the teacher should consider this in deciding how much support is necessary or whether an easier book should be provided.

### Answer key

| | | |
|---|---|---|
| 1. rules | 12. return | 22. lawmaking |
| 2. regulates | 13. include | 23. simple |
| 3. people | 14. in | 24. of |
| 4. they | 15. nation | 25. from |
| 5. do | 16. an | 26. country |
| 6. possible | 17. laws | 27. political |
| 7. people | 18. man | 28. with |
| 8. peace | 19. fastest | 29. How |
| 9. other | 20. make | 30. on |
| 10. the | 21. democracy | 31. for |
| 11. the | | |

### Scoring

Independent Level — 57%

Instruction Level — 44%–57%

Frustration Level — Below 44%

## EXHIBIT 6-2.    Graph for Estimating Readability*

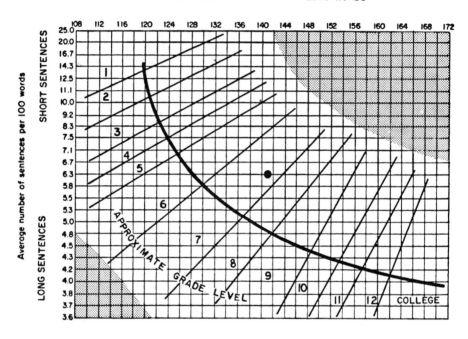

Average number of syllables per 100 words

SHORT WORDS                     LONG WORDS

DIRECTIONS:  Randomly select 3 one hundred word passages from a book or an article. Plot average
            number of syllables and average number of sentences per 100 words on graph to
            determine the grade level of the material. Choose more passages per book if great
            variability is observed and conclude that the book has uneven readability. Few books
            will fall in gray area but when they do grade level scores are invalid.

|            |                   | SYLLABLES | SENTENCES |
|------------|-------------------|-----------|-----------|
| EXAMPLE:   | 1st Hundred Words | 124       | 6.6       |
|            | 2nd Hundred Words | 141       | 5.5       |
|            | 3rd Hundred Words | 158       | 6.8       |
|            | AVERAGE           | 141       | 6.3       |

READABILITY 7th GRADE (see dot plotted on graph)

*By Edward Fry, Rutgers University Reading Center, New Jersey. Reprinted by permission.

# EXHIBIT 6-3.  Sample of Rewritten Material (first revision)

| Original | Comments | Revision I |
|---|---|---|
| The Constitution has successfully survived the years as the supreme law of the land for two main reasons. First, it lays down rules of procedure that must be followed even when critical circumstances arise. Second, it is a "living" document, flexible enough to meet the changing needs of a growing nation. By a number of means, as you will see, Americans have been able to adapt the Constitution to changing times. So it is that the Constitution works as well today for an industrialized nation of fifty states and a population approaching 200,000,000 people as it once worked for an agricultural nation of thirteen states and 4,000,000 people. | Doublespace.<br><br>Shorten sentences.<br>Number paragraphs.<br><br>Reduce number of modifying clauses.<br><br>Maintain concept by including illustration.<br><br>Clarify abstraction with illustration.<br><br>Start new paragraph to break up block of print (if logic is not destroyed). Retain "difficult" but germane terms.<br><br>Change a long, involved sentence into several short ones. | The Constitution is the *highest* law of this country. It has been the highest, or the supreme law of the United States since the year 1791. That is almost 200 years! Why has the Constitution survived so very long? There are several reasons. One reason is that it tells the rules that the country must follow at all times, in good times and in difficult times. This means that there is never a time when anyone can say, "Well, we will not use the Constitution this month. We will just ignore it." No. The Constitution must be used at all times.<br><br>A second reason why the Constitution has lasted is that it can be changed when the country changes. It is *flexible*. The U.S.A. has changed in many ways since 1791. Our population today is about 200,000,000. In 1791 our population was about 4,000,000. In 1791 we had thirteen states. Today we have fifty. We have changed from a nation of farms in 1791 to a nation of industry today. When the country was changing, the Constitution was changing, too. Because the Constitution is flexible, it works as well for us today as it did in 1791. |

(From Todd and Cutti, *Rise of the American Nation*)

# EXHIBIT 6-4. Sample of Rewritten Material (second revision)

| Revision I | Comments | Revision II |
|---|---|---|
| The Constitution is the *highest* law of this country. It has been the highest, or the supreme law of the United States since the year 1791. That is almost 200 years! Why has the Constitution survived so very long? There are several reasons. One reason is that it tells the rules that the country must follow at all times, in good times and in difficult times. This means that there is never a time when anyone can say, "Well, we will not use the Constitution this month. We will just ignore it." No. The Constitution must be used at all times. | Shorten paragraph length if logic permits. | 1. The most *important* law in the U.S.A. is the 2. Constitution. It is the *supreme* law of the 3. United States. 4. The Constitution was written in the year 5. 1791. Why has the Constitution *survived* for 6. so long? There are two main reasons. 7. One reason the Constitution has *survived* is 8. that it tells us the rules that must be used at 9. all times. We can never say, "We will not use 10. the Constitution today." No. We must 11. always use it. |
| | Replace abstract word. | |
| | Present 'new' multi-syllable word in syllables. | |
| | Retain vital vocabulary. | |
| | Repetition reinforces the idea. | |
| | Organizational word clue. | |
| A second reason why the Constitution has lasted is that it can be changed when the country changes. It is *flexible*. The U.S.A. has changed in many ways since 1791. Our population today is about 200,000,000. In 1791 our population was about 4,000,000. Today we have fifty. We have changed from a nation of farms in 1791 to a nation of industry today. When the country was changing, the Constitution was changing, too. Because the Constitution is flexible, it works as well for us today as it did in 1791. | Numerals can replace words. | 12. A second reason it has *survived* is that it can 13. be changed. It is *flexible*. The U.S. has 14. changed in many ways since 1791. 15. *For example,* our population in 1791 was 16. about 4,000,000. Today our nation's population is about 200,000,000. In 1791 we had 13 18. states. Today we have 50 states. In 1791 19. most people worked on farms, but today 20. *most people work in industry.* 21. When the U.S.A. changed, the Constitution 22. changed, too. That is why the Constitution 23. works as well for us today as it did in 1791. |
| | Reduce abstract to concrete. | |

# EXHIBIT 6–5. Sample of Rewritten Material (third revision)

| Revision II | Comments | Revision III |
|---|---|---|
| 1. The most important law in the U.S.A. is the<br>2. Constitution. It is the *supreme* law of the<br>3. United States.<br>4. The Constitution was written in the year<br>5. 1791. Why has the Constitution *survived* for<br>6. so long? There are two main reasons.<br>7. One reason the Constitution has *survived* is<br>8. that it tells us the rules that must be used at<br>9. all times. We can never say, "We will not use<br>10. the Constitution today." No. We must<br>11. always use it.<br>12. A second reason it has *survived* is that it can<br>13. be changed. It is *flexible*. The U. S. has<br>14. changed in many ways since 1791.<br>15. *For example*, our population in 1791 was<br>16. about 4,000,000. Today our nation's popula-<br>17. tion is about 200,000,000. In 1791 we had 13<br>18. states. Today we have 50 states. In 1791<br>19. most people worked on farms, but today<br>20. *most people work in industry.*<br>21. When the U.S.A. changed, the Constitution<br>22. changed, too. That is why the Constitution<br>23. works as well for us today as it did in 1791. | Shorten paragraphs.<br><br>Reduce from abstract to concrete.<br><br>Replace referent pronouns with repetition of noun.<br><br>Retain vital vocabulary but give synonym.<br><br>Use format to express organization of ideas. | The most important law of the U.S.A. is the Constitution. It is the *supreme* law of the United States.<br>The Constitution is almost 200 years old! How can we use this one law for so many years? Why did the Constitution *survive?* The Constitution stayed alive because:<br>1. It tells the United States how to run the country at all times. We must use the Constitution in good times and in bad times.<br>2. It can be changed. When the U.S.A. changes, we can change the Constitution.<br>Here are some ways that the United States has changed since 1791: |

| *In 1791* | *Today* |
|---|---|
| Most people were farmers. | Most people work in industry. |
| There were 13 states. | There are 50 states. |
| The population was about 4,000,000. | The population is about 200,000,000. |

## EXHIBIT 6-6.    Study Sheet Based on a Cartoon

*Source:* Permission to reprint by Don Wright, *The Miami News.*

*Instructions:* Study the cartoon and answer the following questions:

1. Who do you think the figure represents?
2. What is he doing?
3. What policy of the United States do you think the badge represents?
4. Why do you think the badge is where it is?
5. What events do you think might have led to the decision depicted in the cartoon?
6. Do you think the badge should ever be picked up and worn again? If your answer is "yes," explain the conditions under which the badge should be worn again. If your answer is "no," explain your reasons for believing that the badge should never again be worn.
7. Write a caption for this cartoon.

*Exhibit 6-7   Study Sheet Based on a Graph*   **131**

## EXHIBIT 6-7.   Study Sheet Based on a Graph

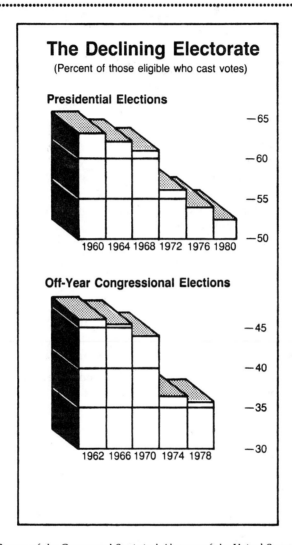

**The Declining Electorate**
(Percent of those eligible who cast votes)

**Presidential Elections**

**Off-Year Congressional Elections**

*Source:* U. S. Bureau of the Census and Statistical Abstract of the United States.

*Instructions:*   Study the graph and answer the following questions:

**Multiple choice**

1. What percentage of those eligible voted in the presidential election of 1960?

   a. 64%   b. 60%   c. 55%   d. 50%

2. What percentage of those eligible voted in the presidential election of 1980?

   a. 64%   b. 60%   c. 52.5%   d. 50%

3. Which statement best compares presidential elections with congressional elections?

   a. More people vote in congressional elections.
   b. More people vote in presidential elections.
   c. About the same vote in both elections.
   d. The percentage of people voting in congressional elections is on the increase.

4. Which is a trend revealed by this graph?

   a. There is an increase of eligible voters who vote in elections.
   b. There is a decrease in the percentage of eligible voters who vote in elections.
   c. The percentage of eligible voters who vote in both elections has remained the same since 1960.
   d. The eligibility of eighteen-year-olds to vote since 1972 has increased interest in elections.

### Opinion essay questions

1. Other democratic nations have a larger turnout of eligible voters. Sweden, for example, has a 90 percent rate. In your opinion, what can be done to increase our rate of voter turnout?

2. In Australia citizens pay a fine if they do not vote. Should the United States have a law penalizing nonvoters?

## BIBLIOGRAPHY

### Books on Reading

Aukerman, Robert C. *Reading in the Secondary School Classroom.* (New York: McGraw Hill, 1972).

Hafner, Lawrence E. *Improving Reading in Secondary Schools—Selected Readings.* (New York: MacMillan Publishing Co., 1967).

Herber, Harold L. *Teaching Reading in the Content Area.* (Englewood Cliffs, New Jersey: Prentice-Hall, 1970).

Shepherd, David L. *Comprehensive High School Reading Methods.* (Columbus, Ohio: Charles E. Merrill Publishing Co., 1973).

Thomas, Ellen Lamar and Robinson, H. Alan, *Improving Reading in Every Class.* (Boston: Allyn and Bacon, 1973).

Viex, Ruth, *Evaluating Reading and Study Skills in the Secondary Classroom.* (Newark, Delaware: International Reading Association, 1968).

**Curriculum Bulletins**

"Reading in the Subject Areas," Chapter 6 in the *Handbook for the Language Arts, Grades 6–12: Reading and Literature* (New York City Board of Education, 1967–1968 Series).

*English Language Arts*–Reading. (New York State Department of Education, Albany, New York, 1968).

*Sequential Levels of Reading Skills: Pre-K through Grade 12* (New York City Board of Education, 1967–1968 Series).

*The Reading Process in the Content Areas.* (Board of Education, School District of Philadelphia Instructional Services, 1973).

*Reading in the Subject Areas, Grades 7, 8 and 9.* (Bureau of Curriculum Development, Board of Education of the City of New York).

# 7

••••••••••••••••••••••••••••••••••••••••••••••••••••••••••••••••••••••••••••••••••••

# Writing Skills

••••••••••••••••••••••••••••••••••••••••••••••••••••••••••••••••••••••••••••••••••••

## WHY THE SOCIAL STUDIES TEACHER
## EMPHASIZES WRITING SKILLS

"I am a social studies teacher, not an English teacher. Why do I have to teach writing?" This question is frequently asked by teachers in our discipline as more and more pressure is being exerted on them. The question deserves an answer.

To start, the teaching of writing has always been part of social studies. The social studies teacher has traditionally asked essay test questions, assigned the writing of essay questions for homework, and required term papers and other assorted written projects. Writing outlines on the board and taking notes have been standard fare in the social studies classroom. In addition, in the past many teachers have made written expression an integral part of a lesson. The new emphasis on writing skills follows from the needs of students whose lack of skills stands in their way of doing these writing activities and from the fact that the social studies teacher in the secondary school can no longer take for granted that students are equipped with the necessary writing skills. Secondary students represent the full range of ability, from slow to bright, from those who need to learn how to spell and write complete sentences to those who muddle sophisticated thoughts in sentence structures that are needlessly complex.

It should bring a sense of professional satisfaction that teachers are being called upon to help students develop a concrete skill. Teachers report immediate, observable improvement in students whom they help to learn writing skills. We strive to instill good citizenship in our students. This is not immediately observable. However, when we help provide our students with the necessary skills to write a letter to their elected representatives, we may feel that we have helped them take a positive step towards good citizenship.

We also help our students in a concrete way when we help them write. Writing does not come naturally to many young people. Even adults who have become professional writers frequently tell of their earlier struggles with writing. One famous author tells of waiting expectantly as an eleven-year-old to show his father his latest poem and then having the bubble burst when his father came home and declared, "This is the worst poem I've ever read." The author admitted that upon reflection the poem was terrible. While this incident has multiple significances, one of its meanings is that accomplished writers are not born, they are made. Social studies teachers can be part of this process.

There is another significance to be drawn from the above incident. For better or worse, the father did provide a reaction to a creative effort. This is a necessary ingredient in helping students to write well. Since so much of social studies writing is of the persuasive or opinionated nature and invites response, a social studies class can bring positive or negative reinforcement. This can be in the form of a teacher's written comment or a classmate's reaction to a point made in a written project read to the class. Opportunities for provocation exist in social studies classes, which are geared for controversy.

It is to be expected that students will enjoy writing more if assignments are based on the students' need to take a position on an emotional issue. Social studies is replete with issues such as euthanasia, abortion, drugs, war and war prevention, and population control. The issues are there, as is the opportunity to express oneself in writing. Moreover, the social studies class provides the student with an evaluative audience.

Learning to write cannot take place in a vacuum. It cannot be mastered in a singular situation, once and for all. Writing is taught effectively within a medium. That medium is the content area.

Once learned in the content area, for example science, writing skills cannot necessarily be transferred to another content area, such as social studies. Nor should we expect the transference of writing skills from subjects within social studies, for example, from history to economics. Educational psychologists tell us that learning how to write in a "content-free" (a nonsocial studies or a nonhistory) course does not automatically insure the transfer of writing proficiency to social studies or history.[1] This is the reason that many colleges divide their freshman writing seminars into disciplines—e. g., writing for science majors, writing for social science majors, writing for business majors. Each discipline emphasizes different writing skills. Writing, therefore, must be taught within all disciplines including social studies.

Finally, there is another compelling reason for being concerned with writing skills. As social studies teachers, we stress thinking skills. Writing and thinking go together. The writing process involves the clarification of thought, the organization of ideas, and the discerning of relationships. Ideas emerge through reflective writing.

# HOW CAN STUDENTS BE MOTIVATED TO WRITE?

"I can't write! I hate to write!" Even students well into their high school years often give this type of response to a written assignment. Indeed, many times in marking final examinations teachers discover that an otherwise excellent student did well on all the objective questions but left the essay portion blank. Teachers have to work at helping students overcome their writing cramps.

Before we discuss the unmotivated student, let us consider the student who is motivated but is a victim of "writing paralysis."

Students who express themselves well orally are frequently not able to convert their thoughts to writing. There is something frightening about writing. Perhaps it is the permanence of writing on a piece of paper which is so disquieting. The teacher must inspire confidence and reassure the students, especially about getting started. Students frequently sit at their desks awaiting a profound thought to begin their essay. They also wish to begin with style and a flourish. If they have read Paine and Rousseau, they may want to begin their essay with something on a par with "These are the times that try men's souls" or "Man is born free, but everywhere he is in chains."

To counter this form of writer's cramp, the teacher has to encourage the student. "The best way to begin is to begin," the teacher advises. "The great opening sentence frequently occurs to the creative writer after the complete essay has been created." The teacher should look around the room to make sure that each student has started promptly when a reasonable time has elapsed after the written assignment has been given. To begin promptly without waiting for a brilliant beginning is one of the suggestions made for students in Exhibit 7-1. Another recommendation gives a standard way to start: "Incorporate key words of the question into the opening sentence."

This solution to the problem of starting an essay presumes that students do want to write. This is not entirely so. Many students do not want to write; making them want to is another concern of the teacher: the problem of motivation.

The best way of looking at the problem of motivation concerning writing skills is to imagine that the teacher has to recreate the invention of writing. When devising strategies for motivating students to write, the teacher has to develop within them a terrific urge to write. For example, an Egyptian boy might have had to send a message to his father telling him that the Nile had crested and that the flood waters were about to sweep down on their farm, while at the same time the boy desired to stem the flow by remaining at the river to reinforce the embankment and control the flooding. Such a boy would have had a great urge to scrawl something on a papyrus leaf. You can try to provide your students with a similar urge.

Adolescent psychology helps at this point. What are adolescents interested in? What will they regard as urgent? Adolescents are interested, among other things, in boy/girl relationships, generational problems, and fairness in interpersonal relations. You may have heard an adolescent praise a teacher by saying, "He is hard but *fair*." Themes of interpersonal relationships, moral dilemmas, and conflicts as to what is fair constantly appear in social studies. As an example, the teacher might role-play a distraught parent (generational problem) finding a note pinned to the pillow of a child who has gone off to a frontier settlement to find fame and fortune or who has joined the children's crusade (or an army) to fight in a foreign war. The teacher would then ask students to write out the contents of the note explaining the runaway child's reasons for leaving, which would be the least that the child could do (sense of fairness). This strategy was incorporated in an actual lesson on the settlement of the Northwest Territory, as shown in Exhibit 7-2. In general, one can say that the strategy worked because the teacher played on the students' emotions. He made the students want to write. They wrote things about the Northwest Territory, about educational and economic opportunities, the prohibition of slavery, and the opportunity to develop a republican form of government that they would have normally not written if the teacher had asked mundanely, "Write an essay about the provisions of the Northwest Ordinance of 1787." The list of writing activities in Exhibit 7-3 contains several suggestions for imaginative strategies that will help motivate students to write.

The most serious cases of writing cramp can be handled with the use of a tape recorder. The teacher should stress that the best writing is based on the spoken word. What we say will look good in writing, if only we can get it down on paper the way we said it. To back up this point, the teacher asks a student a question. The student's response is tape recorded. The teacher then directs the student to write down what he said, using the tape recorder as a dictaphone. Students are generally amazed at how well their spoken words look in writing.

## NEEDED: A SYSTEMATIC APPROACH TO TEACHING WRITING

We teach writing skills by organizing a sequence that goes from the simple to the complex. Unlike riding a bicycle, learning how to write does not mean you always know how to write well. The recommended sequence should be taught in each lesson, included in each course of study, and covered throughout the term. In classical biological evolutionary theory, this sequence was expressed in the phrase "ontogeny recapitulates phylogeny": every individual relived its evolutionary history. We are proposing that every writing lesson recapitulate the learning process in stages. Furthermore, a semester's work should be divided into the same stages.

What are the stages of learning how to write in social studies? The beginning stage is called "narrative," the intermediary stage is called "generalization," and the final stage is called "hypothetical." Note that in Exhibit 7–2 in the lesson about the problems of inflation, the students have three written class assignments following the above taxonomy. 1) As preparation for the lesson, students had to write a transcript of an interview concerning the effects of inflation. This is a simple form of narrative. 2) Students then had to draw conclusions from their interviews. This is a form of generalization. 3) Finally, students had to create a mock interview in which an individual expressed an opinion on an inflation-fighting measure, such as government-enforced ceilings on prices and wages. This is the hypothetical stage of social studies writing.

In similar fashion, using the same breakdown, the teacher can plan units of work and courses of study. For an elective course in Latin-American studies, for example, in the first part of the term one teacher stressed making written answers to information-gathering questions, e. g., What were the mercantile practices of Spanish colonial rule? In the middle third of the term, the students had to apply themselves more frequently to questions that asked them to generalize, e. g., How did the single-crop economic system affect the development of Brazil? The final third of the term saw the teacher emphasizing opinion and conjecture. Students had to write a "State Department White Paper" on the question, "What should be the United States policy towards El Salvador?"

As simple as this recommendation is—going from basic material to the complex—many teachers overwhelm their students early in the term with too sophisticated written assignments and thereby discourage effective writing. Frustration is the biggest obstacle to good writing. A teacher should not stress the most advanced form of writing until the student has gained confidence in mastering the course content.

## THE PARAGRAPH AS THE BASIC ORGANIZING UNIT

Grade-school teachers teach that the sentence is the basic unit of writing. While it is true that some students progress into high school without the ability to write a simple sentence, for the vast majority of high school students, the paragraph is the big stumbling block. Lacking the ability to write paragraphs handicaps many students. Without coherent paragraphs, students' essays reflect scattershot thinking, and their ideas do not emerge. Students have to be taught that the best writing takes place when each sentence contains one basic idea and that a collection of basic ideas around a theme is called a paragraph. Paragraph writing helps students to organize their ideas to form arguments or explanations.

Writing paragraphs also forces students to elaborate with more information, which makes for an interesting presentation. In an essay test, providing more information means a higher grade. In the absence of effective paragraph writing, students will blurt out the information that first occurs to them and their effort will soon be exhausted. When a student writes paragraphs, he or she searches the mind for additional information to round out the paragraph. The paragraph format provides a design for factual exposition or persuasion.

Let us review the structure of a typical paragraph. There are three components: an introductory sentence which announces the topic of the paragraph; two or three development sentences which present the pertinent facts; and the concluding sentence which arrives at a summation or leads to the next paragraph. A diagram that contains the above components should be placed on the chalkboard.

The teacher should then state, "Let's answer a question on the Dred Scott decision. How did it influence sectional tension? Does anyone have an introductory sentence to start us off?" After obtaining one and placing it in the appropriate space, the teacher can ask for a sentence that develops the topic. The teacher then asks for an elaboration. This is placed in the space labeled "development sentences." Then the teacher asks for a statement that wraps it up or provides a lead into the next paragraph. As the paragraph emerges, it looks like the illustration – after erasing the numbers and labels.

The teacher then declares that the next paragraph can begin with a topical sentence on an abolitionist such as John Brown and asks for a suggestion. The process continues until a model essay is developed by the class in paragraph form. All term long, the teacher reminds students how to form paragraphs, indicating on their papers with the mark ¶ where a paragraph should begin, or where one should not have begun, with the mark N¶. By constantly reminding students that paragraphing is necessary, the teacher can train them to think in terms of paragraphs. The student who is trained this way will be immensely helped in doing homework, writing essay examinations, letters, and term papers.

An exercise that can be integrated into a lesson is shown in Exhibit 7–4, on the Dred Scott case. Here the teacher puts a series of sentences containing historical data on the chalkboard or on a duplicated worksheet. The teacher then directs the students to use these sentences in a paragraph.

| Introductory Sentence (Topical Sentence) | 1) |
| Development Sentences | 2)<br>3) |
| Concluding Sentence | 4) |

> *The Dred Scott Case helped to bring on the Civil War. Chief Justice Taney's decision declared that Dred Scott was not a citizen, but property. Moreover, he stated the Missouri Compromise was unconstitutional. This angered the Northern abolitionists and made some of them more fanatical.*

## THE USE OF LINKING WORDS AND PHRASES

To do this kind of writing exercise, leading to cohesive writing ability, students have to be helped in mastering the use of linking words and phrases. Sentences have to be joined together to form thoughts. The words listed on page 142 in the chart on "signals" are the glue. These words link sentences together. In the chapter on reading, the teacher is urged to explain the meaning of linking words such as "however" and "therefore." It is hoped that students will thus anticipate the meaning of a sentence that begins with one of these words. In teaching writing skills, the teacher has to instruct students to use signal words if they, as writers, want to communicate with their readers. Without the use of linking words, the students will not be able to present their thoughts in writing.

When we speak, we signal listeners of a change in meaning through facial expressions, gestures, and inflections in our voice. Remind students that, for example, when they want to present the other side of an argument in oral speech, they indicate they are about to do this by changing their tone of voice. In order to do this in writing, it is necessary to use a phrase such as "on the other hand." The teaching of the use of linking words and phrases is essential in social studies, because a social studies essay has to convey to the reader the thought processes that the writer is undergoing. It must not be merely a collection of unrelated facts.

A simple oral drill at the beginning of the term will help establish the usefulness of linking expressions. The teacher should say to the class, "In history we are interested in causation—what caused a war, inflation, or depression. Whenever I begin a question with the interrogative 'Why,' you should immediately think of an anwer that begins with the preposition 'Because.' Let's practice this."

> Teacher:   Why did the Supreme Court decide that the hostage deal was constitutional? Alfred?
>
> Alfred:   Because, to arrange a deal was part of the President's power to make foreign policy.

The teacher would then explain that whenever students are asked to write on causation, they might begin their essays with "why" questions to be answered with sentences containing the linking word "because."

There are other examples of the thought processes frequently utilized in social studies and of the linking words that can help students express their thoughts in writing:

**Contrast or disagreement**

| | |
|---|---|
| But | In spite of |
| However | Although |
| On the other hand | Conversely |
| In contrast | Nevertheless |

**To show direct relationship** (agreement)

| | |
|---|---|
| Similarly | In addition |
| And | Furthermore |
| Or (choice) | Moreover |

**To announce factual information**
A case in point
To illustrate
An example is

**To reach a conclusion**

| | |
|---|---|
| Consequently | Finally |
| Thus | Hence |
| In conclusion | In summation |

The social studies teacher has to teach students how to use these linking expressions so that they can apply them in written discourse. For example, the teacher might ask, "How would you link these two sentences to show that they express two opposing views?"

1. The Israeli raid of the Osirak nuclear plant in Iraq was a defensive measure.

2. There was no clearcut evidence that the plant was to be used to make a bomb.

The teacher would accept the students' response "however" to be inserted before the second sentence. The teacher would also invite the class to evaluate the usefulness of the insertion of a linking word by asking, "Would the two statements make any sense standing alongside each other without a linking word?"

## ENCOURAGING STUDENTS TO WRITE WITH DETAILS

Did you ever ask a student how he or she liked a motion picture and obtain a one-word response like "Yeah"? The student might want to describe why he or she liked the picture or disliked it, but does not know how. Unfortunately, many adolescents are equally as taciturn in their social studies writing. They over-use pronouns and fail to make antecedents clear. They do not mention specific places, dates, or names of countries. They do not give reasons for their opinions. These editorial marks may be used as a reminder for students:

V = vague

Too gen = too general

NCL = not clear

Beyond such reminders, how do we obtain specificity in student writing? One teacher used this device to convince the students that writing with details makes both listening and reading more interesting:

Which of these descriptions of the movie *Superman* do you like?
a. Like this, baby come from outer space from this planet, you know. He's different, you know. He goes to this city and gets a job. Like he fights them bad guys, you know.

The teacher then said "Do we really know?" The students realized that nothing specific was said.

Another response might have been:

b. A planet by the name of Krypton in a distant galaxy blows up, but before it does they send a child to the planet earth. He has super powers such as the ability to fly and x-ray vision. He gets a job as a reporter in the city of Metropolis and soon fights crime. One criminal is Lex Luthor, an evil scientist.

The teacher would ask the class, "What is the difference between examples **A** and B? The intention is to show that detail can enhance visual imagery and heighten interest.

At this point the student should be ready to write something with specific details. It is a good time to introduce linking words that induce the use of details, such as "An example is." Students will realize that they cannot begin a sentence this way without providing a specific example.

## RESPONDING TO STUDENTS' WRITING

"I would like to help my students write better, but I am drowning under paper!" This is an oft-heard complaint of teachers. Recent research on responding to student writing suggests a redefinition of the teacher's role as an evaluator and also recasts the teacher in a role that is less burdensome. These are the findings:[2]

1. Effective evaluation does not necessarily mean marking up a paper with a lot of corrections in red ink. Indeed, some educational psychologists would recommend that no corrections in style be placed on the student's paper, and that only responses to the substance of the paper be recorded. This is an extreme position, but that it is widely held in some circles should help all teachers rethink how much and what type of interlineation is most effective.
2. Feedback is needed to encourage skilled writing, but the feedback need not be entirely from the teacher. Educational research indicates no significant improvement in writing results obtained when only the teacher reacted to students' writing as compared to feedback from other students. Therefore, the teacher should design evaluation which includes peer feedback. This means allowing time for students to exchange papers and to write their reactions to each other. Students might even correct each other's papers before they are finally handed in to the teacher. These papers will be handed in appreciably improved from the original version, and both the student author and student evaluator learn much in the process.

Another way of providing the student writer with peer evaluation is to assign a brief written task during the daily lesson. As the teacher circulates among the students, he or she selects samples of the completed assignment to be placed on the chalkboard. The author's classmates are asked to react to the student's writing placed on the chalkboard. Peer approval or appraisal is extremely effective in this situation.

When papers are marked by the teacher, it would be useful to maintain a perspective based on the objectives for assigning written work. The main purpose is not the evaluation of cognitive recall. Short-answer objective questions do this better. The purpose is to test students for conceptualization, commitment to ideals and values, organizational ability, and clarity of thought. These affective objectives can be evaluated without going over the students' papers with a fine-tooth comb. A guide to responding to student writing that reflects this reasonable approach can be found in Exhibit 7–5.

A curriculum bulletin published by the New York City Board of Education[3] makes many excellent suggestions on responding to student writing, such as "Positive comments can take the form of a restatement of what the student has said: 'Yes, vaccines do produce antibodies.'" The teacher succeeds in encouraging the student by giving positive feedback on the content of the paper rather than its style.

The holistic method of assessing student writing can be used effectively by teachers in all curriculum areas. In holistic evaluation, the teacher reads quickly through a student's essay to grasp the whole meaning. The teacher might then focus on some particular feature. This has been referred to as "primary trait evaluation." The particular trait evaluated might be the ability to explain causation or to express an opinion on an issue. If the student's main objective is carried out, the teacher need not splatter the paper with red marks which could easily discourage the student in subsequent efforts at writing. Communication by means of interchanging ideas is the main goal.

The dimensions of the problem faced by teachers in developing writing skills warrant an acceptance of this basic idea. It is preferable not to limit the amount of assigned writing by the time a teacher has to mark students' papers. Creative strategies must be found for motivating students to write and for providing feedback. The feedback need not always come from the teacher.

## HOW TO HELP STUDENTS WRITE RESEARCH PAPERS IN SOCIAL STUDIES

*Teacher's Introduction.* When confronted with the assignment to prepare a research paper, many students are confused and apprehensive. If you are going to require your students to write a paper based on several types of sources and including a large number of footnotes, it is advisable to introduce the assignment in two or three lessons rather than overwhelm the students by presenting the entire project during a forty-minute period.

*Lesson I.* Ask the students if they have heard of Sherlock Holmes or Perry Mason. Discuss the idea that a skillful detective hunts for clues and pieces them together to unravel a puzzle and discover the truth. As term-paper writers, the students are also going to search for pieces of information that relate to a particular problem, their research topic. After they have found this information, they are going to fit it together in a logical sequence to solve the problem they have posed.

Just as Sherlock Holmes, a master detective, could solve crimes that were too difficult for others, professional social scientists can offer meaningful solutions to complex problems. Amateur detectives can solve less difficult problems, so high school students should choose topics that can be researched easily.

At this point, the teacher has two choices. You can require students to choose their topic from a preselected list, or you may allow them to go to the library and find a topic on their own. Many students prefer an assigned list because this makes it easier to select a suitable topic. However, if your primary purpose in making this assignment is to teach term-paper writing skills rather than specific content material, it may be more beneficial to allow students to find their own topics. (They may be motivated to work harder on topics that are intrinsically more interesting to them.) In the event you decide to follow this second course, be certain to allow sufficient time in class to discuss methods of choosing a topic and to scrutinize all topics to assure both that they are limited in scope and that local libraries contain adequate materials for students to conduct their research. Sample topics for a ten-page paper might be "Franklin Roosevelt's attempt to pack the Supreme Court" or "the Nazi party's takeover of power in Weimar Germany." A more current topic would be "the reasons for [the current President's] victory in the [latest] election." (Caution students that the selection of a current topic will involve the use of a large number of magazine articles and that authors of articles on controversial topics tend to be more biased.) Emphasize that topics that explore cause and effect tend to be easier to organize and write. Assign students to purchase a pack of 3″ × 5″ index cards which they should bring to the next lesson.

*Lesson II.*    This lesson teaches students how to take notes. Tell students that they should study encyclopedias and indices to books and periodicals to locate information for their paper. Explain the uses of the library card catalogue and demonstrate how to use the footnotes and bibliography of one book to obtain other sources for a topic. Explain to students how they should use the 3″ × 5″ index cards to take down information on their subject. Help students to refine this system of notetaking as much as possible so they can save themselves copying time and unnecessary effort.[3]

*Library Lesson.*    (Optional) If appropriate arrangements can be made, a library lesson focusing on the general area of the course should be arranged. This will not only reinforce instruction students have received concerning library use but also will provide the opportunity to consult with students to determine if they are following proper procedures for obtaining information and library materials.

After students have made one or two visits to the library, instruct them to submit a tentative topic and bibliography. Once they have selected workable topics, they are ready to learn to organize the material and write their paper.

*Lesson III.*    Term-paper organization and writing is a complex skill which requires clear and concise explanation. Explain to students that their term paper should have three parts: an introduction, a body, and a conclusion. The *introduction* discusses the problem and offers several possible solutions. The *body* presents information in a logical order so that the reader can form an intelligent opinion on the subject. The *conclusion* summarizes the point of view that has been formulated in the paper. Both the introduction and the conclusion should normally be written after the body of the paper has been organized.

Instruct students to prepare an outline. Explain that the outline is their "insurance policy" to assure an orderly procession of thought. (If it contains content or organizational weaknesses, an outline will help students find the most effective method of reorganizing their paper.) Inform students that you will collect their outline in about two weeks. Instruct them also to submit their note cards. This step serves two purposes: 1) It enables the teacher to ascertain if students are obtaining the material they need to write their paper. 2) It insures that the students will go to the library and do the research rather than obtain an entire paper through fraudulent means.

Explain the importance of correct footnoting. A good analogy is to compare footnotes to the tags that department stores attach to merchandise. ("Just as a tag on a suit or a dress tells the store clerk the garment's size, price, style number, and manufacturer, a footnote tells the reader the author of your source, its title, the date and place it was published, and the place where you found the information.")

Caution students to be careful about the different kinds of footnotes used for different types of sources. Show them examples by referring to a manual that clearly demonstrates the different types of notes. Define plagiarism and warn students to avoid it by using quotation marks. Explain paraphrasing techniques, and indicate the importance of footnoting information that has been paraphrased. (This is a point that students often fail to grasp.)

If you want to require students to type their papers (a good idea if you are preparing students for college, since most university instructors mandate typed papers), show students a sample page emphasizing the following: doublespacing on the typewriter, the positioning of footnote numbers, the use of quotation marks and single spacing to indicate verbatim quotations, and the absence of quotation marks (but the presence of a footnote number) to indicate paraphrasing.

Outline the requirements for preparing a bibliography. Students often miss the following contrasts between bibliographical and footnote form:

| Footnotes | Bibliography |
|---|---|
| 1. Author's first name preceding the last name | 1. Author's last name followed by first name |
| 2. Indentation of first line (subsequent lines at margin) | 2. First line at margin (indentation of subsequent lines) |
| 3. Notes following the order of material | 3. Entries in alphabetical order according to authors' last names |
| 4. Commas separating most parts of each note | 4. Periods separating most parts of each entry |

*Important Suggestion.*    Since many students tend to procrastinate, it is advisable to establish a reasonable but firm calendar of due dates for each part of the paper you wish to check. A minimum time of six weeks to two months will assure that all students have sufficient time.

### Sample calendar

March 1, 2: Initial explanation of assignment

March 5: Library lesson (optional)

March 10: Tentative topics and bibliographies due

March 15: Return of topics and bibliographies
      Lesson III (organizing, writing, and footnoting)

March 30: Outline and research note cards due

April 5: Outline returned

April 30: Completed paper due

••••••••••••••••••••••••••••••••••••••••••••••••••••••••••••••••••••••••••••••••••••••••••••••••••••

## EXHIBIT 7-1.    Suggestions for Answering Essay Questions

••••••••••••••••••••••••••••••••••••••••••••••••••••••••••••••••••••••••••••••••••••••••••••••••••••

Providing students with a list of suggestions such as this before an essay examination should help in obtaining better results.

### Survey
1. Examine all questions before you make up your mind on your choices.

### Outline
2. Outline the facts that you remember for each essay question under consideration. Choose the questions that were easiest to outline.

### Key Words
3. Underline the key words or phrase(s) in the question statement that provide you with the main ideas, concept, or premise of the question. Be sure to refer to these in your response.

### Time
4. Ration your time. If you have an hour and a half left for three questions, use twenty-five minutes for each question and fifteen minutes to reread your answers and check your paper.

*Exhibit 7-2.  Lessons*    **149**

**Opening Sentence**

5. Incorporate key words and phrases of the question in the first sentence of your essay.

**Paragraph Form**

6. Use paragraph form, indenting the first line of each paragraph. A paragraph has a topic sentence (where you announce what you will be saying), two or three developmental sentences (where you provide your reasoning backed by data), and a concluding sentence (where you tie everything together or provide a lead into the next paragraph).

**Linking Words**

7. Use words to help you tie sentences or clauses together in a logical manner, e. g., *therefore, whereas, however, moreover.*

**Simple Sentence**

8. Try to limit your sentences to one thought whenever possible.

**Facts**

9. Express your opinion but substantiate it with facts, such as names of people, actual events, and statistics (in round figures). You do not have to indicate exact figures and dates. Use opening phrases that will induce you to substantiate that with concrete facts, e. g., a case in point; for example; to illustrate. Present two factual illustrations for every five points.

**Conclusion**

10. Whenever possible, "wrap up" your essay by explaining that you proved or disproved something in a sentence or two at the end of the essay.

Be neat!

Write clearly. Leave margins on both sides of your paper. Skip lines between questions and parts of questions. Number questions and parts of questions. Use only one line to cross out.

••••••••••••••••••••••••••••••••••••••••••••••••••••••••••••••••••••••••••••••••••••••••••••••••

# EXHIBIT 7-2.  Lessons*

••••••••••••••••••••••••••••••••••••••••••••••••••••••••••••••••••••••••••••••••••••••••••••••••

**Social studies.   Problems of organizing the Northwest Territory**

*Preceding Assignment:* Accomplishments under the Articles of Confederation

*Pages 149-57 and 165-67 of these Exhibits 7-2 and 7-5 were first published in *Writing Competently across the Curriculum,* 1980, published by the New York City Board of Education, Office of Curriculum and Support, Division of Curriculum and Instruction, Charlotte Frank, Executive Director. William Dobkin was the social studies specialist in this project.

Read pp. 126–31 in Todd and Curti, *Rise of the American Nation.* Answer one of the following questions in writing.

1. How did Congress succeed in enlarging the territorial boundaries of the new nation in the Treaty of Paris, 1783?

2. How did the acquisition of the Northwest Territory present Congress with a problem? How was the problem solved?

*Aim*

1. Students should be able to discuss the gains made in the Northwest Territories on behalf of democracy by our first national government.

2. Students should be able to write a letter in which they show their understanding of those gains. The topic of the letter will be: "Why I'm Moving to the Northwest Territory."

*Motivation:* The teacher leads a discussion on parent-child relations, based on these questions:

1. Why do parents often say, "I didn't have it so good, but you should have it better!"

2. Why do parents say, "Don't do as I do, do as I say!"

3. How can a nation act like a parent in dealing with a territorial possession?

4. Using the wall map, will you (a student) point out the thirteen original states (the analogous parent) and the new territories (the analogous children)?

*Development: Discussion Questions*

1. By setting aside one square mile in each township in the Northwest Ordinance for free public school education, how were the original states indicating that conditions should be better for people in the territories than for people in the original states?

2. How did the original thirteen states show a willingness to share power?

3. What forms of democracy were guaranteed to people in order for a territory to be admitted into the union as a state?

4. How did the nation say, "Don't do as I do; do as I say!" in the Northwest Ordinance?

*Exhibit 7-2. Lessons* **151**

*Intermediate Summary:* As the students respond to questions on the specific provisions of the Northwest Ordinance of 1787, the teacher develops and places on the board a list of the requirements for going from territory to statehood.

Under 5,000 free adult males — governor and three judges appointed

Over 5,000 free adult males — election of territorial legislature

60,000 free adult males — apply for statehood, with following provisions:

- Prohibition of slavery
- Republican form of government
- Encouragement of free public education

*Final Summary: A Writing Exercise*

1. The teacher states: Imagine this is 1787 and I am your father. I walk into your room to find you have disappeared, leaving a letter on your pillow which begins:

```
                                    September 22, 1787

Dear Mom and Dad,

        I have left for the Northwest Territory to find my
fame and fortune because . . . . .
```

2. Students complete the letter, including at least three reasons for their departure.
3. Students exchange letters and then discuss their reasons for leaving for Ohio or Indiana.

*Followup Activity:* Students, with the teacher, respond to each other's letters in terms of these points:

1. Does the letter show an understanding of the gains in democracy written into the Northwest Ordinance?
2. Are justifications for leaving home expressed clearly?
3. Does the letter need any editing or proofreading?

**Social studies (economics).    How does inflation affect people?**

*Preceding Assignment:* Effects of Inflation on the Economy

Read pp. 235–37 in Antell, *Economics* (Amsco). Respond to these questions with a single-sentence answer.

1. How does inflation affect creditors and debtors differently?
2. How can a business person stay ahead of inflation?
3. Why are persons with fixed income particularly hurt by inflation?

*Aim:* Students should be able to synthesize collected data on the effects of inflation (the problem) in order to write a report on the best possible methods for coping with inflation (the solution).

*Motivation:* (Series of questions put to the students)

1. Why do many people regard inflation as public enemy number one?
2. Why can we refer to it as the "inescapable mugger"?
3. How have you been affected by the 13 percent annual inflation rate noted in the first three months of this year?

*Instructional Materials:*

Text: Antell, *Economics* (Amsco)
Newspaper and magazine articles on inflation and procedures for combatting it on both policy and personal levels.

Example:

Farnsworth, "Lag in Productivity Called Major Peril to Living Standard," *New York Times*, August 13, 1979, p. 1.

Parker, "Gnawing Inflation," *Newsday*, August 16, 1979, p. 69.

"More Punch in Productivity," *Time*, November 13, 1978, p. 93.

*Development:*

1. Teacher asks: How does inflation seem to be affecting some of the people around you?
2. Teacher states: If we had a way of finding out how people in various categories are responding to inflation, we might be able to have a better understanding of problems created by inflation. Therefore,

*Exhibit 7–2. Lessons*   **153**

everyone select one person in each of these categories. (Place categories on board.)

- self-employed professional
- self-employed businessperson
- civil service worker
- worker in the private sector
- unemployed worker
- retired person

3. Those who selected the same category will form a committee to design a questionnaire for interviewing a person in that category.

   The following special instructions should be observed.

   - Give preference to questions that begin with interrogative words, such as "why" and "how."
   - Use questions such as "How are you coping with the high price of food?" (This is intended to obtain a sustained response.)
   - Use a scale (1 to 7) with questions such as "Do you think the government is doing enough to combat inflation?"
   - Offer choices with questions such as "Who is the most to blame for inflation?"
     a. unions          c. oil interests
     b. government      d. big business

4. Instruct students to keep a running transcript of the interview. (In this example, "Q" = question, "A" = answer.)

   Q: How are you coping with inflation?

   A: I'm not. It's wiping me out.

   Q: Whom do you blame most—the government, big business, labor unions, or oil interests?

   A: Government.

   Q: Why?

etc.

*Final Summary:* (Discussion for further enrichment, based on these questions:)

1. How are various people affected differently by inflation?
2. The inflation rate for necessities—housing, health, food and energy— is over 17 percent. How does this affect the poor?

3. Why is it difficult for the president to obtain support for an anti-inflation program from *all* Americans?

4. One economist suggests: "Don't just stand there. The government should *undo* something, which means deregulation." What effect did deregulation have on airfares?

5. On the other hand, other economists suggest stronger government regulations in the form of ceilings on prices and wages. How might these affect inflation? How would these regulations be enforced?

6. Other economists contend that all the government can do is "pray and inveigh." How can the president put pressure on industrial and labor leaders? How effective is "jawboning"?

*Homework Assignment:*

Ask students to write a paragraph in which they sum up the main points of their interview under the title, "My Interview Subject's Reaction to Inflation."

Students will then read their paragraph to their committee, which will draw up a report from the collated findings.

*Writing Enrichment:*

After they complete their first transcript, which was based on an actual interview, students should write a mock interview. In this piece of writing, an "interviewee" with a definite point of reference responds to the following:

- government-enforced ceilings on prices and wages
- increased productivity (efficiency in turning out goods or services, based on hours worked per person)

**Social studies:   Should the soldiers in the French Army have reaffirmed their loyalty to Napoleon upon his return from exile?**

*Preceding Assignment:*

Read pp. 414–21, Mazour and Peoples, *Men and Nations.*
Answer the question below.

How did Napoleon's leadership affect the people of France?
Fill in this chart:

| *Achievements* | *Failures* |
|---|---|
| a. _____ | a. _____ |
| b. _____ | b. _____ |

*Exhibit 7–2.  Lessons*    **155**

c.  _____  c.  _____

d.  _____  d.  _____

*Aim:* (Specific:) The students should be able to assess the leadership of Napoleon Bonaparte. (General:) The students should be able to say how citizens judge leadership.

*Motivation:* (Teacher states to class:) "There is a great deal of public discussion of the strengths and weaknesses of [the current President]. Some people say he is not a leader. Others say he is. What do you think? How would you judge the quality of leadership? What do you look for in a leader?"

The class may list [the current President's] achievements and failures in two columns. The teacher may ask what conclusions can be drawn and how people may have been influenced in deciding whether or not to reelect [the current President]?

*Transition into Lesson:* "The French people had to decide whether or not to follow Napoleon after he returned from his first exile."

*Development:*

1. Some students read or copy on the board their homework lists of Napoleon's achievements and failures. These are discussed and evaluated, and students make individual assessments of Napoleon.

2. Teacher asks a series of pivotal questions before distributing the story "Sergeant Granier's Dilemma."
   a. Why was the decision as to whether or not to follow Napoleon after his escape from Elba a difficult one to make?
   b. What did the French people gain under Napoleon's leadership?
   c. What did they lose under his leadership?

3. Before the students read the story, teacher states:

   "The French soldiers had to decide whether or not to follow Napoleon. Let's read this story and then make individual decisions, as if we were in the French army at that time. We'll make our decisions, write them as an entry in a diary, and then explain our reasoning. As you write in your diary, keep in mind the questions on the board:
   a. Would you follow Napoleon again? Why? Why not?
   b. What quality did Napoleon have that may have swayed the opinions of many soldiers?

c. What effect would the opinion of the other soldiers have on your decision?

d. What effect would the memory of your brother's death have on your decision?

e. How would the total career of Napoleon to that date influence your decision?"

*Application:* Direct students to exchange diary entries and discuss and respond to one another's writing.

Tell students that they may now elaborate on their own diary entries on the basis of the reaction of their peers.

*Final Summary:* (Discussion based on questions:)

1. Based on the reading, what decisions did most soldiers make in response to Napoleon's appeal?

2. Write another entry into "your" diary (Sergeant Granier) twenty years later (1835), in which you recall your decision of 1815 and reflect on its wisdom.

*Alternate Suggestions:*

1. The class may put together a facsimile of an 1815 newspaper, including editorials, letters to the editor, cartoons, news articles, advertisements, want ads, and feature columns—all of these reflecting the social and political climate of the times.

2. The class may stage "Sergeant Granier's Dilemma" as a video vignette, using narration or extension of the dialogue for clarification and characterization.

### SERGEANT GRANIER'S DILEMMA*

Sergeant Granier was sleeping soundly when he was suddenly awakened by the shouting of the captain outside the barracks. "Awake! Awake!" the captain shouted. "Napoleon has escaped and is marching towards Paris." The sergeant could hardly believe what he heard. He knew that after being defeated in 1814, Napoleon was exiled to the island of Elba, off the coast of Italy. But before Sergeant Granier could give this matter any further thought, the captain burst into the barracks. "Sergeant, we have been ordered by the King to join with the entire regiment and march to Grenoble. There we will stop Napoleon and arrest him. He has 1,100 men with him; we will try to avoid a fight, but if we have to . . . ."

*Unpublished fictionalized version of the meeting at Grenoble, by William Dobkin.

*Exhibit 7-3.  Activities*    **157**

The sergeant was already dressed before the captain finished his orders. His men were up also and, before a few minutes had passed, they ate their rations and were marching on the road to Grenoble.

When they reached Grenoble, the familiar figure of Napoleon was waiting for them in a field. He stood there facing the troops who had come to arrest him. The sergeant and the rest of the soldiers stood frozen before the stern figure who had led them to conquest and then defeat. After an embarrassing moment of silence, Napoleon said slowly, "If any one of you wishes to kill his Emperor, he can do so. I am ready for you to fire." The soldiers looked at each other. No one moved.

The sergeant saw that Napoleon's gamble worked. He saw the captain break down and weep. The soldiers now began to cheer Napoleon. "Long live our Emperor!" they shouted. Instead of arresting him, they fell in line and joined ranks with Napoleon's men. The sergeant's own captain urged him to lead his men to join Napoleon with these words: "Granier, join ranks with our leader, our general. He will lead us to glory and honor once again. We will avenge the deaths of our fallen brothers."

Sergeant Granier had heard words like this once before. He had been one of the 600,000 soldiers who marched with Napoleon into Russia. He was lucky to be one of the 50,000 to get out alive. His brother, Pierre, had died on the long march home from Moscow. He would never forget passing a frozen corpse, stopping after a few feet, and then realizing that it was his brother.

And now he had to decide whether or not to follow Napoleon once again.

●●●●●●●●●●●●●●●●●●●●●●●●●●●●●●●●●●●●●●●●●●●●●●●●●●●●●●●●●●●●●●●●●●●●●●●●●●●●●●●●●●●●●●●●●●●●●●●●

# EXHIBIT 7-3.  Activities

●●●●●●●●●●●●●●●●●●●●●●●●●●●●●●●●●●●●●●●●●●●●●●●●●●●●●●●●●●●●●●●●●●●●●●●●●●●●●●●●●●●●●●●●●●●●●●●●

**Social studies**

1. *Make a diary entry.*

   A record of personal experiences, observations, reactions to events, situations, and happenings may be entered in a diary. These entries may be made daily or at frequent intervals.

   The information should contain highlights of the experience and the thoughts, reactions, and observations of the writer.

   Important details and statistical information, as well as the significance of the event, are necessary for the diary entry to have meaning and future utility.

2. *Prepare a news broadcast.*

   Historical events, current situations, and imaginary happenings may serve as a basis for writing a news broadcast.

   The broadcast should contain factual information which answers questions in terms of who, what, when, where, and how.

The information should be written concisely, so that it can be read within a specific time limit, such as fifteen, twenty, or thirty seconds.

No statements of opinion should be included in the news broadcast.

3. *Write an advertisement.*

In a consumer economics class, students may prepare advertisements for publication in a newspaper or for broadcast over the air.

The advertisements could be written for a particular time in history, for the present, or for some time in the future.

Each advertisement may recommend either a product or a service. It should include the name of the product, a description of the item, an emphasis on the best features and/or advantages of the item, the places where purchased or obtained, and the price.

To insure added appeal, endorsements, slogans, and guarantees may be included in the advertisement.

4. *Write an editorial.*

Current issues or problems may be utilized as a basis for writing an editorial.

The editorial should be prepared as if for publication in a newspaper such as the *New York Times*, the *Daily News*, or the *New York Post* or for broadcast over a specific station or channel. It should present a position that might be taken by the specific publisher or station on the issue or problem.

The editorial should contain a brief description of the issue or problem, the arguments for or against the issue, a statement of the writer's or speaker's opinion, and some proof to support the reasons for the position taken.

Counterarguments may be presented but should be proved wrong through specific evidence.

5. *Write a job prospectus.*

In a class on government, the students can describe in writing the constitutional as well as the unwritten requirements for any particular office as if the writer were announcing the position in a want ad.

The job requirements should be stated in order of importance. This will give the students the opportunity to think about the traits most sought in governmental leaders.

6. *Write a letter.*

A letter can be sent to an editor expressing an opinion or to a consulate asking for information about a country. These are examples of letters students can write in social studies which serve a definite purpose.

*Exhibit 7–4. Strategies*    **159**

Another type is the imaginary letter that helps to re-create the emotions experienced by someone living during a historical event:

```
Dear Mom and Dad,

        When you find this letter I will be on my way
to Jerusalem. I'm joining Stephen and the other
children in the Crusade. This is my reason.
```

## EXHIBIT 7–4.  Strategies

Each of these strategies stresses reading or writing as designated. However, since both of these skills are mutually supportive, each strategy contains both reading and writing components.

The strategies were selected because they met these criteria:

1. A major social studies concept was to be developed.
2. The activity could be easily motivated because it is imaginative and creative.
3. The skill could be applied in other learning situations.
4. It would be basic to succeeding in future social studies courses taken by the student (i. e., notetaking and writing paragraphs).

This presentation of skill strategies follows the guide "Minimum Learning Essentials for American Studies — Experimental Edition," published by the New York City Board of Education, Office of Curriculum and Support, Division of Curriculum Instruction (Fall 1980).

**Strategy one**

*Topic:* Why Are Governments Necessary?

*Skill Mode:* Reading

*Objective:* Students will establish a theme for this term's work.

*Reading Support:* "A Ukrainian Family and a Question of Juvenile Law," *New York Times,* September 9, 1980.

*Skill:* Finding the main idea.

*Procedure:*

A. Students will read the article and answer these questions:
   1. Why does Walter Polavcik want to stay in the United States?
   2. What legal dilemmas do the American authorities face?
B. Possible theme: The class can "adopt" Walter and try to explain our country's political system to him.

*Concept:* American ideals attract immigrants to our country.

**Strategy two**

*Topic:* How Does the Declaration of Independence Justify the American Revolution?

*Skill Mode:* Writing

*Objective:* Students will be able to write their own version of the Declaration of Independence, listing three major grievances.

*Reading Support:* Schwartz and O'Connor, *Exploring Our Nation's History,* pp. 86–87.

*Skill:* Writing an imaginary letter to a pen-pal in France in 1776 (the ability to personalize history).

*Procedure:*

Use this outline to assist students in writing their "Dear Pierre" letter:

   I.  Why you are writing this letter
  II.  Why we feel justified in changing governments
III.  Three specific grievances
     A.
     B.
     C.

*Concept:* Our founding fathers had rational goals.

**Strategy three**

*Topic:* How Does a Bill Become a Law?

*Skill Mode:* Reading

*Exhibit 7–4.* *Strategies* **161**

*Objective:* Students will list and explain the major steps in a bill's becoming a law.

*Reading Support:* Abramowitz, *Foundations of Freedom,* pp. 28–31.

*Skill:* Outlining in topic or sentence form to second-level sub-categories, based on a reading selection.

*Procedures:*

Have students read above pages and then fill in this outline:

*How a Bill Becomes a Law*

    I.  Introduction of the bill
        A.
        B.
   II.  Committees
        A.
        B.
        C.
  III.  Sent to each House
        A.
        B.
  IV.  Voting
        A.
        B.
   V.  Conference committee
        A.
        B.
  VI.  Identical bill
 VII.  Presidential action
        A.
        B.
VIII.  Overriding the veto
        A.
        B.

*Writing Support:* Have students write the "biography" of a bill: "Today I was introduced in the Senate by. . . ."

*Concept:* Lawmaking is a painstaking procedure.

**Strategy four**

*Topic:* Is it Possible for One Man to Function Effectively as President?

*Skill Mode:* Writing

*Objective:* Students will be able to write a "people's want-ad" for president of the United States by deciding on the most important qualifications needed for the job.

*Reading Support:* Magruder, *American Government*, pp. 352–58.

*Skill:* Locating details and incorporating them in a written announcement.

*Procedure:*

A. Have students research the following information about the presidency: job description, qualifications, compensation and fringe benefits, personal qualities.

B. Have them complete an ad beginning "Wanted: President of the United States" using this information.

C. Place the best want-ad on the chalkboard and discuss with class.

*Concept:*

The criteria for selecting the president of the United States is based both on constitutional and personal considerations.

**Strategy five**

*Topic:* Is Our Method of Selecting a President Democratic?

*Skill Mode:* Writing

*Objective:* Students will write a short persuasive essay on what is fair (or unfair) about the electoral college system.

*Reading Support:* Magruder, *American Government*, pp. 172–76.

*Skill:* Analyzing and synthesizing data and coming to a conclusion.

*Procedures:*

A. Direct students to this chart reproduced on the chalkboard:

*Exhibit 7-4. Strategies* **163**

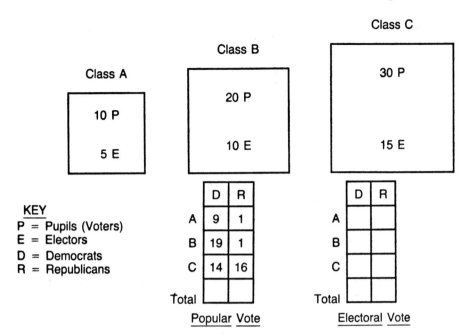

KEY
P = Pupils (Voters)
E = Electors
D = Democrats
R = Republicans

B. Explain that each box represents a class of varying student enrollment in a small school. The school has decided to follow the United States Constitution in holding its election for student-government president.

C. Explain and drill students on the meaning of the symbols (in the Key).

D. Ask students to tally the vote and determine who won the election. (Although the Democrats won the popular vote, the result is a tie in the electoral college.)

E. Change the figure in the "C" class to 32 P. This will result in one candidate's victory in the electoral college without a majority of the popular vote.

F. Have the students write a brief evaluation of the electoral college system.

*Concept:* New ideas are needed to perfect our form of democracy.

**Strategy six**

*Topic:* How Is the President Prevented from Becoming Too Powerful?

*Skill Mode:* Writing

*Objective:* The students will develop a proposal restricting presidential war powers.

*Reading Support:* Magruder, *American Government*, p. 408.

*Skill:* Obtaining specific information and incorporating it into a proposal.

*Procedure:*

A. Question students on unrestrictive powers, constitutional authority, conflict between the president and Congress.

B. Have students read about extension of presidential authority.

C. Invite students to write a similar proposal.

D. Compare students' proposal to the actual War Powers Act (1973).

*Concept:* The power to declare war belongs to Congress and has recently been reaffirmed.

**Strategy seven**

*Topic:* The Dred Scott Decision Increases Polarization

*Skill Mode:* Writing

*Objective:* Students will be able to write a "news dispatch" from notes supplied during a Supreme Court session.

*Reading Support:* James, *The Supreme Court in American Life*, pp. 52–55.

*Skill:* Writing an essay.

*Procedure:*

A. Simulate a mock session of the Supreme Court in 1857 with a panel of students playing Chief Justice Taney and associate justices, Dred Scott, Lt. Emerson (former slave-owner), and Sanford (present slave-owner) and the rest of the class acting as news reporters.

B. Have each witness explain Dred Scott's status in response to questions posed by the justices, i. e., "Where do you reside?" "What laws concerning slavery did you live under?"

C. Place the key words obtained during the intermediate summary on the chalkboard, simulating a reporter's notebook entries. Provide these instructions:

*Exhibit 7–5.* *Evaluation* **165**

The editor of your hometown newspaper has assigned you to cover the Dred Scott case, which will be decided "today." Write a news dispatch from these notes.

| | |
|---|---|
| Dred Scott is not a citizen | Both acts outlawed slavery |
| Dred Scott is property | Both acts are unconstitutional |
| Cannot sue before this court | Cannot deprive citizen of prop- |
| Case cannot be heard | erty without due process |
| *Obiter dictum*-court's thinking | South hails decision |
| Northwest Ordinance, 1787 | Northern abolitionists upset |
| Missouri Compromise, 1820 | Country polarized |

Organize these notes into a written report. To help you organize your report (news dispatch), rearrange the notes on scrap paper before you start to write your first draft. In your dispatch be sure to include all the information in the notes.

D. Place the best dispatch on the chalkboard or project it from a transparency for student evaluation.

*Concept:* The Supreme Court in its decisions has a profound influence on the course of history.

•••••••••••••••••••••••••••••••••••••••••••••••••••••••••••••••••••••••••••••••••••••••••••••••••••

# EXHIBIT 7–5.   Evaluation

•••••••••••••••••••••••••••••••••••••••••••••••••••••••••••••••••••••••••••••••••••••••••••••••••••

### Responding to student writing

It is necessary for student writers to understand that writing is a way of sharing ideas and feelings.

Respond as often as possible to what the writer is trying to communicate, with thoughtful, nonthreatening, supportive comments. Criticism that is too harsh, too frequent, and too early will make students afraid to write again. Indeed, extravagant, unsupported praise can be harmful too.

Obviously not every aspect of writing needs to be responded to in every paper. But in every paper the student should be aware that the teacher is interested in what he or she has to say and is responding as in a two-way conversation.

If the student's ideas are meager or misguided, we know we have more work to do in our content area—more explaining, more reading, more thinking, more talking.

But if the student's difficulty is in expressing his or her ideas on paper, the best remedy is to encourage frequent short reports that give practice.

## Comments on Content

Positive comments can take the form of a restatement of what the student has said: "Yes, the Equal Rights Amendment has met with stiff resistance in some states."

Or, the teacher can express interest and encourage further communication by sharing his or her point of view: "You are concerned about nuclear weapons. I, too, feel that they are a threat to our civilization."

Sometimes leading questions may clarify thinking, jog memory, or stimulate ideas: "What caused this?" "When did those conditions exist?"

If the writing is unclear, ask for clarification. "Which laws are you talking about?" "Who is to blame?"

Approach both overblown generalities and inchoate garbles with: "What do you mean?" "Is this so?" "How does this follow?" "What is your proof?" "If . . . is true, how can . . . be so?"

## Comments on Organization

If the paper lacks organization, number some of the sentences in the paper and write: "Which of these sentences go together?" "Which of these sentences should you write first? Last?"

If the paper lacks unity, you might write: "How is this sentence related to your topic?"

Limit your questions about content and organization to one or two areas.

## Comments on Mechanics and Technical Errors

Finally, attend to the mechanics and technical errors. Correct gross errors, but not many. Too many corrections discourage students; too few communicate an unrealistic sense of perfection.

"Don't forget to put in your periods." "I don't know exactly what you mean when you don't show me where your sentence ends." "Please read your paper over before handing it in. You've made a number of careless errors in spelling."

## Overall Guidelines for the Teacher

Aim at correcting one error at a time, for individuals or the class. If many of the students need help in one area, emphasize it before they write and comment on this one writing skill on the papers that follow.

Don't feel guilty about not indicating every error. There seems to be no correlation between increased ability to write and intensive marking and correction.

If a number of the students failed to write on the topic assigned, was it because the assignment itself was ambiguous? Were the students able to understand the question or the assignment?

If a student's writing was unorganized or inadequately developed, was it lack of knowledge or interest in the particular topic? Did the writer make a plan before writing or simply put down ideas as they came to mind? Did the writer know how to organize and develop the report or narrative or argument?

Did the writer reread and edit the paper? Do the errors in spelling, capitalization, and so forth stem from carelessness or lack of knowledge?

Did the writer have the opportunity to reread and revise?

## ENDNOTES

1. David Ausubel, *Educational Psychology: A Cognitive View* (New York: Holt, Rinehart, and Winston, 1968), pp. 147–65.
2. An excellent source for research findings about teaching writing is Don Murray, *A Writer Teaches Writing* (Boston, Mass.: Houghton Mifflin, 1968).
3. *Writing Competently across the Curriculum*, New York City Board of Education, Office of Curriculum and Support, Division of Curriculum and Instruction, 1980, Charlotte Frank, Executive Director; William Dobkin, social studies specialist.

# 8

••••••••••••••••••••••••••••••••••••••••••••••••••••••••••••••••••••••••••••••

# Media

••••••••••••••••••••••••••••••••••••••••••••••••••••••••••••••••••••••••••••••

## WHY USE MEDIA?

There is no such thing as a media lesson. *All* lessons use media to a certain degree. For example, most social studies teachers use the chalkboard in outlining a lesson. There is an oral component in all discussions, lectures, forums, and student reporting. The question should not be whether or not to use an audiovisual approach in planning a lesson. Rather, it is to discover the best available media to achieve the goals of the lesson and to reach optimum pupil learning.

How do children learn? It is difficult to provide an acceptable answer to this question. We can, however, recognize that some forms of teaching approaches are more likely to succeed than others. Edgar Dale (a leading audiovisual specialist, many years ago) developed a cone or pyramid schema in evaluating learning experiences in relation to retention of learning. The base of the cone represented those experiences that were far removed from the student's interest and involvement. Reading a dry, nonillustrated text is an example. The apex of the cone represented those direct, "inquiry and discovery" experiences involved in manipulating real things, engaging in trips, etc. Thus, at the top of the cone, we find that most students retained learning experiences when they were exposed to an audiovisual approach.

To test this hypothesis, ask your students to name the stars of popular television programs. Ask them to repeat the words of the most popular songs that they are continuously hearing. Then ask them to repeat the name of the principal of their school or the main idea of the last lesson. Today's students have been exposed to multimedia communications almost from infancy. The average child watches twenty-five hours of television each week. Associating oral expression with a visual image is natural for them and has become an important component of their learning style. Students receive information this

169

way outside of the classroom. It should not be unnatural for them to be involved in receiving some of their information through media in the classroom.

Does this mean that children should watch television all day in school or see motion pictures during every social studies lesson? The answer obviously is no. It is not the aim of the school to duplicate the experiences that a child may engage in at home. The implications for successful teaching are more subtle. They involve the use of media within a lesson to motivate, summarize, give information, provide data for interpretation, and invite comparisons.

Watching a film for twenty-five minutes of a class may be counterproductive, but viewing just three to five minutes of an appropriate section of that same film might help more than half the class understand the concept involved in the lesson. One need not view an entire filmstrip — a few frames may be enough. By using the overhead projector, transparencies, and overlays, one might vitalize a lesson in geography or present data to an economics class. The techniques that may be employed are endless. An imaginative teacher can invent new and different ways to employ those learning materials which are available, and produce new ones.

The use of media is not only important in the acquisition of information and the production of attitudinal changes — a necessary skills component is also involved. We can expose children to different conflicting written expressions and ask them to search for the truth. Children have to learn to become visually literate and to search for the truth when confronted with conflicting visual evidence. This is an increasing responsibility of teachers as students receive more and more information through visual communication.

To summarize, children learn and retain what they learn through various media. Therefore, the classroom approach should be media-oriented, employing a variety of approaches using print and nonprint materials in helping children learn. In addition, just as children need to be taught skills so they can interpret and draw conclusions after being exposed to print information, they must also acquire similar critical thinking skills after being exposed to nonprint information.


## TYPES OF MEDIA


### The Textbook

One of the most frequently used media forms is the textbook. Although the modern trend is not to use the traditional single hardcover text but a number of paperback books, the importance of the textbook has not been minimized. The average text is generally full of color photographs, charts, diagrams, suggested activities, time lines and many other useful illustrations. It can be used as a means of preparing the class for a future lesson or as a measure for reinforcing a lesson already taught. As resource material, the text should never be overlooked. Students can utilize a text as common ground for the class or as a reading resource for supplementary work. Because of its importance, a text-book should be wisely chosen in terms of readability, content, and student appeal. However useful the text may be, it should never be used as the exclusive source of instruction.

## The Chalkboard

This is probably the most frequently used form of audiovisual instruction. Since it is accessible and commonly used, it has been looked upon by both students and teachers as a necessary part of every lesson. The importance of careful planning and selective use should always be remembered by the teacher. Many students look at material on the chalkboard as the highlight of the lesson and, therefore, this information should be illustrated in logical sequence, clearly written, and presented in such a way as to serve as a source of future reference. Typically, the aim of the lesson should be clearly presented—followed by major points, new vocabulary, suggested readings related to the topic, and any assignments given along with relevant instruction and date for completion. The chalkboard should be used discriminately to avoid overloading it. The chalkboard should elucidate the key information offered in a lesson and should reflect the cooperative efforts of both the student and teacher.

## Tape Recorder, Cassette Player

One of the most popular forms of entertainment for students today is the tape recorder or its more compact version, the cassette player. The advantageous aspects of this form of media are its compact size, simple operation, and reusable nature. Today the process has been even more simplified through the use of cartridge tapes that do not require threading and are available in different lengths. They can easily be used, erased, and reused. Students now have the opportunity to tape radio broadcasts, teachers' lessons, lectures, and homemade recordings. A popular use for this has also been the interview process. Currently, oral history has become recognized and respected as an activity that can easily be handled by students through the use of the cassette or tape recorder. Sometimes the effects of hearing one's own voice can, in itself, be a very meaningful experience for a student. The recorder offers a wealth of possible activities and should not be overlooked as a valuable and enriching form of media.

## Video Tape

A significant leap above the tape recorder is the video-tape recorder (or VTR). The VTR allows the teacher to record or play back TV programs and movies directly from, or to, a TV monitor. When used strictly for educational purposes, teachers may record significant TV programs that may not have been broadcast at the time needed, so that they may be played back during appropriate class times. Unlike film, video tape may be recorded over and used again and again. With various features, action may be speeded up, slowed down or "frozen" (stopped) at any place desired. Thus, while showing a program with a moral dilemma, the teacher could stop the action at a crucial point and ask the students what they would do. Another optional feature allows the teacher with an easily operated VTR camera to enable students to make their own video taped productions of such things as news casts, plays or documentaries. Unlike film, which has to be sent out for developing and processing and may only be used once, video tapes may be replayed immediately and redone if necessary.

### Silent and Sound Filmstrips

Perhaps one of the most often used media forms is the filmstrip. The quality of the materials being produced today is often very good. They come in a variety of ways: filmstrips that offer a short verbal description of the frames presented; and noncaptioned filmstrips that rely upon the student's ability to interpret the picture or the teacher to read a prepared statement given in the kit. The artistry, vivid colors, and life-like productions capture the imagination of the students and allow them to participate actively in the situation presented. Although this form of media is most attractive to teachers, its use should be carefully planned. The materials should not be forced; rather, it should fit neatly into the development of the topic. All materials should be previewed by the teacher and, in doing so, the reading level and the interest of the students should be considered. The lesson should never be just the showing of a film; rather, the film should be preceded by introductory remarks, followed by a summary of important points and reactions of the students. Organized activities may flow from this exercise in the form of group discussion, debate, research projects, role-playing, and written or oral reports.

All schools should develop an inventory of these valuable devices and supplement their supply regularly.

### Slide Projectors

Hundreds of thousands of pictures of various places and people are available at little or no cost to social studies teachers in the form of $2 \times 2$-inch mounted slides. Although many are commercially prepared, the majority are slides taken by all kinds of amateur photographers. While commercially prepared slides can bring exotic places right into the classroom, a teacher's own slides can be equally effective. A quick canvas of your school's staff might turn up fascinating slides that can be borrowed or copied for school use. Any of these 2×2-inch mounted slides can be projected on any standard projector or a filmstrip projector with an adapter. Some slide projectors can hold up to 140 slides; adapted filmstrip projectors usually can hold less than twenty at a time, with some only able to hold one or two.

## Opaque Projector

This device also allows students the opportunity to view important materials. Teachers may present parts of books, pictures, articles, charts, maps, diagrams, written work, or photographs by placing them within this machine. Basically, it operates on the principle of magnification and allows an entire class to view materials that would be very difficult or impossible to duplicate. Teachers should mount materials on a dark background which will improve the illumination of the material and allow for easier viewing. Although improvements have been made, these machines tend to be heavy, and it is recommended that they be placed on a movable stand to allow for greater mobility.

## Overhead Projector

In many ways, the overhead projector is the best invention for teachers since chalk! In fact, it can literally replace chalk. Transparencies made by various methods can be projected onto a screen in normal room light with the teacher in front of the room, facing the students at all times. Transparencies are made primarily in two ways:

*1. Pen-and-Pencil Method.*   Using felt-tip pens, china markers, or specially made pencils, one or more colors can be used to write directly on pieces of transparent acetate — either attached to the projector on a roll or on individually cut pieces. Everything from a simple content outline to a multi-colored map can be quickly and easily made and projected. These transparencies can be retained or erased with a damp cloth or tissue.

*2. Heat-Transfer Process.*   A variety of office copying machines utilizing a heat-transfer process can make transparencies. With specially treated acetate, originals can be duplicated into permanent transparencies in seconds. These transparencies can be made in a variety of colors. Additional colors can be added using the pen-and-pencil method. Pages from most books, pencil drawings, and mimeographed copies all can be turned into transparencies. In this manner, a mimeographed outline map can be made into a transparency so that students can fill in information as the teacher writes it on the transparency.

Teachers may choose to use transparencies in the development of topics. These materials are very convenient, since they may be reused as often as possible and are sometimes accompanied with overlays (placing one upon the other). They are easily stored, inexpensive, and come in a variety of colors for special effects. Teachers may make their own materials by simply writing on a piece of acetate with a wax or grease pencil. The acetate can easily be wiped clean and used in the future. These machines should be mounted upon a table equipped with rollers to allow adequate mobility. Their greatest appeal is the ease in which materials may be presented and changed. Teachers may make additions to the transparency during the course of the lesson as students follow along from their seats.

## Spirit-Duplicated Materials

Every lesson has learning needs that may not be satisfied in the text or not properly explained in a film. It becomes necessary for the teacher to fill the void by preparing materials that can be easily prepared and distributed. The use of rexograph stencils has satisfied this need. A teacher may prepare the needed information by simply writing with a pen or typing on a stencil. This stencil may be placed on a spirit-duplicating machine that may either be automatic or manual. In any event, the required number of copies can be made in a matter of minutes. This process is particularly helpful in those situations where slow learners find the vocabulary of the text too difficult. Gifted students may be supplied with supplementary materials (i. e., reading lists, quotations, charts, diagrams, maps) where, again, the text is found lacking. Youngsters find this process particularly helpful in their preparation of materials which they are to prepare at home and bring to school for duplication. Through the use of these materials, teachers may provide information tailored to the specific needs of their students in an expeditious manner.

## Multimedia Materials

The current trend leans towards the use of many audiovisual media simultaneously. Much of the material available today includes filmstrips, records, or cassette tapes and readers. Here again, the effectiveness of the materials depends upon the thoroughness of the planning on the part of the teacher and the appropriateness of the material to the level of the students. Teachers should acquaint themselves with available audiovisual equipment and use it for the benefit of their students.

Prepared records or tapes are synchronized with the film and audible signals are provided so that the film may progress equally with the narration. Workbooks generally accompany these kits and include suggested activities and questions for inquiry. Teachers should preview these materials carefully and integrate their use neatly into the development of the topic. The materials should supplement the instruction of the teacher and not replace it.

## Maps and Globes

Maps and globes are the audiovisual materials most often associated with social studies. Flat maps are commonly found in social studies classrooms illustrating such varied information as historical development or the relationship of geography to history and the other social sciences. They assist the learner in viewing important spatial relationships and allow the teacher to present a total picture showing the relationship of the topic to the world. Maps may be written on with chalk or marker and wiped clean for future use. Overlays are available that allow the teacher to place one map upon another, further illustrating a specific point. Maps may be purchased in convenient groupings, providing a complete study. Inflatable globes are now available that facilitate storage and use.

## Audiovisual Equipment

*Cassette-filmstrip projector.* Allows for use of filmstrip and cassette in one operation. Easily operated and stored. Perfect for classroom use.

*Record-filmstrip projector.* Allows for use of filmstrip and record in one operation. Easily operated and stored. Perfect for classroom use.

*Filmstrip-cassette viewer.* Allows for use of filmstrip and cassette in one operation. Perfect for independent study or individual use. Operates on push-button controls and may easily be used by students.

*Sound-film loop viewer.* Allows for use of film loop with a cassette providing the sound. May be stopped on any given frame and can easily be used by individual students or in small group projects.

*Slide projector.* Either manual or with remote control. Allows students to view color slides in a very convenient manner. Slide trays accommodate a hundred or more slides and are easily stored.

*Thermal copy machine.* Makes copies of color and black-and-white transparencies, spirit masters, and mimeograph stencils. Very simple to operate and is portable.

## Computers

Few pieces of equipment have the potential for revolutionizing the field of social studies education as does the recent introduction of computers to the classroom. Properly understood for what they are able to do, these computers, like any other multimedia device, can provide an exciting new dimension to the study of social studies concerns and be a useful adjunct to any classroom experience.

Fortunately for the typical social studies classroom teacher, a thorough understanding of how computers work or how to program them is not necessary. In fact, only two terms — hardware (the physical equipment such as the keyboard, display unit, or printer) and software (the computer program or step-by-step instructions that operate the computer) — are required. There are many software programs currently available (see Exhibit 8-3), and many more on the way. Teachers need only know which program suits their needs and whether or not it will work with the type of system (hardware) available in their school.

In an article devoted to the educational use of computers, two instructional uses for the social studies could be identified:[1] drill and practice, and simulation.

The first type is that of drill and practice. These programs provide

> the student with a series of questions to be answered or problems to be solved. Typically, drill and practice programs reinforce basic skills.
>
> Not all drill and practice programs are structured in the same way, however. Some simply display a particular number of questions and tally a student's right and wrong answers. . . . Most . . . provide some form of feedback to the student. The feedback will vary from program to program — from something as simple as "Correct" to a more elaborate pictorial reward for the right answer.

Programs asking the student to identify state capitals, countries, or names of presidents are of this type. As students choose an answer, they get immediate feedback as to the accuracy of their recall.

The second type of available program identified in the same article falls into the simulation category. These

> simulations model real-life or fantastic situations which otherwise might be impossible or impractical to bring to the classroom. . . . For example, . . . a student might role-play a presidential candidate, a stockmarket tycoon, or a ruler of an ancient kingdom. Landing on the moon, charting the open seas and excavating an archeological site are other possible classroom activities.

Other simulations recreate historical events or ask students to predict the impact changes to a situation might produce (e. g., what might happen to the inflation rate if taxes were increased?).

The final type of available program for the social studies teacher falls into the rapid computation category. Students are able to gather data (e. g., responses to an opinionaire) and then compute response patterns (e. g, do more adults than teenagers favor raising the draft age?).

Computers, like any other teaching device, must be thought of as a means to an end. They are not substitutes for a well-thought-out lesson. How they are used, and for what purpose, is what teaching social studies is all about.[2]

## What to Do Once You Know How to Do It

Knowing how to use multimedia tools is only part of the problem. You must also know when to use a particular tool. While every social studies lesson can use some type of multimedia instruction, the teacher should look for the most appropriate form. Media are only a tool to assist the teacher in teaching.

Some lessons revolve around a particular medium, such as film—one that might introduce and motivate students to learn a unit or give details on one specific section of a unit.

Media more frequently are used during a lesson to motivate students and emphasize details. Whenever an important place or person is discussed, a picture can be used for illustration.

## Teacher-Developed Materials

Teachers often travel and return with their own photographs or slides. Too often, however, these photographs or slides are used in a type of travelogue lesson that may be titled, "Look what I saw and did on my trip." Such a lesson neither involves the student creatively nor makes the student feel that these pictures are an integral part of the classwork. However, with a little care and preparation, these photographs, slides, and picture postcards can become rewardingly integrated into classroom work and can be used to create informative and thought-provoking discussions.

Photographs, slides, or picture postcards from any city, town, or countryside, whether near home or halfway around the world, can be put to effective classroom use. Ideally, teachers should plan ahead while on the trip and shoot subjects they feel will be valuable in the classroom. Right now there must be mounds of film shot without prior thought, gathering dust in closets and cabinets of teachers' homes instead of being fruitfully used.

Never use your total set of pictures in one lesson. One to a maximum of ten pictures will serve to involve the students in discussion. More than ten pictures will take up too much time to show and will put the students in a passive role rather than an active question-and-comment role.

Pictures used in one lesson should stick to one topic. For example, the topic of economic activity could cover anything from shops to outdoor markets to fishing boats, cruise ships, farms, or plantations—or just one of these.

Select shots that lend themselves to questions or interpretations. Sometimes one picture alone can do this. For example, a picture of a marketplace can be used for a discussion on "Why do so many people from the countryside come here?" However, since most of us, not being professional photographers, are not likely to take that "one fantastic shot," a short series of pictures on the same subject — several views of the marketplace, for example — will also work very well.

### Evaluating Commercial Media

*Caveat emptor* is not an unfamiliar phrase to social studies teachers. It is a phrase that they must be mindful of in the selection and evaluation of commercially prepared audiovisual materials.

First, the market is glutted with materials. Twenty years ago, there were a handful of producers. Today, as a result of the acceptance of audiovisual materials in the classroom and the recent availability of federal funds, there are many hundreds of producing companies. Of course, every salesperson claims that his or her materials are the finest and surely will work with your students. We, as consumers of instructional materials, have every right to be bewildered. Though there is now a beginning movement of sorts to provide *learner verification* for instructional materials, there is some doubt whether or not this concept is feasible.

Second, one must caution prospective evaluators and purchasers of the axiom, "Don't be the first or the last to buy." When a course of study becomes popular, a new elective is considered, a new program is introduced, or a new device is marketed, there are producers who will rush to provide materials for the teacher so that the immediate need presented by the innovation can be met. Generally, the educational quality of this initial burst of material is poor. Wait for a short while and a better selection will be available for your limited dollars.

Third, be careful when examining the all-inclusive claims of producers. They have taken the concept of interdisciplinary learning to an exaggerated extreme. A filmstrip may be offered for five or six subject areas and sometimes from grades pre-K–adult.

Frequently, commercially produced material is "overstacked" and/or "overpacked." Overstacked material tries to present too much content in the form of wordy title frames or narrations. Most probably, no frame in a media presentation should have more than twenty or twenty-five words to accompany it either in captions or narration. An effective media presentation allows the visual presentation to carry a large portion of the information. Some media presentations rely solely on the visual presentation exclusively and are very effective. Controlling the amount of information imparted verbally allows time for reflection and the full impact of the graphic presentation. Another deficiency to be noted is "packing." If the presentation both feeds and digests the learning material for the student with definite conclusions, an opportunity to engage the students' reflective ability is being missed. Propaganda, especially in free materials, is to be carefully considered in previewing media material. Learning material should always pass the does-it-help-the-student-think test.

What can one do to meet these problems? Each school or department can establish a materials-evaluation committee. This committee would solicit and preview as many relevant and available materials as possible. Members of the committee may be rotated annually so that as many teachers as possible have an opportunity to preview and evaluate new materials. A form should be established similar to the one illustrated below. Each school may vary the questions to suit its own goals.

A program such as this has many advantages. The form is easy to fill out. The information can be filed and is easily retrievable. Only those materials

School _____ Department _____

1.  Title _____

2.  Type of medium:  16 mm _____     Filmstrip _____

    Sound _____     Silent _____

    Transparency _____     Slide _____

    Tape _____     Game _____

    Kit _____

3.  Length _____ Color or B/W_____

4.  Cost _____

5.  Producer _____

6.  Vendor _____

7.  Is the material accurate?        Yes _____    No _____

8.  Is the material appropriate?     Yes _____    No _____

    Grade level _____

9.  Is the material current?         Yes _____    No _____

10. Is the organization clear and logically presented?

                                        Yes _____    No _____

11. Is the material technically acceptable?

                                        Yes _____    No _____

12. Is the content presented at a pace that allows for reflection?

                                        Yes _____    No _____

13. Is the material suitable for individual instruction?

                                        Yes _____    No _____

                          Class use?    Yes _____    No _____

                          Both?         Yes _____    No _____

14. Was the material tried out with students?

                                        Yes _____    No _____

15. Do you recommend purchase?

    Highly recommended?_____

    Recommended? _____

    Not recommended?_____

16. Comments_____

    _____

    _____

    _____

17. Evaluator _____

18. Date _____

that are highly recommended should be ordered. When monies become available that must be spent quickly, a file of highly recommended previewed materials is available. Finally, teachers are exposed to the newest commercial materials and receive training in material selection.

Most commercial producers are anxious to provide preview materials to potential purchasers. If the school or department head does not abuse the preview privilege, he or she can look forward to vendor cooperation. Yes—this does involve administrative problems in soliciting and receiving materials, distributing them, retrieving the materials and evaluation forms, and returning the materials. The price, however, is small in comparison to what one might pay in ordering materials from a catalog, finding that they are inappropriate, and having them gather dust on a storeroom shelf.

## Types of Innovative Media and Their Uses

What are innovative uses of media? Certainly, any usage that moves away from the traditional showing of a film or filmstrips straight through without any kind of development or pause for interaction would approach that definition. The filmstrip, for example, is essentially a visual lecture. How does one provide an opportunity for the student to be involved in the learning process? One approach is to use selected frames on the filmstrip to present evidence or to help the teacher make the point. Thus, the film can be used for discovery. Can a student perceive evidence in a particular frame? Try showing the filmstrip without the accompanying sound. Can the students put together a narration that would show that they are able to use the filmstrip as a summary of what they have learned? Or vice versa—play only the sound. Students should be able to describe the kind of pictures that they would expect to see. Then show the filmstrip with the sound. Were their expectations met? If yes, you have reinforced instruction. If not, why not? It could be that the filmstrip was inadequate or that the students did not learn all you had hoped they would learn. In this manner, students can use pictorial media to examine

*Source:* Reprinted by permission from Educational Audio Visual Inc.

visual and auditory evidence, draw hypotheses, and then move to other materials to find supportive evidence. One example of single-concept filmstrips, strips of a small number of frames that teach a particular idea or concept, is Olcott-Forward's *Indians View Americans, Americans View Indians* (distributed by Educational Audio-Visual, Pleasantville, New York). In this media kit, one finds a two-frame filmstrip — that's right — two frames. In the first frame, one sees an Indian looking at his land — the forest, the deer, the stream. Students get a sense of the values in the Indian's culture and the things of great importance to this culture. The second, and concluding, frame is that of a settler viewing the same land. What does he see? Tree stumps; the land cleared, put under cultivation, fenced with grazing animals. How different are the values? How different are the cultures? A natural question — could these two cultures live together?

*16mm Sound Film.*    Can movies also be used in unusual patterns? Take as an example the film *Pompeii* (distributed by Learning Corporation of America, 1350 Avenue of the Americas, New York, New York 10020). As the credits for the film unroll against the background of ancient structures, the voice-over narration says, "Once there was a city; it was a city of common people, of lawyers, doctors, workers, etc. It was a city of. . ." (and goes on describing the type of city). "The name of the city was Pompeii." Turning off the lamp in the projector, one can still get the audio, and as the voice describes that it was a city of this and that, the sound is turned off a moment before the identifying name, Pompeii, is uttered. What a potential discussion! The city as described could be any city. Students may take it as a contemporary city. One can interject, "What has happened to this city?" The students might hypothesize war, bombing, destruction of one means or another. One can introduce whether this destruction might have been avoided. Then, and only then, does the film begin, and students see a Pompeii with many, possibly frightening, parallels to the city in which they live. The film can become a true learning experience.

Or take *Napoleon: Once There Was a Dictator*, distributed by Learning Corporation of America. Of course, the film can be used to summarize the rise of Napoleon or to introduce students to the study of this great leader. But at the very beginning of the film, there are a series of short scenes where Napoleon, accompanied by one or two aides, is hurrying to Paris — about to see whether he can take over the government. He stops at a country tavern. An old soldier, one leg gone, recognizes him and totters over to the leader, quaveringly saluting him and saying, "My general, I would follow you to the ends of the earth." Stop the action. What was there about Napoleon that should have had a soldier, maimed in his service, so willing to serve under this man again? The whole question of qualities of leadership — of charisma — enters into the picture. The lesson can develop the qualities of leadership and what makes for a great leader. This concept-oriented lesson can take place when parts of a film are used for their own particular purposes.

*Exhibit 8–1. Excerpts from Observations*     **183**

Innovation in the use of media means knowing how to use any teaching material for the purposes the teacher envisions. By knowing the desired outcomes, one realizes that one doesn't want to teach only about Napoleon, but about the qualities of leadership, the means people use to gain power, the justification of methods. Then parts of different media can be used to illustrate and lead students to these desired outcomes. It means moving away from the view of media as another type of lesson, and to a view that the media experience can be integrated as part and parcel of any social studies lesson.

•••••••••••••••••••••••••••••••••••••••••••••••••••••••••••••••••••••••••••••••••••••••••••••••••••••••••

## EXHIBIT 8–1.   Excerpts from Observations

•••••••••••••••••••••••••••••••••••••••••••••••••••••••••••••••••••••••••••••••••••••••••••••••••••••••••

The following are excerpts from supervisory observations:

During the last module of the session, the teacher showed a single slide which he had prepared, depicting a policeman standing over a bleeding boy. He asked students for their interpretation of the photo. The first responses were that the boy had been shot by a policeman; that there had been a riot; that the picture had been taken in the South; and that the boy probably had been stealing. He asked for explanations of each interpretation. Then a student observed that perhaps the boy had been hit either by a car or a bicycle. Other similar responses followed.

The teacher then asked a number of provocative questions: How might older people, like your parents or grandparents, interpret the picture? How would the socio-economic background of people influence their interpretation of the picture? The teacher elicited from the students the fact that these were all individual interpretations of the same scene. He underscored the importance of objective criteria.

•  •  •

The teacher asked each pupil to draw a picture showing what slavery was like. Then she held up some of the student drawings so that the class could develop a composite description of conditions under slavery according to the members of the class. Next, she showed the class a few slides of drawings depicting slavery conditions. The class formulated a list of conditions shown in these pictures. Finally, the two views of slavery were compared. This lesson was intended as an introductory lesson on slavery.

This lesson is an example of the inquiry technique. In this meeting she offered the children divergent views of slavery, from their own drawings and her own 35mm color slides of old drawings and paintings of slavery. Given the contradiction of views, she next planned to pose the question, "What additional data do we need to answer the question: What was slavery really like?" The pupils would develop the list of kinds of information they need and sources they can use to help them answer the question. Now, they'll be off on their inquiry, prepared to challenge and question as they go. Used properly, this exercise can be a marvelous example of helping students in developing critical thinking skills, research ability, and respect for the opinions of others.

The motivating activity of drawing their own pictures of slavery was very successful. All of the pupils were involved. The motivation was an intrinsic part of the lesson and a point of reference throughout the period.

• • •

After all the words have been spoken about multimedia lessons, this lesson combines superior technique with the use of the filmstrip, overhead projector, chart, and newspaper articles.

Reference to a series of newspaper headlines brought ready acknowledgment of "What are the causes of the population problem?" as the aim. Then, projection of three graphs on the overhead projector led to skill development activities with the students identifying the type of graph, the information presented, and the trends shown. These skills were developed through questions such as "What factors do we gather from looking at the chart?"

Not content with developing students' skills, the teacher also led them through an analysis of supply and demand as it applied to Indian food production. Dietary charts were utilized to show the comparative protein intake of Indians and Americans, and one or two frames from a filmstrip of a traditional village were used to let students see the items (bullocks pulling a plow, crude implements, inadequate irrigation) that limit food production.

• • •

By projecting a transparency of a cartoon showing a big battleship representing the reactionary powers of post-Napoleonic Europe and a small rowboat representing nationalism, the teacher hoped to develop in his students cartoon-interpreting skills and, at the same time, motivate them to examine the conflict between these two forces. The use of the medium to illustrate and present learning not only leads to variety of instruction, but it also acts to quicken student interest.

• • •

The teacher used the recording of a song from *West Side Story*, wherein Puerto Ricans sing of their two views of their island and of the reasons for coming to the continental United States, to lead students to a statement of the aim: "Why did immigrants come to America?" This media approach was not only successful in involving the students in the questions raised, but was also followed up by the teacher showing a selected number of frames from a filmstrip asking students to look at each picture and try to read into it the factors that caused people to leave their homelands. The hypotheses thus raised became the subject for the students to prove during the class session. This was a most successful approach; it was dramatic, and it made students feel involved in the introduction to the immigrant experience.

## EXHIBIT 8-2.   Lesson Plan

*Aim:*

How do Buddhist monks play a part in the life of Asia?

*Exhibit 8–2. Lesson Plan* **185**

*Materials:*

Slide projector and screen. The following slides (incorporate the titles at the bottom of each slide when you make them up).

1. Title — *Buddhist Monks* (hand-made)
2. *Buddhist Monks at Ankgor Wat, Cambodia* (from a photograph in a book)
3. *Buddhist Monk at the Temple of the Reclining Buddha, Bangkok, Thailand* (from a postcard)
4. *Buddhist Monk, Chao Phyraya River, Bangkok, Thailand* (from a personal photograph)
5. *Monks Begging and Praying* (hand-drawn by the teacher)
6. *Monk Teaching* (hand-drawn by the teacher)

*Objectives:*

1. The student should be able to identify a Buddhist monk.
2. The student should be able to identify the duties of a Buddhist monk and the reasons for these duties.
3. The student should be able to discuss why someone becomes a Buddhist monk.
4. The student should be able to suggest how Buddhist monks help in Asian life.
5. The student should be able to role-play a Buddhist monk and be able to write a composition entitled: "A Day in My Life as a Buddhist Monk."
6. The student should be able to compare the role of a Buddhist monk with that of other religious leaders.

**Procedure**

*Motivation:*

Show slides straight through, having students read the titles. Why are some people in the pictures dressed differently than others?

*Pivotal Questions:*

1. How can you tell who is a Buddhist monk?
2. From the pictures, what do you think Buddhist monks do? Why do they do these things?

3. Why does someone become a Buddhist monk?

4. Why do you see many monks in the streets of Asian cities?

5. How do you think Buddhist monks help Asian life?

6. How can you compare the role of a Buddhist monk with the role of the religious leaders with whom you are familiar—such as a priest, minister, or rabbi?

*Conclusion:*

Why are Buddhist monks important people in Asia?

*Homework:*

Pretend you are a Buddhist monk. Write a composition entitled: "A Day in My Life as a Buddhist Monk."

••••••••••••••••••••••••••••••••••••••••••••••••••••••••••••••••••••••••••••••••••••••••••••••••••••••

# EXHIBIT 8-3.   Microcomputer Materials

••••••••••••••••••••••••••••••••••••••••••••••••••••••••••••••••••••••••••••••••••••••••••••••••••••••

(The following list is intended to convey to the reader an indication of the variety of material commercially available. Listing does not constitute endorsement by the Association of Teachers of Social Studies/United Federation of Teachers, New York City.)

THREE MILE ISLAND

APPLE II/APPLE II Plus/48K (Diskette)

This simulation game allows students to manage a nuclear facility. With a goal of supplying electricity profitably, students will see such results of various management policies as loss of the operating license, radiation leaks, and closing of the facility. The program is applicable to general science, ecology, and political science.

SOCIAL STUDIES I

APPLE II with Applesoft/32K (Diskette)
Printer — optional

This diskette offers a variety of programs that simulate such key social studies topics as elections, policy formation, and world resources. Teacher's notes, suggested activities. Produced by the Minnesota Educational Computing Consortium.

*Exhibit 8-3. Microcomputer Materials* **187**

LIMITS – simulates future world resources.
ELECT 1, 2, and 3 – simulates presidential elections.
POLICY – simulates impact of special-interest groups on policy formation.
USPOP – projects U.S. population.
ENERGY and FUTURE – deal with future energy supplies.

## SOCIAL STUDIES II

APPLE II with Applesoft/32K (Diskette)
Printer – optional

This diskette provides drill and practice and simulation programs in a variety of social studies topics. Teacher's notes include background information, suggested activities. Produced by the Minnesota Educational Computing Consortium.

STATES 1 and 2 – drill and practice on U.S. states and capitals
COUNTRY – capitals of various countries.
CONTINENT – identifies continents and countries
MINNAG – explores agricultural factors in an American state.
BARGAIN – simulates the collective bargaining process.
FAIL SAFE – simulates a nuclear-war situation (based on the book).
CRISIS – simulates Berlin confrontation.

## UNITED STATES ENERGY: ENVIRONMENT and ECONOMIC PROBLEMS

TRS-80/Model III (Diskette)

This simulation program allows students to study the formation of public policy by examining the interaction of the United States economy, energy supply and demand, and the physical environment. The public policy model used in the simulation consists of societal, group, and individual values and goals; government structures and processes; and the nonpolitical environment – the economy, the physical environment, and the energy system. The program provides data for modeling the nonpolitical environment, so that students can look at the implications of various goals, structures, and processes. The program includes five copies of the fifty-two-page student manual and a teacher's manual.

## HAIL TO THE CHIEF

APPLE II Plus with Applesoft/48K (Diskette)
Atari 400/800/40K (Diskette)

This program simulates a presidential election in which the student player runs against a computer-generated candidate. The player sets up a strategy and carries it out for a simulated, nine-week campaign. Tactics include television or magazine advertisements, campaign travels, news conferences, debates, and polls. Included are four models of varying complexity; each can be used at ten levels of difficulty. The more complex models introduce the influence of incumbency, campaign finance, and spending limits. Includes comprehensive manual.

## EASTERN FRONT, 1941

Atari 400/800/16K (Cassette)/32K (Diskette)
Joystick

This war game simulates Hitler's 1941 drive into Russia, emphasizing tactical planning and a military-campaign approach to the problems of moving men and equipment — on the German side — into place against computer-directed Russian units. The program can be used by one student or by a team. Teacher's notes include instructions and historical background.

### ENDNOTES

1. "How Educators Use Microcomputers," *Electronic Learning* (Jan./Feb. 1982), pp. 22–24.
2. For a comprehensive discussion of computers and the social studies, as well as an annotated bibliography of microcomputer programs, see *Social Education*, May, 1983.

# 9

## Simulation Activities

A panel discussion at a recent conference of social studies educators was mellifluously entitled "Stimulation by Simulation." The section planners certainly deserve credit for a well-turned phrase. But the title alone would have failed to attract a sizeable audience had simulation not already received attention from teachers anxious to improve classroom instruction. The conference participants were no doubt searching for solutions to the reticence, alienation, and boredom commonly ascribed to today's student population. Simulation, if not a panacea for these problems, nevertheless involves students actively in the educational process. Its emphases on problem solving, participant interaction, and decision making are key elements of the new social studies.

As with many educational innovations, simulation is not easily definable. Numerous labels, often used interchangeably, have been applied to this mode. The most common are simulation and simulation games. One writer refers to simulation as "a selective representation of reality, containing only those elements of reality that the designer deems relevant to his purpose."[1] Another speaks of "models of reality simplified for classroom use."[2] But is there a difference between simulation and simulation games? Authorities are in disagreement. Jack. E. Cousins has argued that the element of winning or losing is needed for a simulation to be considered a game.[3] On the other hand, Ray Glazier uses different definitional criteria in describing two types of simulation games: (a) traditional "gamey games," which lend themselves to easily quantifiable subject matter, and employ such hardware as cards, spinners, dice, and game boards, and (b) role-playing simulations, which stress qualitative factors usually associated with social studies. Elaborating on the differences between these typologies, Glazier states:

> The first type (gamey games) emphasizes manipulation of concrete variables, while the second (role-playing simulations) emphasizes human factors like: persuasion, power, communication, resource control, planning and forecasting,

community decision-making, strategy trade-offs, and "psyching out" actions of others.[4]

A difficulty with Glazier's analysis lies in the fact that some gamey games employ role-playing and that some role-playing simulations make use of hardware. For the classroom teacher, however, haggling over terminology is less important than a knowledge of what simulation games do, how they operate, and how to select, modify, or design them. The terms simulation and simulation games will therefore be used interchangeably in this chapter.

Teachers, especially those in traditional schools, are often frightened away from simulation games because of the radical change in their classroom role. Use of this technique requires the teacher to act as game facilitator rather than as a dispenser of knowledge. In most games, the teacher reads the directions, makes certain the rules and regulations are properly followed, and helps to move the game along. Some teachers feel threatened by this role change because they are no longer the central figure in the classroom. Moreover, those who believe their primary function is to cover a given body of subject matter will be unwilling converts to methodologies that deviate from the one-lesson, one-period lockstep.

It is true that some games require many participants and are designed to last for days or even weeks. But others involve only a few players and take one or two class sessions to complete. Games may be simple yet provide a sound basis for cognitive and affective learning. Conversely, a poorly constructed game of a week's duration would represent a terrible misuse of instructional resources. We would argue that the importance of the game's educational objectives in the total course of study should determine the amount of time a teacher devotes to this learning activity or to any other, for that matter.

Simulation is by no means universally acclaimed as a trouble-free teaching tool. Critics have alluded to the overly complex nature of some games now on the market. Others stress the notion that no simulation game can genuinely duplicate a social situation. Still another basis for criticism centers on the dangers of improper student orientation. In gamey games, winning may become the major operating factor—to the detriment of learning. Moreover, participants in role-playing simulation games often play themselves instead of their designated roles. Also, some students may not take games seriously. Such a youngster in a war-peace simulation, for example, might initiate an atomic holocaust and merely lose the game or have to pay an innocuous penalty.

Teachers would be well advised to avoid these pitfalls as they prepare to employ simulation in the classroom. Against the negatives, however, are these positives to consider: simulation games bring a sense of reality to otherwise abstract situations. Students take an active part in the learning process rather than a passive one; many who rarely speak during traditional lessons become quite vocal. Youngsters may learn to empathize, compete constructively, and cooperate. Critical thinking skills and decision-making abilities are enhanced.

Finally, simulation lends itself to a variety of uses in the teacher's instructional scheme. It may be used not only for substantive teaching, but also as a motivational or diagnostic device or as a culminating activity for a larger unit of study. In summary, the authors believe that nothing in teaching is devoid of risk, and that simulation offers sufficient rewards for its inclusion among the methodologies used in the classroom.

Commercial simulation games abound in today's educational market. Many of them are excellent instructional tools. But budgetary problems and bureaucratic delay may inhibit their purchase and use. Ideally, teacher-created games would solve this problem and, of necessity, reflect the abilities and needs of students in a given class, course, or school. The premium on creativity and the personal satisfaction implicit in the development of new material would contribute significantly to teacher enthusiasm in the classroom and, hopefully, to more effective instruction. Of course, designing of original games calls for a great amount of time, effort, and knowledge. Not all teachers will find it practical to engage in this type of creative activity, at least not until they have tested and mastered a sampling of the games presently available. A summary of practical hints for using simulation games in the classroom is presented in Exhibit 9-1.

A prerequisite for the use of simulation games in the classroom is an understanding of the essential elements of simulation. These are briefly summarized and discussed in the sections below. Reference will be made to the simulation game *New Vigilantes* (see Exhibit 9-2), as well as to other games, at appropriate points in the text. A list of commercial simulation games is presented at the end of this chapter.

## OBJECTIVES*

Every learning activity, including simulation games, must have clear educational objectives. Without specific objectives, evaluation is impossible. Robert F. Mager has defined objective as "an *intent* communicated by a statement describing a proposed change in a learner—a statement of what the learner is to be like when he has successfully completed a learning experience."[5] The first step in simulation game design is the setting of objectives. What is it the game will teach? Objectives may be cognitive (ideas, concepts, and basic reasoning) or affective (values, morals, emotions, and attitudes) or both. Cognitive objectives might include concepts such as nationalism, megalopolis, or balance of power; an affective objective might stress empathy for the problems confronting a particular ethnic group.

In analyzing simulation games, it is important to distinguish between learning objectives and game objectives. The latter refers to the goals of the players within the game framework. In *Napoli*, for example, the goal of each

*For a detailed discussion of objectives, see Chapter 1.

participant is to be reelected at the end of the simulation by working toward the passage or defeat of a series of bills. One of the learning objectives of this game, however, is for the players to be able to identify the conflicting pressures on legislators. The game objective of *New Vigilantes* is the gaining of support for acceptance or for rejection of the establishment of a citizens' patrol; a learning objective is to have students arrive at a hypothesis about the relationship between public safety and individual rights. In short, game objectives are the means by which the ends (learning objectives) are achieved.

## THE CONTENT MODEL AND GAME SETTING

The content model in simulation games is that portion of reality that is being re-created for classroom use. Such models, of course, cannot duplicate all of the aspects of the real-life situation. Therefore, only those variables that are regarded as significant and relevant to the game's educational objectives are included. For example, *Napoli* is a re-creation of the United States Congress, but instead of fifty states there are eight. Because it would have been impossible to reproduce every element of the legislative process, the focus on logrolling and reelection tactics selectively reduces the game to practical proportions. Such selectivity is common to the content models of all simulation games. In brief, models should be realistic and manageable.

The content model may also contain elements outside the players' ability to influence or control. These external factors are usually lumped together under the rubric of chance or contingency devices, including dice, cards, and spinners. In a good simulation game, the device used approximates the probability existing in the real-life situation. In *New Vigilantes*, a designated player selects a contingency card at a crucial point in the game to introduce that element of chance occurrence that often exists in the real world.

The game setting refers to the background information given to the players at the outset. Such information might include the event, organizational body, or social situation being simulated, the geographic location (if relevant), and the time period (past, present, or future). The relationship between the time in the real world and in the simulation game should be clear to participants. The setting may reflect actual historical events (e. g., the Korean War in *Dangerous Parallel*) or fictitious events, as in *Crisis*. Of course, real-life simulation games, whether past or present, place greater strictures on the kind of information provided the players. In *New Vigilantes*, the "neighborhood profile" and "scenario" comprise the setting.

## INTERACTION

The realism of most simulation games is shaped primarily by the kind of player interaction built into the content model. Samuel A. Livingston has observed that game designers must be aware of how each player's actions can affect the other players: "The interactions can be co-operative or competitive (or both); they can be deterministic or probabilistic."[6] Accordingly, some games permit considerable freedom of action by the participants, whereas others, such as *Dangerous Parallel* and *Confrontation: The Cuban Missile Crisis*, are highly structured and allow for little or restricted kinds of interaction.

In some games, the interaction is affected by unequal possession of resources. Resources are the things players use to influence the game's outcome. These may be abstract qualities (such as status or ability) or tangible objects (such as money, chips, or land). *Economics* puts a premium on astute trading by opposing teams to gain a certain number of points. In *Notsob*, players receive discrete information in the form of memoranda, which differ in impact and value and add to the excitement. *Starpower* produces a three-tiered society based on an inequitable distribution of wealth, which usually results in rebellion by the lower classes. Other simulations, such as *The Balloon Game*, generate interaction through intrinsic fun appeal.

## ROLES

William A. Nesbitt has pointed out that simulation games and role-playing are often confused, primarily because most games involve role-playing.[7] But there is an important distinction between the two. Role-playing may be defined as the assumption of another person's identity. In simulation games, a social situation is re-created, whereas in role-playing, a student may simply act the part of an individual in a nonsituational context. For example, we ask students to role-play when we pose such questions as, "If you were president of the United States in 1932, how would you have dealt with the unemployment problem?" or "Imagine you are a World War II veteran attending an American Legion convention. How would you vote on the issue of universal amnesty for draft evaders?" Merely personalizing questions — as good a technique as that is — does not comprise a simulation. For this to occur, a social situation must be re-created. Quite conceivably, of course, a full-scale game could be designed around each of the questions cited above.

If students have had little or no experience with role-playing simulations, they should be oriented on the nature of role-playing a day or two before the actual game. Awareness of what a role is and how it operates may be taught through a series of brief exercises. Before *New Vigilantes* was played, for example, students were asked to define "law and order" personally and from the differing perspectives of a police officer, a crime victim, and a political activist. Similarities and differences in responses were analyzed by the teacher and class to determine whether role-playing had occurred.

Another orientation technique is to examine a specific situational role in depth. Such a case might involve a state legislator about to vote on ratification of the Equal Rights Amendment. On the basis of information contained in a role guide, students should be able to predict the lawmaker's vote. This may be easily accomplished if the legislator is described simply as a male chauvinist with conservative antecedents. A more complex role description, however, could indicate the difficulties of a legislator who must consider the wishes of his or her constituency, his or her personal values and aspirations, and the policies of his or her political party before making a decision. Students would thus be shown that role-playing may involve varying degrees of predictability. Regardless of technique used, such prior orientation will reduce the likelihood that students will play themselves rather than their designated roles during the game.

To the fullest extent possible, the entire class should participate functionally in role-playing simulations. Games that require only a few players are less desirable as instructional tools. If possible, teachers may add new roles or duplicate existing ones to maximize participation. Some games also ask students to perform necessary logistical services, such as time keeping or recording, which have no counterparts in real-life situations.

If the teacher is writing an original game, the number and type of roles to create will depend primarily on the simulation model and, to a lesser extent, on the size of the class. Only those roles that directly affect the course of the game should be considered for inclusion. The typing of role descriptions on index cards will allow players to consult them unobtrusively while the game is in progress. Furthermore, role tags, with the game name of the player and other identifying data, should be worn conspicuously by each participant in the simulation.

Roles may be markedly different or exactly alike for all players. The only role in *Notsob* is that of ambassador; on the other hand, a wide variety exists in *New Vigilantes*. Some roles allow great latitude of action. Participants may be assigned open or ambiguous roles which do not mandate specific stands on given issues. Others are highly structured and leave little room for individual decision making. Some games, of course, provide for no roles at all. In *Starpower*, students participate as members of a team but do not assume different identities.

Role guides should include sufficient information for the player to make an educated guess as to how the person portrayed would react to a given set of stimuli. Depending on the sophistication of the class and the objectives of the designer, some roles may have conflicting pressures built in to increase the complexity of decision making for the players. One such example from *New Vigilantes* is George Freese, whose history suggests opposition to the citizens' patrol, but whose financial and familial pressures are such that he may defer to the views of Harrison Schuyler, a likely patrol proponent. Freese is thus confronted with a moral dilemma. Will he opt for principle or expediency? Can he reconcile the two?

Simulation games will also more accurately reflect reality if a disparity of player resources (power, wealth, and prestige) has been written into the role descriptions. For example, each player in *Decide* receives a specific number of weighted resource points, according to the role. *New Vigilantes*, which seemingly duplicates a parliamentary, one-person, one-vote situation, actually provides the potential for bloc voting. Harrison Schuyler technically may cast one vote, but his status as potential employer, mortgage holder, and political campaign contributor will probably sway the decisions of other players.

## RULES

Simulation game rules set the limits of legitimate action by the players. Who they represent, what their goals and resources are, the sequence of events and time limits, what the players can or cannot do during each phase of the simulation — all these must be clearly delineated. Rules are among the major criteria in assessing a game's suitability. They should be concise and understandable. Teachers must be thoroughly familiar with them and be able to field questions from the class prior to the game's start. The reading of a long list of instructions, however, tends to cause confusion and destroy interest. On the other hand, insufficient information would also produce student misunderstanding. Following the initial tryout of *New Vigilantes*, for example, some rudimentary rules of parliamentary procedure had to be added because no provision had been made originally for instructing the players in the orderly functioning of public meetings.

Game rules should reflect the real-life situation as nearly as possible. As Judith Gillespie has written, "Rules are used effectively when they do not distort strategies or outcomes." For example, if the rules overemphasize chance, distortion will occur. Gillespie's illustration of the misuse of chance in an electoral college game bears repetition:

> The problem of the game is to determine how candidates gain electoral votes. The major concept is votes per state, and the major rule for determining states won is the correct answers to random questions about the three branches of government. In this case chance can be effectively used as a rule for determining which questions students must answer, but unfortunately chance also determines which *states* are gained by candidates. In this way, the Democrats can sweep the Midwest and the Republicans the South without any problem. Thus, the chance rule completely distorts the strategic aspects of election campaigning.[8]

Teachers may sometimes fail to detect such rule deficiencies before the game is actually played. Trial runs will more likely highlight weaknesses, if any. In such cases, necessary revisions should be made, suitable to the game's educational objectives and to the students' needs and abilities.

## THE DEBRIEFING

The debriefing, or postgame discussion, is probably the most crucial aspect of the simulation. "It is here that everyone, including the teacher," comments Glazier, "finds out what took place and why."[9] The debriefing allows the teacher to evaluate the game's success or failure. Authorities are divided on the extent to which the game session itself is productive of true learning, but most would agree that the debriefing, if properly executed, clarifies the events and underlying concepts involved in the simulation. "In a sense," Gillespie has written, "the debriefing session represents a 'mini' game in and of itself: a re-creation of the fundamental structure of the gaming situation. In addition, the session often uses applications such as case studies, suggestions for exploration of reading material, or the student's own experience to draw out and reapply the information learned."[10]

The debriefing session should never be terminated because of lack of time. If necessary, it should be continued in subsequent class meetings.

Various debriefing strategies are available. Some employ a series of teacher-directed questions that focus on the players' evaluation of their experiences in the game. For example, students may be asked to describe what major thoughts and considerations governed their actions during the game. What strategies did they use to achieve their goals? Could they predict the behavior of others? Who played their roles best? Who influenced them the most?

A related level of debriefing might deal with the players' analysis of the overall simulation. Discussion of the game's realism, its strengths and weaknesses, and its possible improvement helps the teacher in evaluating the game.

Moreover, this approach may enhance the self-esteem of students by encouraging them to analyze critically a major classroom activity.

Another debriefing strategy, and probably the most important, involves questions that prompt students to consider the broad conceptual issues raised by the game. In *Metfab*, students play roles as various members of the board of directors of a company that must decide in which one of several cities to locate a new plant. To evaluate the learning of cost-and-profit concepts, for example, the following debriefing question is posed: "How important are least cost and maximum profit considerations as influences on manufacturing-location decisions?" *New Vigilantes* seeks to familiarize students with the concept of the rule of law in a democratic society. Consequently, these questions are included in the postgame discussion: To what extent may the neighborhood patrol be likened to a posse in the Old West? If law enforcement is ineffective, should citizens have the right to assume police powers? Should constitutional guarantees be suspended in communities with high crime rates?

In order to determine whether the game's educational goals have been achieved, debriefing questions should be related to specific objectives. The following examples from *New Vigilantes* illustrate how this may be done:

*Exhibit 9-1. Using Simulation Games in the Classroom* **197**

| Objective | Debriefing questions |
|---|---|
| Students will be able to formulate a hypothesis about the conflict between public safety and individual constitutional rights. | Would it be possible to safeguard individual rights and still lower the crime rate in the community in the game? If not, which is it more important to protect: individual rights or public safety? |
| Students will be able to determine the values which influenced them and other players in making decisions about the citizens' patrol. | Why did you vote either to support or to reject the formation of the citizens' patrol? How did the values and beliefs of the person you portrayed influence your decisions? What other values were expressed by different players in your group? In other groups? |

Evaluating achievement of game objectives may include activities in addition to questioning. In *Police Patrol*, affective learnings are measured by means of pregame and postgame attitude surveys.

Finally, debriefing strategies need not be used in their entirety. Teachers may select, modify, or substitute their own questions and activities. Nevertheless, the debriefing should set the stage for future learning activities or class lessons. In *New Vigilantes*, the exercise where students discuss the effectiveness of various methods of crime prevention and place them in rank order can serve as an introduction to a unit on crime prevention. The use of case studies, guest speakers, panel discussions, and individual research about real neighborhood patrols could follow the simulation game.

•••••••••••••••••••••••••••••••••••••••••••••••••••••••••••••••••••••••••••••••••••••••••••••••

# EXHIBIT 9-1.   Using Simulation Games in the Classroom: Summary of Practical Hints

•••••••••••••••••••••••••••••••••••••••••••••••••••••••••••••••••••••••••••••••••••••••••••••••

1. The physical structure of the playing area influences the game's effectiveness. If the simulation requires much player movement, do not play it in a classroom with fixed furniture.

2. Because some games produce considerable noise and seeming confusion, be sure to notify your supervisor and neighboring colleagues, in advance, that you have scheduled a simulation. Otherwise, the proceedings may be misinterpreted as an incipient riot.

3. A full contingent of players is necessary for a successful simulation game. If too many students are absent on the day of the game, postpone it.

4. Avoid reading long lists of instructions to the class in the initial phase of the game. This tends to destroy interest, and is generally a poor way to motivate students.

5. Game materials that may be recycled are preferable to expensive consumable ones. Be sure to have materials available in sufficient quantities for all players.

6. In designing original games, avoid spending too much time constructing elaborate materials such as boards, pictures, and spinners. Building in the kind of player interaction that motivates students and makes the game "tick" deserves the bulk of your attention.

7. If not already available in commercial games, role descriptions should be typed on index cards for easy player reference.

8. Wearing of name tags will facilitate player interaction during role-playing simulation games. Self-stick labels are recommended.

9. If you are planning a simulation activity for the first time, orient students on the nature of role-playing a day or two before the actual game.

10. Students should participate actively during most of the game. Long periods of inaction or games that involve too few students should be avoided.

11. The teacher's most important function during the game's playing is to make certain that students are doing what is expected of them to the best of their abilities. Circulate around the room while the game is in progress and lend a helping hand to individuals or groups when necessary.

12. Contingency cards should never be used by the teacher to "rig" the outcome of the game. Such manipulation would be the antithesis of a true simulation.

13. If you design or try a simulation game that works, share it with your colleagues. The best way to do this is to play the game with them at a department or grade meeting. If lack of time is a stumbling block, play an abbreviated version of the game.

••••••••••••••••••••••••••••••••••••••••••••••••••••••••••••••••••••••••••••••••••••••••••••••••••

## EXHIBIT 9–2.   New Vigilantes: A Simulation Game

••••••••••••••••••••••••••••••••••••••••••••••••••••••••••••••••••••••••••••••••••••••••••••••••••

### I.   Introduction

Few public questions generate as much heat and as little light as the crime issue. *New Vigilantes* deals with community response to a rising crime rate. It

*Exhibit 9–2. New Vigilantes: A Simulation Game* **199**

raises issues of seminal importance: individual rights vs. public safety, the rule of law, alternative methods of crime prevention, the limits of police power, community mores, and decision making in a democracy. These are matters with which students — as well as adults — should come to grips, or at least think about rationally.

*New Vigilantes* is suited for students in grades 9 through 12 and for such courses as American Studies, Urban Law, Government, Sociology, and Criminology. It may be used at the beginning or at the end of a unit on crime prevention, and serve either as a motivational device or as a summary.

The game is designed for twenty-two students. Players will be divided into three groups: *concerned citizens, businessmen,* and *police.* Additional roles within these categories may be created in lots of three, with an equal number of extra youngsters joining each group. If several students are left over, they could play themselves or serve as evaluators, and give a detailed oral report to the class during the debriefing session.

## II.  Objectives

By playing the game, the following objectives will be achieved by the students:

  A. Students will be able to determine the values that influenced them and other players in making decisions about the citizens' patrol.

  B. Students will be able to describe and evaluate the effectiveness of the various strategies used to influence the players' decisions concerning the citizens' patrol.

  C. Students will be able to list and explain the reasons for the rise of vigilante groups in recent years.

  D. Students will be able to formulate a hypothesis about the conflict between public safety and individual constitutional rights.

  E. Students will be able to explain the relationship between the suggested powers of the citizens' patrol and the maintenance of the rule of law.

## III.  Materials

### A.  *Neighborhood Profile:*

A middle-class neighborhood in the town of Cityville is undergoing a rapid change in population. During the last two years, employment opportunities have declined markedly with the closing of one of Cityville's largest firms, a plant that had manufactured rocket parts for the United States moon program. Many residents have departed for "greener pastures" in the suburbs. At the same time, a large number of young unskilled and semiskilled workers and their families have moved into newly constructed housing projects in the area.

Many of the remaining inhabitants are senior citizens whose children now live elsewhere.

Numerous efforts to stabilize the neighborhood and to encourage longtime residents to remain have not succeeded. A rapid rise in crime, especially street crime and store robberies, has accompanied the population shifts. Stores are closed by 7:00 P.M. and very few people venture out of their homes at night because of the rising crime rate.

### B.   Problem Scenario:

There has been a great increase in violent crime and drug addiction over the past few months in this middle-class neighborhood in Cityville. Two months ago, an elderly shopowner and his wife were murdered during an attempted robbery. Last Monday, Mary Warren, a six-year-old girl, disappeared while returning home from school. After two days of intensive searching by the police, she was found dead in a vacant lot on the other side of town. Mary had been sexually assaulted and murdered. Enraged neighborhood leaders have besieged the mayor's office, demanding that decisive action be taken to avert future incidents of this type. In response, the mayor claimed that his hands were tied because no additional money was available to expand the Cityville police force.

A four-hour meeting was held at the community center several nights ago. Many community leaders and residents expressed their views on the reasons for the rising crime rate and what could be done about it. Shortly before 11:00 P.M., Robert Underwood, president of the Cityville Chamber of Commerce, distributed copies of his plan for a neighborhood citizens' patrol. In addition, Carolyn Loggia, a lawyer, handed out an information flyer on some state and federal laws governing citizens' arrests and gun control.

Owing to the lateness of the hour, the proposals were tabled until the following week. Mr. Underwood urged the participants to consider his proposals in the interim. He also promised to donate $25,000 to pay the expenses involved in establishing and supplying the patrol.

### C.   Proposals Worksheet:

Proposal A   A community patrol shall be set up in the neighborhood.

Proposal B   The patrol shall consist of representatives from the neighborhood.

1. The patrol shall:
   a.   Patrol the neighborhood in groups of four (by car).
   b.   Report all suspected crimes to the police by two-way radio.
   c.   Wear uniforms.

*Exhibit 9-2. New Vigilantes: A Simulation Game* **201**

2. The patrol shall be empowered to:
   a. Stop and question people suspected of criminal wrongdoing.
   b. Carry weapons (nightsticks, attack dogs, and guns).
   c. Make arrests.

---

My views on Proposal A are as follows:

I feel this way because:

    1.

    2.

My views on Proposal B are as follows:

I feel this way because:

    1.

    2.

---

### D.  Information Flyer on Arrests and Weapons Laws

State laws governing arrest —

The following conditions must exist before a private citizen may arrest a suspect without a warrant:

1. He or she has reasonable grounds for believing the arrestee is guilty.

2. A felony has been committed.

A private citizen has no authority to arrest a suspect for the committing of a misdemeanor without a warrant.

Laws governing weapons —

1. "A well-regulated militia, being necessary to the security of a free state, the right of the people to keep and bear arms shall not be infringed."

   *Amendment II, Bill of Rights*
   *United States Constitution*

2. According to state law, all guns must be licensed. All concealed weapons are illegal.

3. A mail-order buyer of a handgun (a pistol or revolver) must file a notarized statement that he or she is over eighteen years of age and has not been convicted of a felony or have a history of mental illness.
   *Federal Gun Control Act, 1968*

### E.  Contingency Cards:

1. In a neighboring city in the same state, a suspected criminal was apprehended and beaten by a group of citizens. Upon further investigation by the police, he was found to be innocent — the victim of mistaken identity.

2. The Cityville police commissioner announced at an unscheduled news conference tonight that he would ask the mayor and city council for authority to train any newly created citizens' patrol.

3. The television evening news has just reported the fatal stabbing of a teenage youth during an altercation between rival gangs in Cityville Park.

4. Responding to popular pressure, the state legislature today approved an emergency allocation of funds for a 10-percent increase in the size of local police forces.

*Exhibit 9-2. New Vigilantes: A Simulation Game* **203**

## IV. Directions for administration

### A. *Preliminary Exercise* (Omit if class has experience with previous role-playing simulation games.)

Students must be familiar with the requirements of role-playing before they can participate in *New Vigilantes*. A day before the game, inform students they are to play the role of a police officer in a brief exercise. Ask them to define the phrase "law and order" as a policeman might. After they have written their answers on a sheet of paper, ask them to define the same phrase, but now as a young mother with small children would. Repeat for the following roles: ex-convict, lawyer, army sergeant, and social worker. Individual responses should then be discussed by the teacher and class, and the nature of role-playing clarified. If necessary, devote additional time to youngsters who still respond as themselves.

### B. *Orientation*

Explain to the students they will role-play community residents faced with the problem of a rising crime rate. Distribute game materials to the class:

1. Neighborhood profile*
2. Problem scenario
3. Individual role-description cards and name tags
4. Proposals worksheet
5. Information flyer on arrests and weapons laws

After the students have read all of the handouts, briefly summarize the game procedures. Emphasize the point that their chief task during the meetings will be to reach a majority decision concerning the Underwood proposals. Answer any questions from the class at this time.

### C. *Phase I: Individual Decision Making* (Suggested time: 10 minutes)

1. Direct students to read and complete the proposals worksheet. Remind them to answer according to their assigned roles. If a player has a totally negative response to Proposal A, he should not go on to Proposal B.

---

*For schools in urban locations, an alternate way to present the neighborhood profile is through a slide show prepared by the students. A few weeks before the simulation game, have one or two student volunteers take a series of color slide photographs of scenes that match the profile. Subsequently, the teacher and students should collaborate on the selection of the most appropriate slides. During the game, play a tape recording of the profile as the slides are shown to the class. The slide show could also be enriched by accompanying music at appropriate points.

2. While the students work on the proposals, circulate around the room and spot-check individuals for possible out-of-role responses. Where necessary, suggest a rethinking of position in accordance with the role description.

D. *Phase II: Small-group Meetings* (Suggested time: 40–60 minutes)

1. The next step in the sequence is small-group meetings, during which time individual responses will be analyzed and discussed by the other players in the group. Majority-vote decisions of the group should be reached on Proposal A and on Proposal B (if "A" is approved).

2. Form three groups, at different corners of the room, with these headings: *concerned citizens, businessmen,* and *police.* Students should report to the group indicated on their role cards.

3. Each group should select a leader, who will conduct discussion and voting and later speak for the group at the main neighborhood meeting.

4. The leader will ask the group's members, in turn, to present and explain their reactions to Proposal A. Individuals may introduce amendments to the proposal. The leader should encourage cross-discussion aimed at securing a consensus of the group. (If consensus is reached, bloc voting will occur at the neighborhood meeting. See Phase III, below.) When, at the leader's discretion, discussion is complete, a vote should be taken on the proposal. (Amendments, if any, should be voted on before the main proposal.) If "A" is rejected by the group, no position should be taken on Proposal B. If the group's decision is reached by a slim majority, a minority report (consisting of a sentence or two) may be drawn up that will also be presented at the neighborhood meeting.

5. If "A" is passed (with or without amendments), repeat the above procedures for Proposal B.

6. Groups may send messages to other groups offering compromises or deals in an attempt to gain broader-based support for their position. Each group may discuss or vote on any other group's suggestion or compromise.

E. *Phase III: The Neighborhood Meeting* (Suggested time: 40–60 minutes)

1. The next phase of the simulation game is the main neighborhood meeting. Because of its complex responsibilities, the teacher may choose to play the role of the chairperson. If a student is used, however, a role card should have been written in advance and given

*Exhibit 9-2. New Vigilantes: A Simulation Game* **205**

to the designated player at the beginning of the game. Appoint a secretary to keep track of the motions, debate, and votes. A tape recording of the proceedings would be valuable as a motivational device and as an evaluation tool during the debriefing.

2. A minute or two before the end of the game's small-group phase, the chairperson should alert the players to the imminent convening of the main meeting. (If a gavel is available, its use would add a touch of realism to the game.) Upon calling the neigborhood meeting to order, the chairperson should briefly review the rules for debate. A dittoed worksheet or overhead transparency projector may be used for on-going reference to the following rules of parliamentary procedure:

   a. Anyone wishing to speak at the meeting must be recognized by the chairperson. Individuals should stand when speaking.

   b. Each person is limited to a one-minute presentation each time he or she speaks.

   c. All remarks must pertain to the proposal or amendment under consideration.

   d. Amendments may be offered to the original resolution. If an amendment is proposed, it must be seconded before it can be discussed. If it is not seconded, it may not be discussed. If it is seconded, it must be discussed and voted upon before another amendment can be offered or before the original proposal can once again become the focus of debate. Any amendments to the original proposal accepted by majority vote will be considered defeated if the original proposal to which they are attached is later defeated.

   e. No new proposals or resolutions will be accepted until the original proposal and its amendments (if any) are either accepted or rejected. If the original proposal is accepted, a new proposal or resolution may be introduced.

   f. Each resident of Cityville will have one vote.* (No outsider may vote.)

   g. A tally of 50 percent plus one vote is needed to pass any proposal or amendment.

3. The chairperson should call on the three group leaders to present the official positions of their respective constituencies on Proposal A. Each leader's presentation, including proposed amendments and minority reports, is limited to one minute.

4. Following these opening statements, the chairperson should move acceptance of Proposal A. After a second has been obtained, the floor will be open for general discussion and debate. Amendments, if any, may be proposed and discussed at this time.

---

*Although it appears that each individual has one vote, the game players have unequal resources and some individuals control more than one vote. Moreover, the potential for bloc voting has been incorporated into the small-group sessions.

5. After the debate, but before a vote is taken on amendments or on the original proposal, the chairperson should order a five-minute recess. This will afford players an opportunity to use their resources to round up support for their group's stand on "A." Because all three groups will be lobbying, it is suggested that each maintain a minimum of two members at its home base. The wearing of name tags is especially important now because players will be singling out specific individuals for bargaining and discussion.

6. The student who has been designated to draw a contingency card will do so during the recess. Upon selecting the card, the student should give it to the chairperson, who will then announce the "news" to the players. The impact of this information may lead players to reconsider their positions and possibly contribute to the emergence of new groupings. Five more minutes should therefore be alloted for a continuation of individual and group lobbying.

7. After reconvening the meeting, the chairperson should call the question and conduct a vote on Proposal A. If any amendments have been offered, these should be voted on first. Fifty percent plus one vote is needed to carry.

8. If the motion to create a patrol is carried, go on to Phase IV. If it is defeated, the game ends at this point.

F. *Phase IV: Group Interaction* (Suggested time: 5 minutes)

After Proposal A has been accepted in some form, players are given the opportunity to circulate for the purpose of gaining allies for their group's stand on Proposal B. As in Section 5 for Phase III, each group should maintain a minimum of two members at its home base.

G. *Phase V: Discussion and Vote on Proposal B* (Suggested time: 20–30 minutes)

1. Now that the players have voted to create a citizens' patrol, its functioning, personnel, and powers will have to be decided. The same rules that applied in Phase III are to be enforced.

2. The chairperson will call on each group leader for a one-minute presentation of the group's predetermined position on Proposal B. Minority reports and amendments may be included.

3. After these statements, the chairperson will throw open the floor for general discussion and debate. When several minutes have elapsed, the chairperson should ask for specific motions from the floor, which must be seconded and voted upon in order.

*Exhibit 9-2. New Vigilantes: A Simulation Game* **207**

Because of the complexity of Proposal B, individual motions must be entertained for each step. For example, the chairperson will first ask for a motion from the floor concerning the patrol's composition. Once that has been carried, he or she should ask for separate motions establishing each of the patrol's specific powers (i. e., a motion to make arrests, a motion to carry weapons). Only one such motion may be discussed at a time.

4. The game ends when:
   a. The personnel and powers of the patrol are agreed upon, or when
   b. No agreement can be reached on either of the above. If the latter is the case, the chairperson will bring down the gavel, stating there is no hope for agreement, and adjourn the meeting.

*H. The Debriefing* (Suggested time: 40–60 minutes)

The following questions are offered as suggestions for discussion during the debriefing. The teacher should feel free to modify, delete, or add questions according to his or her objectives and to the needs and academic level of the class.

1. Why did you vote either to support or to reject the formation of the citizens' patrol? (If the teacher wants to do an in-depth evaluation of decision making, he or she may distribute copies of several roles to the entire class and conduct a discussion on the various factors influencing the decisions such individuals would be likely to reach.)
   a. How did the values and beliefs of the person you portrayed in the game influence your decisions?
   b. What other values were expressed by different players in your group? In other groups?
   c. Were your decisions in the game influenced by forces other than the personal preferences of the individual you role-played? Explain.
   d. What strategies did you use to gain support for your views? How did you attempt to influence other people in the game? How did they attempt to influence you?
   e. Cite the contingency cards that were not used during the game. Ask students to explain if their positions would have changed had one of these cards been drawn.
2. To what extent would people at a real neighborhood meeting have acted the way the players did during the simulation game? Explain.
   a. Did you enjoy playing the game? Why? Why not?
   b. To what extent was the game worth the classroom time and effort spent in playing it?
   c. How could this simulation game have been improved?

3. What were the most important issues involved in the game?

    a. Are there any traditional American values or constitutional rights that might be in conflict with the establishment of a citizens' patrol? Were there any powers you would be unwilling to give the patrol? Why? Why not?

    b. Would it be possible to safeguard individual rights and still lower the crime rate in the community described in the game? If not, which is it more important to protect: individual rights or public safety? Why?

    c. To what extent may the neighborhood patrol be likened to a posse in the Old West?

    d. If law enforcement is ineffective, should citizens have the right to assume police powers? Should constitutional guarantees be suspended in communities with high crime rates?

    e. How do you account for the increase in such citizens' patrols in recent years?

[This simulation game can serve as an introduction or as a culmination to a study of crime prevention. The following question and exercise will help to link *New Vigilantes* to other aspects of crime prevention or criminal justice.]

4. Can you think of any solutions to rising crime rates other than the formation of citizens' patrols?

5. Listed below are suggested approaches to deal with the problem of crime in the United States. Rate these approaches in descending order from the best to the worst, and be prepared to justify your ranking:

    a. Better street lighting

    b. Evening curfews for teenagers

    c. More police patrols

    d. Better neighborhood housing

    e. More civic pride

    f. Private paid guards

    g. More and better employment opportunities

    h. Stricter laws for drug pushers

    i. Additional community centers

    j. Additional police telephone boxes in the streets

    k. Longer prison terms for street crimes

    l. Restoration of the death penalty for all persons convicted of first-degree murder

    m. A "good samaritan" law, providing monetary rewards for those citizens who aid crime victims

    n. Making it a criminal offense not to report a crime to the police

*Exhibit 9–2. New Vigilantes: A Simulation Game* **209**

## V. Role descriptions

### *Group I: Business—Peter Friend*

Your name is Peter Friend. You are an ex-Marine and former prizefighter who has had several encounters with the authorities, mainly for civil disorders. For the last ten years, you have been part-owner of a florist shop in the neighborhood. You are heavily indebted to Harrison Schuyler's bank and would have been unable to start your business without this loan. You are an active member of the National Rifle Association. Last fall, two men attempted to rob your shop. You shot one of the men and beat the other so severely he had to be hospitalized. You believe every man must be prepared to defend himself in whatever way he can.

### *Group I: Business—Perry Martin*

Your name is Perry Martin. You are black and have invested all your savings in a candy store. You are afraid to send your two young children out of the house since Mary Warren was killed. You want to support any action that will make the streets safer for your family, but are afraid black people will be indiscriminately harassed by a citizens' patrol.

### *Group I: Business—Timothy Shinewald*

Your name is Timothy Shinewald. You own both a real estate firm and the largest department store in Cityville, employing over four hundred people. You contribute regularly to many charities, and are considered one of the most influential persons in Cityville. After your store was burglarized last year, you arranged for the installation of intricate anticrime devices. It is your belief that more anticrime devices in homes and better street lighting will lower the rising crime rate.

You are Greta Swenson's landlord. Although she has been late in paying her rent in the last few months, you have seen fit not to initiate eviction proceedings. You are sure you can control her vote at the meeting.

### *Group I: Business—Stanley Carson*

Your name is Stanley Carson. You and your wife operate a sporting-goods business. Your store has been burglarized twice. On one occasion a few months ago, you were injured, but not seriously, during an attempted holdup by a lone gunman. You now close your store everyday at 5:00 P.M. Profits have fallen sharply, and there has been an increase in shoplifting in your store. You feel there must be a strong neighborhood patrol.

### Group I: Business — Shirley Greene

Your name is Shirley Greene. You took over management of your husband's hardware store after his death five years ago. You were the only member of your family to survive the concentration camps of World War II. Citizens wearing uniforms, carrying weapons, and stopping people in the street remind you of Nazi Germany, and you are against giving these powers to a citizens' patrol.

### Group I: Business — Harrison Schuyler III

Your name is Harrison Schuyler III. You are president of the Cityville Savings and Loan Association, the largest bank in the neighborhood. Your bank has helped to finance many local businesses, and you are greatly concerned that the rise in crime will hurt your investments.

You feel that any action, including the formation of a neighborhood patrol, should be taken if it will reduce crime. Although you officially have one vote, you are very much aware of your power to influence other people at the meeting. You have contributed heavily to Councilman Crawford's election campaign. Your bank holds mortgages on Peter Friend's florist shop and on Shirley Greene's hardware store. You also know that George Freese has applied for a job at the Cityville Savings and Loan Association.

### Group II: Concerned citizens — William Cunningham

Your name is William Cunningham. You are a former member of the Black Panther Party. You are not a community resident, but are at the meeting to see that black people receive justice. You do not trust the police and think they will do nothing to apprehend Mary Warren's killer. On three occasions, you were arrested for participating in civil disobedience actions. It is your view that racism and capitalism are the real causes of crime.

### Group II: Concerned citizens — Billy Brown

Your name is Billy Brown. You are leader of a gang called the Young Avengers. For the past year, your gang has been involved in a drug rehabilitation program. You have set up a patrol of your members which hunts down and forces drug pushers out of the neighborhood. You feel that with more patrols and a tougher policy towards drug dealers, the rate of street crime will be lowered.

You have tremendous respect for Dan Ramirez, a social worker who has been working with your gang for the last two months. He has persuaded you to return to high school, and you will soon receive your diploma. In addition, he helped your mother find a job. You think of Ramirez as a "big brother" and have constantly sought his advice.

*Exhibit 9-2. New Vigilantes: A Simulation Game* **211**

### Group II: Concerned citizens — Carolyn Loggia

Your name is Carolyn Loggia. You are a civil rights lawyer who is very much concerned with the protection of individual rights and liberties. You have been studying the neighborhood situation closely over the past year, even more so since the Warren murder. You believe that justice should be served, but that never — under any circumstances — should the law be taken into private hands. You have declared publicly: "We must be especially careful that the powers of any citizens' group not violate the rights of the individual."

### Group II: Concerned citizens — George Freese

Your name is George Freese. You are a twenty-five-year-old graduate of the University of California at Berkeley, where you majored in accounting. You are married, with an infant daughter. While a student at Berkeley, you were arrested several times for taking part in antiwar demonstrations. You have lived in Cityville for a year but have been unemployed for the last two months. Your wife has persuaded you to apply for a position in Harrison Schuyler's bank. She has urged you not to antagonize Schuyler at the meeting.

### Group II: Concerned citizens — Dan Ramirez

Your name is Dan Ramirez. You are a social worker with advanced degrees in sociology. For the past two years, you have worked with youngsters in the neighborhood, and especially with street gangs. You believe that the underlying cause of crime is poverty. It is your conviction that stronger efforts must be made to stabilize the neighborhood and to keep people who have lived in Cityville for many years from running to the suburbs.

### Group II: Concerned citizens — John Crawford

Your name is John Crawford. You are a member of the City Council in Cityville. It is an election year, and you are anxious not to alienate any bloc of potential supporters. You are particularly interested in gaining liberal support in your community. Your own instincts are against a citizens' patrol, which you fear will lead to serious violations of civil liberty, but you also do not want to lose the political support of such powerful individuals as Timothy Shinewald and Harrison Schuyler III.

### Group II: Concerned citizens — Greta Swenson

Your name is Greta Swenson. You are an elderly widow who lives on the ground floor of a three-family house. You have been mugged twice in the last year: the first time, your purse was stolen while you waited for a bus; the second time, you were accosted by an assailant outside your house. You were knocked to the ground and suffered a concussion and a broken wrist. Your hospital bills after this second incident were exorbitant, and it has been difficult for you to pay your rent. Timothy Shinewald, your landlord, has been very considerate in permitting you to be late in your rent payments. You believe the crime problems began when the neighborhood started to change. You are particularly upset by the groups of boisterous teenagers who loiter in the schoolyard near your house.

### Group II: Concerned citizens — Reverend Matthew Collins

Your name is Reverend Matthew Collins. Your church is located three blocks from the community center. For the past few years, you have attempted to dissuade members of your congregation from moving out of the neighborhood. You are a pacifist and hate violence of any kind. In your church's newsletter you have written: "No citizen should carry weapons. Violence only breeds more violence." After your church was vandalized last month, however, your congregation asked you to demand more police protection.

### Group II: Concerned citizens — Gloria Warren

Your name is Gloria Warren. You are the mother of the little girl who was murdered. You are deeply aggrieved over her death, but you felt compelled to attend tonight's meeting. You have sought solace in Reverend Collins' church. You have great respect for him as a man of the cloth, and would not think of disagreeing with his wishes. Meanwhile, you do not allow your two older daughters to leave your house without an accompanying adult. You are not sure what should be done to prevent crime, but you want the murderer of your little girl apprehended and punished.

### Group III: Police — Nicholas Bailey

Your name is Nicholas Bailey. You are deputy chief of police in Cityville. The chief has asked you to represent the department at the neighborhood meeting. You have mixed feelings about the wisdom of a citizens' patrol and are interested in hearing the views of the other police officers whom you have chosen to attend the meeting with you. Although the police have been advised by the chairperson that they will be allowed five votes at the meeting tonight, you and the chief are very concerned that your group vote as a bloc and that there be no open disagreement among the police.

### Group III: Police — Charles Robinson

Your name is Charles Robinson. You are a black sergeant assigned to the homicide division. You hold a degree in criminology from the state university.

*Exhibit 9–2. New Vigilantes: A Simulation Game* **213**

For the past few years, you have lived in a middle-income apartment house in the neighborhood. You hope to be promoted to detective rank in the near future and have great respect for the ability and views of Captain Higham.

### Group III: Police — Ralph Biemer

Your name is Ralph Biemer. You are an officer who has been on the force for ten years, most of which were spent walking a beat in the neighborhood. Many of the residents know you by your first name. You believe that the best way to prevent crime is by having police on the beat who know the residents personally. You are working for a promotion and are concerned that you not say anything that will offend your superior officers.

### Group III: Police — Wilma Crownover

Your name is Wilma Crownover. You are the commander of a newly formed division of the Cityville Police Department that investigates sex crimes. You are undecided as to the wisdom of a citizens' patrol.

### Group III: Police — Joseph Ryerson

Your name is Joseph Ryerson. You are a black community relations officer who has been on the force for five years. Recently, you organized a "rap" group of police and civilians which meets periodically to discuss community problems. You like the idea of a citizens' patrol, which in your view can be the "eyes and ears" of the police.

### Group III: Police — Andrew Higham

Your name is Andrew Higham. You are the captain of the local precinct and a law school graduate. You believe that science is the key to effective crime prevention. You were instrumental in persuading the city council to provide funds for the installation of a sophisticated computer system in the police department. You are a specialist in safety devices for the prevention of burglary. You believe the Cityville police are understaffed but regard a citizens' patrol as a potential hindrance to successful law-enforcement.

### Group III: Police — Sheldon Snyder

Your name is Sheldon Snyder. You are a twenty-year veteran on the force who has received three departmental decorations for bravery. You believe that only a tough policy of "cracking skulls and putting fear in the hearts of criminals" can lower the crime rate.

## ENDNOTES

1. William A. Nesbitt, *Simulation Games for the Social Studies Classroom* (New York: The Foreign Policy Association, 1971), pp. 4–5.
2. Jack E. Cousins, "Simulations and Simulation Games," in *Human Interaction in Education*, ed. Gene Stanford and Albert E. Roark (Boston: Allyn and Bacon, Inc., 1974), p. 214.
3. Ibid., p. 213.
4. Ray Glazier. *How to Design Educational Games* (Cambridge, Mass.: Abt Associates, 1969), pp. 4–5.
5. Robert F. Mager, *Preparing Instructional Objectives* (Belmont, Calif. Fearon Publishers, 1962), p. 3.
6. Samuel A. Livingston, "How to Design A Simulation Game," [mimeographed] (distributed by Academic Games Associates, 430 East 33 Street, Baltimore, Maryland 21218; 1972), p. 1.
7. Nesbitt, *Simulation Games*, pp. 5–6.
8. Judith A. Gillespie, "Analyzing and Evaluating Classroom Games" [mimeographed], p. 16.
9. Glazier, *How to Design Educational Games*, p. 6.
10. Gillespie, "Analyzing and Evaluating Classroom Games," p. 20.

## BIBLIOGRAPHY

### I. Simulation Games

(The following list is intended to convey to the reader an indication of the vast number and variety of games commercially available. Listing does not constitute endorsement by the Association of Teachers of Social Studies in the City of New York.)

*Bafa Bafa*.    Time: 90 minutes: Grade level: 7–12. Players: 18–36. This is a simulation that deals with the meaning of the term culture. The game prepares players to live and communicate in a foreign culture and to deal more effectively with subcultures such as the Puerto Ricans and the blacks in our society. [Simile II, 1150 Silverado Road, P.O. Box 1023, LaJolla, California 92037]

*Consumer*.    Time: 90–150 minutes. Grade level: 7–12. Players: 11–34. This game is concerned with installment buying and the problems of consumers with limited credit to buy the necessities of life. Students learn to negotiate contracts, calculate interest rates, and budget limited resources. [Western Publishing Co., Inc., 850 3rd Avenue, New York, New York 10022]

*Crisis*.    Time: 2–4 hours. Grade level: 10–12. Players: 35. Six fictional nations deal with the problem of maintaining a world supply of an important mineral. They become involved in a tense situation in a mining area, which threatens world peace. [Simile II]

*Democracy*.    Time: 30 minutes. Grade level: 10–12. Players: 6–11. This game deals with decision making as it pertains to the legislative process. As legislators, students are confronted with the various forces that influence their decisions. [Bobbs-Merrill Co., Inc., 4300 West 62 Street, Indianapolis, Indiana 46206]

*Edplan.*  Time: 2 hours. Grade level: 10–12. Players: 29–36. This simulation concerns educational planning. Students must deal with costs, alternative programs, and benefits. Methods of finance such as bond issues and taxation are investigated while planning educational programs. [Games Central, Abt Associates, Inc., 55 Wheeler Street, Cambridge, Massachusetts 02138]

*Ghetto.*  Time: 2–4 hours. Grade level: 10–12. Players: 7–10. This is a board game where students face the problems of the urban poor in their attempts to improve their situation. The players confront poverty, family commitments, lack of funds, limited educational opportunities, and crime. They must invest their resources wisely if they are to improve their situation in life. [Western Publishing Co., Inc.]

*Guns or Butter.*  Time: 90 minutes. Grade level: 7–12. Players: 18–28. Players analyze the reasons behind the development of an armaments race. They play the roles of national leaders who are attempting to increase their real wealth while securing their nations against attack. [Simile II]

*Herstory.*  Time: 1–2 hours. Grade level: 9–12. Paired students investigate different male-female relationships that develop in the nuclear family, the collective family, and androgynous marriage. They deal with problems of domestic work allocation and decision making, while studying the history and status of women. [Interact, P.O. Box 262, Lakeside, California 92040]

*Innocent Until.*  Time: 5–11 hours. Grade level: 7–12. Players: 13–32. This is a role-play courtroom dramatization of a manslaughter case involving the killing of a star high school athlete by an intoxicated automobile driver. Students confront conflicting testimony in various roles as jurors, attorneys, witnesses, and prosecutors. Players gain insight into judicial procedure. [Games Central – see Edplan]

*Police Patrol.*  Time: 150 minutes. Grade level: 7–12. Players: 20–35. Players explore their attitudes towards police and investigate the complexities of contemporary law enforcement. Students plan small group incidents involving police, and gain insight into the pressures and problems that police officers face today. [Constitutional Rights Foundation, 609 South Grand Avenue, Los Angeles, California 90017]

*Sitte.*  Time: 2–4 hours. Grade level: 7–12. Players: 35. In this game, five interest groups attempt to use their influence to produce changes in the city of Sitte. The groups are: Business, Government, Taxpayers Association, and Ad Hoc Committee for Parks and Trees. Players must face the consequences of their actions according to predetermined criteria. They learn the importance of forming coalitions to effect community change. [Simile II]

*Starpower.*  Time: 150 minutes. Grade level: 7–12. Players: 18–35. Game participants progress from one level of a three-tiered society to another by acquiring wealth (chips) through trading with other participants. The group with the most wealth is given the opportunity to make game rules. The other two groups subsequently experience the frustrations of oppressed groups because the wealthiest group establishes rules that favor themselves. The game usually ends with some kind of rebellion by the excluded groups. [Simile II]

*Strike.*  Grade level: 7–12. Players: 35. In this game, a strike occurs when three major steel companies and three local unions cannot reach contractual agreement. Players gain awareness of the complexities involved in labor-management relations, the public effects of private enterprise, the role of mediators, and the relationship between government and industry. [Interact]

*The Union Divides.*  Time: 4–10 hours. Grade level: 7–12. Players: 16–42. This is a game in which students play the roles of state governors trying to prevent the outbreak of civil war in the late 1850s. The major crises of the period are presented through a series of recordings. At the end of the game, students should be able to discuss whether the Civil War was inevitable. [Olcott Forward, Inc., 24 Popham Road, Scarsdale, New York]

## II. Books

Abt, Clark C. *Serious Games.* New York: Viking Press, 1970.

Boocock, Sarane S. and Schild, E. O., eds. *Simulation Games in Learning.* Beverly Hills: Sage Publications, 1968.

Caillois, Roger. *Man, Play, and Games.* New York: Free Press, 1961.

Carlson, Elliot. *Learning Through Games.* Washington, D. C.· Public Affairs Press, 1968.

Charles, Cheryl L. and Stadsklev, Ronald, eds. *Learning with Games.* Boulder, Colo.: Social Science Consortium, 1973.

Glazier, Ray. *How to Design Educational Games.* Cambridge, Mass.: Abt Associates, 1969.

Guetzkow, Harold S., ed. *Simulation in Social Science: Readings.* Englewood Cliffs, N. J.: Prentice-Hall, 1962.

Inbar, Michael and Stoll, Clarice S. *Simulation and Gaming in Social Sciences.* New York: Free Press, 1972.

Nesbitt, William A. *Simulation Games for the Social Studies Classroom.* New York: The Foreign Policy Association, 1971.

Shubik, Martin, ed. *Game Theory and Related Approaches to Social Behavior.* New York: John Wiley & Sons, 1964.

Stanford, Gene and Roark, Albert E., eds. *Human Interaction in Education.* Boston: Allyn and Bacon, Inc., 1974.

Tansey, P. J. and Unwin, O. *Simulation and Gaming in Education.* New York: Harper & Row, 1969.

Taylor, John L. and Walford, Rex. *Simulation in the Classroom.* Baltimore: Penguin Books, 1972.

Zuckerman, David W. and Horn, Robert. *The Guide to Simulation Games for Education and Training.* Cambridge, Mass.: Information Resources, 1973.

## III. Articles

Abt, Clark C., "War Gaming." *International Science and Technology* XXXII (1969): 29–37.

Boocock, Sarane S. "An Experimental Study of the Learning Effects of Two Games with Simulated Environments." *American Behavioral Scientist* X (October 1966): 8–17.

DeKock, Paul. "Simulations and Changes in Racial Attitudes." *Social Education* XXXIII (February 1969): 181–85.

Donahay, A. "Social Studies Games: New Learning Tool." *Instructor* LXXVIII (August 1967): 172–73.

Gillespie, Judith A. "Analyzing and Evaluating Classroom Games." *Social Education* XXXVI (January 1972): 33–34, 94.

Gunn, Angus M. "Simulation: The Game of 'Section.'" *Social Education* XXXIII (February 1969): 193–94.

McKenny, James L. and Dill, William. "Influences on Learning in Simulation Games." *American Behavioral Scientist* X (October 1966): 18–28.

Shirts, R. Garry. "Simulations, Games, and Related Activities for Elementary Classrooms." *Social Education* XXXV (March 1971): 300–304.

Thorpe, Gerald L. "A Brief Survey of Research in Learning Through the Use of Simulation Games." *High School Journal* XXI (April 1971): 454–69.

# 10

••••••••••••••••••••••••••••••••••••••••••••••••••••••••••••••••••••••••••••

# Testing and Evaluation

••••••••••••••••••••••••••••••••••••••••••••••••••••••••••••••••••••••••••••

How does the social studies teacher define evaluation? Too often, the definition incorporates only one factor — testing. It is the intention of this chapter to describe evaluation within a much broader framework and to explore its various functions. We will examine the relationship between evaluation and objectives. It will also be necessary to understand the criteria for effective evaluation. Illustrations of evaluative techniques and instruments will be given in order to demonstrate the panoply of available evaluatory techniques. Our definition of evaluation, therefore, involves a comprehensive determination of what is taking place in a learning situation.

## THE PURPOSE OF EVALUATION

Evaluation does not exist in a vacuum but is a process within a larger model. It cannot be separated from the total teaching-learning experience both within and outside of the classroom. Evaluation must be an integral part of the teaching-learning model and not something that happens at the end in order to assign grades. Its primary purpose is to determine the extent to which previously stated objectives have been achieved. As a result of evaluation, teachers should be able to make midcourse corrections within the developing learning situation.

### Functions and Characteristics of Evaluation

Evaluation in the social studies must be comprehensive. Objectives can be redefined as a result of students' success or lack of achievement. The social studies instructional program including teaching units and various learning activities can be reassessed as a result of the evaluation process. Students are

**219**

made aware of their own progress. In order to accomplish these purposes, good evaluation encompasses a wide range of techniques. It is a cooperative effort that includes input by students. Individual growth must be an important function of all evaluation.

Bloom, Hastings, and Madaus' sum up the comprehensiveness of evaluation in the following manner:

1. Evaluation is a method of acquiring and processing needed to improve the students' learning and the teaching.
2. Evaluation includes a great variety of evidence beyond the usual paper-and-pencil examination.
3. Evaluation is an aid in clarifying the significant goals and objectives of education and is a process for determining the extent to which students are developing in these desired ways.
4. Evaluation is a system of quality control which helps determine along every step of the process whether the process is successful or not.

### More Than Testing for Knowledge

Evaluation is most frequently used for the purpose of grading and classifying students. The instrument most closely associated with this goal is the written test, often comprised of objective-type short-answer questions. Testing alone has not contributed to improvement of the teaching-learning process. Not too many years ago, the mastery of subject matter was considered the major goal of the social studies. Achievement of this objective was measured by the ability of students to memorize information. While the objectives are much broader today, there are teachers who regard facts and information as of primary importance, and their evaluation is therefore reflected by paper-and-pencil tests. With the realization that there are different kinds of learning objectives, varied outcomes are to be expected and these must be evaluated.

Too often we measure what is easiest to evaluate. It is a simple task to find out if students know what year the Philippines received its independence from the United States. It becomes more difficult to evaluate the understanding of a concept such as the nationalistic aspiration which led to independence. Even more difficult is the evaluation of values. Because the memorization of facts can easily be measured with use of an objective-type written test, it becomes simple to allow evaluation to influence the objectives. This must not be the case. Understandings, generalizations, attitudes, and social behavior are all important in the social studies. While they are more difficult to assess than facts and information, they nevertheless must be included as important objectives.

Predetermined evaluation, in the form of convenient objective written tests, cannot be the basis for establishing goals. Neither can they become the determinants of teaching methods and strategies. Teachers must not adapt their procedures to what can most easily be evaluated. Evaluation should not dictate methodology. Evaluation is an outgrowth of social studies objectives and teaching strategies. It is part of the total model.

### Diagnostic, Formative, and Summative Evaluation

Evaluation must take place throughout the entire teaching-learning process. It is not something that takes place prior to the distribution of report cards. Frequently the practice in many schools is that at the end of a grading period, the students are subjected to tests. We use grades as a system of rewards and punishment. For those who have achieved according to the established objectives the results are favorable. Those who did not score well are assigned poorer grades. This type of evaluation is merely a check on pupils' test performance. It is true that this is one function, but there are many functions of evaluation. Another function is diagnosis.

Diagnostic evaluation, usually in the form of a test, often occurs prior to the learning experience. The teacher attempts to determine what the learner brings to the classroom. Used in this way, the purpose of evaluation is for placement. Diagnosis can help the teacher understand the readiness of the pupils for learning tasks, to determine the place of entry into a learning experience, and to know what kind of preparation to undertake prior to introducing the students to a new unit. A teacher can determine how much a student knows about the United Nations, or what the student's attitude towards the United Nations might be before the unit on it begins. Diagnostic evaluation can be in the form of pretests, standardized achievement tests, standardized diagnostic tests, observation, and checklists.

Formative evaluation occurs all throughout the learning experience. The purpose is not to grade the student but to determine deficiencies in order to remedy them. An immediate consequence of formative evaluation is the restructuring of instruction to permit remediation to take place. It occurs at frequent intervals and is necessary whenever new material has been completed. Within a social studies unit, there should be many new concepts and skills so formative evaluation should occur frequently. The teacher would not want to proceed before mastery of the preceding tasks was accomplished. Formative evaluation concentrates on providing feedback to students.

Summative evaluation is concerned with an overall assessment of student achievement and has as its primary purpose, the assignment of grades. This is usually associated with testing at the completion of a unit of study or after the entire course. The tests can be of the teacher-made variety, such as unit tests and final examinations, or may be standardized such as a system-wide or state-wide examination.

## A Total Process

Effective evaluation must be diagnostic, formative, and summative in scope. Too often it has been entirely summative, occurring when the class finishes a unit or a course of study. Besides serving as a device for assigning grades, this type of evaluation occurs too late to help the group that was evaluated. Final assessment does not lend itself to remediation. Evaluation must not only keep students continuously aware of their progress, but teachers must continuously be able to reassess their objectives and strategies.

Diagnostic, formative, and summative evaluation are all related to each other. Formative evaluation has a similar function to diagnostic. Both are involved in determining where students have weaknesses and need to be helped. Diagnostic attempts to pinpoint areas in need of remedy prior to the introduction of a learning experience. Formative has the same purpose during the course of the learning experience. Summative evaluation is closely related to both in that the final learning experience is shaped by possible changes introduced because of diagnostic and formative evaluation.

Teachers must come to regard evaluation as an integral part of the teaching-learning process. It is not something that happens when we finish a unit; it is not solely for the purpose of assigning grades, and it should never be used with the intention of punishing students. Michaelis describes the integration of evaluation into the learning experience as something constantly going on: "This means simply that throughout the day, from day to day, and from week to week throughout the year, constant and continuous appraisals must be made. . . ."[2] Evaluation will never be utilized to its total potential unless teachers are fully aware of its full range of purposes.

## EVALUATION AND SOCIAL STUDIES OBJECTIVES

The primary responsibility for evaluation rests with the individual teacher. The teacher must be concerned with three basic questions:

1. What do I evaluate?
2. How do I evaluate?
3. How do I use the results of the evaluation to improve teaching and learning?

Questions two and three will be dealt with in the following pages. The first question is directly related to objectives in the social studies and we have stated that a basic purpose of evaluation is to determine the extent to which objectives have been achieved. To evaluate properly, we want to know what knowledge and understandings the students should be able to demonstrate. What skills should the students possess? What attitudes and values should be exhibited? What type of teaching-learning process is the class to participate in? It is only by identifying objectives and stating them specifically that we can have a clear understanding of what will take place in the classroom. This will then set the stage for effective evaluation.

## Changing Social Studies Objectives

Social-studies objectives have been undergoing changes throughout the twentieth century. By the end of the First World War, the social studies consisted of three basic disciplines: history, geography, and government. They were taught using a chronological approach. Objectives were geared toward the mastery of content which was reflected by having students memorize a great deal of factual information. Evaluation consisted of a regurgitation of these facts, and objective-type test questions comprised the measuring instruments.

The Depression years brought about significant changes. Influenced by the progressive movements in education, the social studies were now involved with citizenship education and education for life. Critical thinking began to be emphasized.

The later part of the 1950s saw greater changes in the social studies than in any prior period. Achievements by the Russians in their space program brought forth many questions and criticisms of American education. Reforms in school mathematics and science programs were effected and these curricula developments had a profound influence on social studies. What emerged were the "new social studies" programs of the 1960s. Bruner and others offered the structure of the disciplines as content for social studies curricula. Organization of curriculum was based on concepts and generalizations as building blocks. Discovery and inquiry became important processes in the teaching-learning experience.

## The New Social Studies, Objectives, and Evaluation

What was the significance of the recent social studies reforms upon evaluation? Teachers now had to concern themselves with not only what knowledge students acquired but *how* they acquired it. The process of learning, including inquiry and problem solving skills, has become an important objective and therefore requires careful evaluation.

The ability to solve problems and think critically is an important objective in the social studies. It is reasonable to assume that within a few days after remembering the provisions of the Northwest Ordinance, the average student will forget them. Perhaps they will be forgotten within a few hours. Twenty years from now students will remember little of the content covered in class, but they will have to find the solutions to many problems. We must stress the ability to apply knowledge to problem situations. Then we evaluate that ability.

It often becomes easy for teachers to accept the importance of developing critical thinking on a philosophical level. Who would speak out and say that retention of facts alone and not higher-level cognitive skills is important? Most of us would agree that both are significant. However, how might teachers react to and evaluate the following hypothetical situation?

> *Teacher:* "In what year did Magellan begin his voyage around the world?"
>
> *Pupil:* "I don't know. But I do know how to find out. I'll go to the library, look in the card catalogue under M, find a book about Magellan, look in the table of contents for his voyage, and read that in the year. . . ."

How would you evaluate this student? If we are interested only in an immediate answer, the score would be a poor one. On the other hand, the student has the tools necessary to find the answer. As a matter of fact, the student really doesn't need a teacher to acquire simple factual information. The social studies today are concerned with more than just information. Evaluation must include all levels of cognitive skills as well as those in the affective domain.

## Categorizing Objectives

Traditionally social-studies objectives (and the evaluation of those objectives) have fallen into three areas: knowledge, attitudes, and skills. With the work by Bloom,[3] Krathwohl,[4] and others, objectives are now usually classified in the cognitive and affective domains. The cognitive category includes knowledge, intellectual abilities, and skills, while the affective category incorporates both attitudes and values. Chapter 1 of this text presents a more detailed explanation of the nature of social studies objectives.

## Specific Objectives for More Effective Evaluation

Once objectives have been decided upon, methodology and evaluation can be developed. The more precise the objectives, the easier the evaluation task becomes. The trend in recent years has been toward behaviorally stated objectives. This calls for the stating of instructional objectives in terms of pupil behavior that can readily be observed and measured. Mager[5] presents an anecdote that illustrates the importance of behavioral objectives:

> *Tutor:* "You can't measure the effects of what I do."
>
> *Student:* "Why not?"
>
> *Tutor:* "They're intangible."

*Student:* "Oh? Why should I pay for intangible results?"

*Tutor:* "Because I've been trained and licensed to practice."

*Student:* "Hmmmm . . . all right. Here's your money."

*Tutor:* "Where? I don't see it."

*Student:* "Of course not — it's intangible."

Evaluation can be facilitated if there is some degree of behavior specified. Lofty and vague objectives provide poor guidelines for evaluation. Acknowledging the difficulty of measuring the affective domain doesn't mean we must not attempt to evaluate as objectively as possible. Social studies teachers cannot abdicate their responsibility with regard to values and other nonknowledge objectives. Perhaps some measure of specificity will help.

*Framework for Effective Evaluation.* The effectiveness of evaluation depends on several factors: the establishment of a clear purpose for evaluation, careful planning based upon purpose, the adequacy of the measurement techniques used for evaluation, and the extent to which evaluation techniques facilitate future program planning.

### Establishing a purpose

The first and perhaps most important step in evaluation is the establishment of a clear and meaningful purpose by reflecting upon the decisions and judgments that are to be made based on the data that will be collected. In order to arrive at a clear and meaningful purpose (goal) for evaluation, the following steps should be taken by the teacher:

1. *Identify the type of information that is desired.* In order to identify the type of information desired the teacher must first focus upon the broad domain to be assessed. The next step is to specify the exact nature of the desired information: for example, the ability of the student to form concepts.

2. *Describe what will be learned from the gathered information.* A delineation of the information expected to be acquired through testing will further aid in the establishment of a clear purpose. For example, the teacher should decide whether the test information will be used for diagnostic purposes, for normative reference, or to assess student feeling towards a particular topic.

3. *Explain the relatedness of the collected data to the total picture of evaluation.* As no single measuring instrument can present a complete picture of evaluation, teachers should be able to state how the particular evaluative instrument being used is related to the total evaluation scheme. That is, what contribution does this assessment make to

an overall evaluation system? Is it diagnostic, formative, or summative in nature?

Following the establishment of a clear purpose for evaluation is the planning phase. This should be greatly facilitated once clear, specific goals have been determined. Appropriate planning of evaluation is crucial and should relate directly to the purpose set forth by the teacher. Unfortunately, in many cases teachers plan their measuring devices at the last moment, resulting in assessment techniques and instruments that do not adequately meet the educational objectives that were defined.

### Planning

In planning for evaluation, the teacher should be able to:

1. *Identify the type of assessment technique that will yield the most comprehensive data.* While tests are generally the most popular measuring devices used by teachers, a variety of instruments such as attitude scales, observational checklists, and open-ended questions, may be effectively employed for the assessment of educational objectives. The type of instrument used will depend upon the nature and scope of the desired data.

2. *Select or produce items that accurately represent the important teaching objectives.* If, for example, a teacher wishes to evaluate student achievement in a particular subject, items of moderate difficulty can be used, related to the content studied, which will differentiate among student achievement levels. On the other hand, if the purpose of testing is to determine whether or not students have mastered basic skills such as locating geographical sites on a map, the items selected should reflect a minimum proficiency in the desired skill. Tests derived for the measurement of attitudes or values must contain items that allow students to express their varying feelings.

3. *Determine at which point during the semester the particular assessment technique and instrument will be used.* While evaluation is frequently viewed as the final step in teaching to culminate a unit of work, this need not be so. Evaluation should be considered both prior to and during an instructional unit as well as after completion of the unit. It is often useful to plan a pretest/posttest in order to determine whether a change has taken place in the student's cognitive or affective behavior.

*Basic Characteristics of Assessment Devices.*    The effectiveness of any measuring, be it a short-answer test, essay examination, or attitude scale, depends upon its reliability, validity, and employability. While a detailed discussion of these three characteristics is beyond the scope of this text, several points will be made to assist teachers in planning for evaluation.

### Validity

A measuring device is said to be valid to the extent that it measures what it purports to measure. In order to be a valid measure of classroom achievement, a teacher-made test must contain items that correspond to the teaching objectives. The items should assess the essential objectives of instruction, and the test content should accurately reflect the emphasis given to the various topics. Care must also be exercised to balance the items among the various types and levels of instructional objectives.

Teachers must concern themselves not only with the material or content of instruction but also with the thought processes they wish their students to engage in (e. g., memorize, recognize, compare, contrast, analyze, apply). Use of Bloom's *Taxonomy of Educational Objectives*, volumes I and II, in preparing test items would assist in writing items with greater content validity.

The notion of validity can also be applied to instruments that purport to assess affective domain objectives. Teachers who wish to sample student attitudes must be certain that the items that they select for an attitude scale accurately reflect the domain of the attitude in question.

### Reliability

Reliability deals with the degree of consistency of test results or the level of consistency between two measures of the same thing. If a teacher administers a reliable achievement test and shortly thereafter readministers an equivalent form of the same test, students should score roughly the same as they did during the first testing period. Likewise, an attitude test readministered after a brief interval should reveal attitudes that are consistent with those of the mutual test period (assuming that nothing has transpired that would alter these attitudes).

All measuring devices lack some degree of reliability. It is up to the teacher to try to construct measuring devices that achieve the highest degree of reliability. Among several factors that may act to make a test less reliable are: the length of the test, the ambiguity of directions and questions, and an overload of items that are too difficult or too easy. As an illustration, a one-item test on the Civil War would be highly unreliable. Some students may know a great deal about the topic and yet it is possible that they will not know this particular answer. Similarly, others may know very little about the topic and yet correctly guess the answer.

It should be pointed out that a test can be valid only if it is reliable; however, it can be highly reliable and yet not be valid. If a teacher prepared a test on complex conceptual information that was not covered during the semester, the majority of students would probably do poorly on such a test.

Readministering the same test a short time later would most likely yield the same results. Such a test would be reliable (consistent) but would not meet the criteria of content validity.

### Employability

The third characteristic of any measuring device is its employability. This refers to the ease of administering the device, the time required, the energy expended to collect the data, and the ease with which the data can be interpreted. Before administering any assessment device, teachers should ascertain that the directions are clear, check for flaws, and make sure that favorable testing conditions exist.

*The Instruments of Evaluation.*   Since evaluation is multipurposed, it may rely on a variety of instruments and techniques. The instrument or instruments to be used will depend upon the specific objectives to be measured. It is the classroom teacher who has primary responsibility for the selection of the evaluation device. It is possible that specific situations may call for a variety of techniques. Therefore the teacher must be continuously aware of what has to be measured and the appropriate tools for evaluating specific objectives.

In the following exhibits we have attempted to describe some basic instruments and techniques of evaluation. The selection is based on what is commonly used in classrooms as well as suggestions for consideration by the teacher. The list is by no means conclusive. We have not, for example, attempted to elaborate on standardized tests. The conclusion of this chapter contains a list of sources which can be referred to for additional information.

**Commonly used measuring instruments and techniques**

| *For cognitive objectives* | *For affective objectives* |
|---|---|
| Objective tests | Attitude scales |
| Essay tests | Opinion polls |
| Observation | Questionnaires |
| Group discussion | Open-ended questions |
| Interviews | Open-mindedness scales |
| Samples of students' work | Observation |
| (projects, book reports, | Group discussion |
| research papers) | Anecdotal records |
|  | Interviews |
|  | Role playing |

*1. Tests and Test Construction.*   Test items can take many forms, as can be seen in tests constructed by teachers and by teachers and students and in standardized tests. Tests have various purposes and should be utilized to measure all levels of cognition, including inquiry skills. This section deals with various forms of test items and suggests how one form may be used for multiple purposes. It is important that teachers recognize that objective questions can be used to evaluate more than simple recall or recognition. Objective items as well as essays can incorporate the application of information to situations that involve critical thinking.

One test should consist of a variety of items, including both objective items and essay questions. In the construction of questions, teachers should consult models provided by system-wide, state-wide, and standardized tests.[6]

A. Objective Items

1. Alternative Response

This type of item presents the test-taker with two alternatives. A statement is given or a picture or diagram is presented that is to be judged as true or false, or fact or opinion. While there are other variations, alternative-response items seem to be the most commonly used by teachers. This type of question is fairly easy to write and to score and enables a wide variety of information to be sampled quickly. However, the element of guessing detracts from the reliability of true-false items, and it is difficult to construct items that accurately measure higher levels of thinking.

In writing alternative-response items, teachers should keep the following points in mind:

—Avoid using specific determiners, such as *always* or *never.*

—Avoid using terms that denote an indefinite degree of amount, such as *often* or *a lot.*

—Avoid items for which more than two plausible responses may be made. Be certain that the item is definitely true or false, or fact or opinion.

—It is best to state the sentence in simple terms as a positive declarative statement. The use of double negatives and difficult phrasing should be avoided.

a. *Retention of Knowledge*

In the space provided before the statement, write *true* or *false.*

__The United States acquired both East and West Florida from Spain.

__President Lincoln's assassination brought a speedy end to the Civil War.

b. *Application of Concepts*

After reading each statement, circle whether it is true or false.

If the Cascade Mountains were 500 miles further east, western Oregon would have an increased rainfall.

c. *Fact and Opinion*

In the following list, some sentences are facts, while others are opinions. Indicate whether you think each sentence is a fact or an opinion by placing an *F* or an *O* before each sentence.

__United States involvement in Indochina was in the best interest of our country.

__South Vietnam was a former French colony.

2. Multiple Choice

Multiple choice can be extremely versatile and effective. A partial condition (stem) is presented as an incomplete statement, and several response alternatives (options) are offered. Among the options is the correct answer and a series of distractors. The following suggestions are offered for writing multiple-choice items:

—Write clearly. State the central issue in the stem and be sure that each question is easy to read and comprehend.

—Avoid lifting items directly from the textbook, as this encourages memorization.

—For each item, arrange the choices in some logical order (alphabetically, chronologically). Care should also be exercised to randomize the correct order.

—As in other types of items, all options should be plausible. Alternative responses should be homogeneous in content, form, and grammatical structure.

*a. Sequencing*

In the space provided, choose the best answer for the question. Which sequence best shows the historical development of a nineteenth-century colonial power?

a. Nationalism, imperialism, industrialization

b. Imperialism, nationalism, industrialization

c. Nationalism, industrialization, imperialism

d. Industrialization, imperialism, nationalism'

*b. Reference Skills*

Directions: You are sent to the library to find answers to questions 1 through 4. Which of the sources under "reference shelf" would you use? Place the letter of the best source next to each question.

*Reference Shelf*

A. An atlas

B. *Who's Who in America*

C. *World Almanac*

D. An encyclopedia

E. *Reader's Guide to Periodical Literature*

__1. Which team won the world series last year?

__2. Which states border on Wyoming?

__3. Which magazines published articles about water pollution last year?

__4. What did Alexander the Great do to be called "great"?

*c. Interpreting and Applying Geographical Data and Concepts*

The map, Figure 10-1, shows an imaginary continent. The principal

FIGURE 10-1.   *Map of Islandia*

*Source:* Reprinted by permission from *Iowa Tests of Basic Skills*, The Riverside Publishing Company.

cities appear in alphabetical order, beginning near the top.

Which of the following is *not* a true statement about Islandia?

1. Much of the western coast is mountainous.

2. The northern part of the continent is in the tropics.

3. Much of the continent lies below the equator.

4. The complete continent is shown on the map.

Where does the point 32°S, 63°W fall?

1. In the ocean

2. In the mountains

3. In a lake
4. Not on the map

## 3. Matching

Matching exercises present students with two lists and ask them to match each item from one list with an item from the other list. Matching questions usually require students to associate names, dates, events, and persons; terms and definitions, causes and effects. This type of test item can be quite versatile. Apart from the standard two-column appearance, matching questions can involve matching items with map locations or diagram parts.

In preparing matching items for tests, the following steps should be followed:

— List and number the stimulus items on the left; options associated with these items should be listed and numbered on the right. The list of options should contain more possible responses than required to complete the exercise.

— Each exercise should contain homogeneous material. Do not "mix apples and oranges" by placing, for example, names of people and places on the same list. All options should seem plausible.

— To facilitate test taking, arrange items and options in a systematic fashion. Thus, dates should be arranged chronologically and names alphabetically.

— Include all items and options on a sample page.

— Provide clear instructions to students.

— Indicate whether items can be used more than once or whether there is only one correct answer.

### a. *Categorization*

In the space before each of the responsibilities, write the letter of the branch of government that carries it out.

| RESPONSIBILITIES | BRANCHES |
|---|---|
| __1. Makes laws | A. Executive |
| __2. Interprets laws | |
| __3. Enforces laws | B. Judicial |
| __4. Appropriates money | |
| __5. Prepares budget | C. Legislative[7] |

### b. *Association*

In the space before each name in Column I, place the number of the phrase in Column II that most closely corresponds to it.

| COLUMN I | COLUMN II |
|---|---|
| __ A. Samuel Adams | 1. Freedom of the press |
| __ B. Nathaniel Bacon | 2. Policy of salutary neglect |
| __ C. Benjamin Franklin | 3. French aid in Revolutionary War |
| __ D. Alexander Hamilton | 4. Critic of Articles of Confederation at Annapolis Convention |
| __ E. Thomas Jefferson | |
| __ F. James Madison | 5. Father of the Constitution |
| __ G. Tom Paine | 6. Debtors' revolt in Massachusetts |
| __ H. Daniel Shays | 7. Mayflower Compact |
| __ I. Robert Walpole | 8. Committee of Correspondence |
| __ J. Peter Zenger | 9. Rebellion in Virginia |
| | 10. Tory leader during Revolution |
| | 11. *Common Sense* |
| | 12. Declaration of Independence |

## B. Essay Questions

Essay items can best be applied in measuring the high-level skills of critical thinking. They involve not only knowledge of specific facts but an ability to select, organize, and apply those facts to specific situations. They are also essential in evaluating an understanding of concepts. Essays can be comprehensive in nature, covering a wide range of subject matter and offering a choice to those answering. Essay questions can also be constructed so that they measure knowledge and understanding of very specific content areas.

Teachers must be aware of certain basic considerations in constructing good essay questions. Questions such as "Describe the provisions of the Treaty of Guadalupe Hidalgo of 1848" would be more effective as short-answer items. On the other hand, a question that asks the student to evaluate the fairness of the treaty does lend itself to the essay format. Questions must clearly identify the purpose for which they are asked. Ambiguous, vague, or general questions confuse the student and are difficult to measure.

*Poor:* Discuss the origins of the cold war.

*Better:* Assume that Winston Churchill, Nikita Khrushchev, and Harry Truman were invited to our class on "The Origins of the Cold War."

How would each of these men be likely to present the subject? What events or ideas might each select as the most significant causal factor?

On which points, if any, would they probably agree? (Support your statements with facts, data, or other evidence.)[8]

*Poor:* Explain why you think the United Nations has been a success or a failure.

*Better:* An important function of the United Nations is to help settle disputes between nations. Describe how one dispute was handled successfully, pointing out how the settlement illustrates a strength of the United Nations. Describe also how one dispute was handled unsuccessfully, pointing out how this illustrates a general weakness of the United Nations. Your essay should be about 300–400 words in length (two or three pages in longhand).[9]

While essay questions have the major advantages of being able to evaluate high-level thinking skills and of allowing students to be expressive and imaginative, they do have disadvantages. They are difficult to grade with regard to objectivity and are time-consuming to read. Essays permit a narrower sampling than do objective items. They can encourage students to be wordy and often result in bluffing. However, since critical thinking and inquiry skills are so important in social studies, essays must form an important part of the evaluation procedure.

Essays can be developed around hypothetical situations:

Base your answers to essay question no. 2 on the hypothetical situation given below.

The military government of Omega has been in power since January, when it overthrew the democratically elected president in a bloodless coup. The new president, General Hector Ramir, is demanding that the United States corporations that hold investments and properties in Omega pay back taxes to his government.

The corporations have so far refused to yield to General Ramir's demands, with the result that the General has given the corporations thirty days in which to meet his demands. Should the corporations refuse, Ramir has been authorized to seize and nationalize the properties and assets of the United States corporations. The corporations have appealed to the United States State Department and the president for assistance.

a. Based on the situation and your knowledge of foreign affairs, judge the seriousness of the threat in terms of the legitimate interests of the United States government. (3 pts.)

b. In its response to the appeals of the corporations, the United States government would probably decide on an immediate action to take, along with a series of follow up actions if the immediate action did not result in the desired outcome.

1. From the list of possible actions below, select the one that you think the United States government should take as the immediate action and indicate the outcome the government would desire from this action. (3 pts.)

2. If the immediate action does not result in the desired outcome, consider the actions below and indicate which further actions might be taken. In your answer, describe the decisions that would be involved. Support your choices by citing specific historical examples of similar decision making in the handling of foreign affairs. (9 pts.)

*Actions*

A. Do nothing
B. Intervene with armed forces
C. Conduct bilateral negotiations
D. Invoke economic sanctions
E. Request assistance from the United Nations
F. Break diplomatic relations[10]

Essays can be used to determine an awareness of conflicting values in society:

Below is a collection of paired phrases about urban living:

1. Respect for civic law
   Freedom to do exactly what I want
2. A city that's easy to walk around
   A city that's easy to drive around
3. Varied neighborhoods
   Neighbors who are just like me
4. Cleaner, faster subways and buses
   Lower bus and subway fares
5. Immediate end to air pollution
   More power stations
6. Lower rents
   A fair break for landlords
7. More jobs for city dwellers
   No commercial zoning near dwellings
8. No parades disrupting traffic flow
   More parades promoting civic pride

a. State a valid generalization based on all eight pairs of phrases. (3 pts.)

b. Select two sets of paired phrases and for each pair selected, explain the basic issue involved in the phrases. (6 pts.)

c. For one of the pairs selected in answer to b, describe a different, workable process that two of the following persons might use in attempting to solve the issue: (6 pts.)

1. The mayor
2. A citizen who is a civic leader
3. A local business person[11]

The first two examples are comprehensive in nature and allow students to incorporate knowledge from many periods. Sometimes we want to measure knowledge of specific periods:

When a nation has severe financial problems, sacrifices have to be made. The debate over Hamilton's financial plan was over who would make these sacrifices. Hamilton's scheme placed the burden on those less able to bear it, whereas his opponents wanted the burden to fall on those best able to bear it.

1. Identify and explain those arguments used by the opponents of Hamilton's plan that could be used to support the above statement.

2. Identify and explain those arguments used by the proponents of Hamilton's financial plan that could be used to oppose the above argument.

3. Explain whether you believe that this statement is a valid description of the issue between the opponents and proponents of Hamilton's financial plan.[12]

Essays can be used to measure various inquiry skills. For example, if teachers want to evaluate the ability to formulate hypotheses, one way would be to ask the following questions dealing with documentary evidence:

(Students are given Pericles' "Oration in Praise of Athens" from Thucydides' *History of the Peloponnesian War*.)

1. What hypothesis would you form about Athenian values from this speech?

2. What questions would you ask to begin validating this hypothesis?[13]

### A word about reading

The importance of reading as a prerequisite for successful learning in social studies has been stressed elsewhere in this book. While it is understood that every social studies teacher cannot be a reading specialist, it is essential that social studies teachers assist students in every possible way to develop and improve reading skills. Evaluation is the first step in this process. Early in the term, teachers must be made aware of students' areas of specific skills — deficiencies as well as interest areas. Diagnostic evaluation aids teachers in structuring lessons, in grouping students for instruction, and in referring students for additional reading assistance. Students also should receive corrective feedback from the teacher to see if they are gaining the necessary skills.

A variety of assessment techniques are available to teachers who wish to gain a comprehensive picture of their students' reading skills and interests. Among these devices are: standardized reading tests, informed-teacher tests, oral reading passages, samples of students' work, and interest inventories. Those interested in learning more about diagnosis and evaluation in reading can refer to the sources listed at the end of this chapter for further reading and to Chapter 6.

### Communicating criteria

In Chapter 1 of this handbook, the teacher was urged to communicate curriculum objectives to his or her clientele, the students and their parents. It was also recommended that these objectives be arrived at through an interaction between the teacher and the students. Because of the close relationship between course objectives and criteria of evaluation, it is similarly recommended that criteria of evaluation be clearly fixed in the students' minds at the beginning of a school term. In some instances, it might be appropriate to "negotiate" these criteria. Some teachers ask students individually to assign a percentage of weighted importance to the various means of evaluating students. The results are collected and class percentages are arrived at. The teacher then "rounds out" the percentages. The students now feel that the way they are marked has not been forced on them, but that they had a say on how they will be evaluated. An eleventh-grade class, with their teacher, arrived at this breakdown:

| | |
|---|---|
| Tests and Quizzes | 60% |
| Class Participation | 15% |
| "Front and Center" Project | 15% |
| Notebook and Homework | 10% |
| Total | 100% |

Teachers report that when they allow their students to negotiate their own criteria, they invariably arrive at a very fair breakdown. The obvious advantage of this system is that students know in advance exactly what is expected of them.

2. *Other Approaches.*    Tests are not the only instruments that can be used to measure cognitive skills. In the day-to-day activities of the classroom, teachers must constantly evaluate. Observation, group discussion, interviews, and samples of students' work can all be utilized.

### A. Observation

This is a very important evaluative technique because the teacher has the opportunity to watch students perform each day. Students can be observed participating in a variety of experiences. Observation continuously takes place but in order to use it most effectively, teachers must know what they are looking for, have some system for observing, and attempt to use the data collected in an objective manner. To facilitate this, teachers might list which cognitive skills they would like to see demonstrated during the course of the lesson. Rather than observing everyone in the class, certain individuals could be singled out for intensive study. Specific situations can be established, such as asking students to do research, so that specific skills can be observed. The key to using observation as an evaluative technique is to combine it with a record of what is being observed. Teachers cannot depend on memory. Written records may take the form of checklists, rating devices, and anecdotal records. These will be dealt with shortly in regard to evaluating the affective domain.

### B. Group discussion

Group discussion can be used effectively in allowing students to participate in the evaluation process. Based on learning goals that are clearly established, this is a way for students to appraise the progress they are making. Many teachers set aside some time in every social studies class for students to evaluate the work they are doing. Discussions can also clarify goals and achievements with regard to special projects, small-group work, and field trips. It is very important that standards be set so that the students have a guide for evaluating their work.

### C. Interviews

Interviews or conferences with students are another aid in evaluating progress being made. These can serve as a diagnostic tool for determining individual problems. Interviews can be informal and can often occur spontaneously. They can also be formal and involve questionnaires, scales, or other instruments that the teacher has worked out prior to meeting with the student. A rapport must be established with the student in either case. The interview will only have value if there is a clear purpose and both the teacher and student participate. Domination by the teacher will not help in evaluation. As in the case of observation, some form of recordkeeping is essential.

### D. Samples of students' work

Work done by individual students can be very helpful in assessing achievement. This is usually in the form of written samples and involves assignments carried out in the classroom or outside of school. Because this type of work is often done on a daily basis, it may present difficulties in measuring progress. The teacher needs to compare student work over a period of time. It can prove helpful to establish folders for each student and collect samples at regular intervals. Teachers must work out a system for evaluating daily work because it becomes an impossible task to check every student's work each day. In addition, written work in the form of book reports, research papers, preparation for debates or panel discussions, and projects should all be part of the evaluation process.

## Measuring Affective Objectives

Although the affective domain has received increased attention during the past decade, most teachers neglect to evaluate affective objectives. Assessment of affective objectives presents greater difficulty than does measurement of cognitive behaviors. There is a lack of readily available valid and reliable instruments, and teachers are not familiar with affective assessment techniques and measures. Some teachers feel that students' affective responses are private and that accurate assessment is questionable due to students' "faking" socially desirable attitudes and values.

In spite of these shortcomings, teachers should concern themselves with measuring students' affective responses. If teachers neglect this affective domain they have no evidence on which to base modifications of their teaching strategies and their curriculum content. Also, by measuring and discussing student attitudes, teachers can encourage the reflective testing of beliefs. Analysis of students' affective responses can help learners to understand the sources of their attitudes. Teachers can provide students with new data in order to help them reconcile value conflicts.

Since no single method or technique can provide a total picture of the affective domain, it is best to consider the use of several instruments and techniques. In many cases, preservation of student anonymity will give the teacher a more accurate measure of the affective dimension being studied.

Attitudes and values can be measured through use of the following, independently or as part of a test: attitude scales, opinion polls, questionnaires, open-ended questions, openmindedness scales, checklists, observation, group discussion, anecdotal records, interviews, and role-playing. The methods presented in this section were selected because of their wide use in and applicability to the social studies classroom.

*1. Attitude and Value Scales.*     Several techniques are available for measuring attitudes. The following measuring devices assume that subjective attitudes can be measured by quantitative techniques, so that each student's affective response can be presented by some numerical score.

### A. Likert scale

The Likert scale can be made up of a series of opinion statements about some issue. Usually the statements are divided between positive and negative expressions of an attitude towards some object.[14] Students indicate on a five-point scale whether or not they agree with each statement. "Strongly agree" with a favorable statement would receive a score of 5, as would "strongly disagree" with an unfavorable statement.

> *Example:* Indicate whether you strongly agree (SA), agree (A), are undecided (?), disagree (D), or strongly disagree (SD), with the statements given.
>
> SA   A   ?   D   SD       1. People should be allowed to move into any neighborhood they choose.
>
> SA   A   ?   D   SD       2. A person should refuse to rent to anyone he or she doesn't like.
>
> *or*
>
> SA   A   ?   D   SD       1. This class is a waste of time.
>
> SA   A   ?   D   SD       2. I enjoy reading about history.

### B. The semantic differential scale

While the Likert scale measures the extent to which individuals agree with various opinion statements, the semantic differential devised by Osgood, Suci, and Tannenbaum measures how individuals judge a particular concept on a set of semantic scales.[15] The scales are composed of a series of bipolar adjectives. Each scale is assigned values ranging from one to seven for the seven positions on interposed ordinal scales.

Weighting of responses involves identifying those adjective pairs for which one adjective seems to be clearly desired over the other. A value of seven is assigned to that side of the semantic scale. The remaining spaces are assigned values ranging from six to one, with the most negative response receiving a value of one, and the most neutral response receiving a value of four.

*Example:*

United Nations

| | | | | | | | |
|---|---|---|---|---|---|---|---|
| Useful | ____: | ____: | ____: | ____: | ____: | ____: | ____Useless |
| Fair | ____: | ____: | ____: | ____: | ____: | ____: | ____Unfair |
| Meaningful | ____: | ____: | ____: | ____: | ____: | ____: | ____Meaningless |
| Important | ____: | ____: | ____: | ____: | ____: | ____: | ____Unimportant |
| Good | ____: | ____: | ____: | ____: | ____: | ____: | ____Bad |
| Valuable | ____: | ____: | ____: | ____: | ____: | ____: | ____Worthless |
| Successful | ____: | ____: | ____: | ____: | ____: | ____: | ____Unsuccessful |

### C. Measuring values

Scaling devices can be used to explore students' values. Simon, Howe, and Kirschenbaum (1972) have employed a values continuum that permits students to indicate their positions on a certain issue.

*Example:*

1. What should the United States attitude be on involvement with other countries?

Help every country even if not asked to do so

Help no country

Complete isolation [16]

Sometimes a single scale can be used to measure a variety of student values on a particular issue.

*Example:*

Place the following workers on the strike scale shown below. Justify your choice by providing a brief statement for your reason.

| Absolute and unlimited | A | / | B | / | C | / | D | / | E | Absolutely no right to strike |
|---|---|---|---|---|---|---|---|---|---|---|

1. Public school teachers
2. Police officers
3. Soldiers
4. Commercial pilots
5. Workers in a toy factory
6. Dairy farmers
7. Radio-TV announcers
8. Gas-station attendants
9. Physicians
10. Toll collectors
11. Auto manufacturers
12. Bank tellers
13. Private-school teachers
14. Astronauts
15. Baseball players
16. Bus drivers
17. Workers in a defense plant
18. Workers in a clothing factory

| | |
|---|---|
| 19. Grave diggers | 22. Stevedores |
| 20. Telephone operators | 23. Office workers or secretaries |
| 21. Firemen | 24. Postal-delivery workers[17] |

*2. Measuring Opinion.*    Opinion surveys or polls are usually concerned with replies to specific questions. Respondents simply check yes or no for each question.

*Example:*

Opinion Poll                                          Yes    No

1. Should our state implement odd/even-day fuel purchasing and similar emergency measures in order to conserve fuel and energy resources?                                                  ( )  ( )

2. Would you be in favor of gasoline rationing?          ( )  ( )

3. Do you favor public financing of election campaigns of all candidates for elective office?                                          ( )  ( )

4. Do you believe that limitations should be placed on campaign spending by candidates for elective office?                       ( )  ( )

*3. Questionnaires.*    These are most useful for determining interests and attitudes of students. Direct questions are prepared, and the responses are usually presented in a yes-no format. Situations can be listed or described and students can write in whether they like or dislike them. A questionnaire can also be designed in terms of paired comparisons, asking students to make a preference choice between two listings. Questionnaires can be used effectively at the end of a unit of work to determine those activities in which students prefer to take part. If used before and after a unit or course, they can help the teacher to assess the extent to which students' opinions or attitudes were influenced.

#### A. Questions about political interest

Directions: After reading each question, select the answer that best describes your political behavior.

1. How often do you read newspaper articles about public affairs and politics? (A) Almost daily (B) Two or three times a week (C) Three or four times a month (D) A few times a year (E) Never

2. How often do you read about public affairs or politics in magazines? (A) Almost daily (B) Two or three times a week (C) Three or four times a month (D) A few times a year (E) Never

3. How often do you talk about politics with members of your family? (A) Almost daily (B) Two or three times a week (C) Three or four times a month (D) A few times a year (E) Never

4. How often do you talk about politics with your friends outside of class? (A) Almost daily (B) Two or three times a week (C) Three or four times a month (D) A few times a year (E) Never

5. How often do you watch television about public affairs, politics, and the news? (A) Almost daily (B) Two or three times a week (C) Three or four times a month (D) A few times a year (E) Never

6. How often do you participate in political activities such as election campaigns, demonstrations, political letter writing, and meetings of political organizations? (A) Almost daily (B) Two or three times a week (C) Three or four times a month (D) A few times a year (E) Never[18]

**B. Questions about public safety**

How afraid of crime are we? This questionnaire is designed to help students discover the extent to which they worry about crime as compared with other problems. Discuss how students in different communities might respond to these questions. (For example, in a rural farming community, in a small town, in a wealthy suburb, in a wealthy section of a big city, or in a poor section of a big city.)

A. Rank the following problems according to how much you worry about them. For example, if you worry about bee stings most, rank that as number 1, and so on.

____Being well liked                ____Getting a good job after
                                        school
____Pollution                       ____A nuclear war
____Bee stings                      ____Auto accidents
____Getting robbed or shot          ____Inflation
____Dropping out of school          ____Illness

B. Which of the following activities do you feel quite safe doing? (If you feel safe, make a check.)
   1. ____Riding public transportation at night.
   2. ____Riding public transportation during the day.
   3. ____Walking around your block at 10 P.M.
   4. ____Leaving your home or apartment unlocked at night.
   5. ____Leaving a car parked on the street overnight.
   6. ____Shopping in your neighborhood during the afternoon.
   7. ____Walking to and from school.
   8. ____Leaving a fifty-dollar coat in your school locker.

9. ____Leaving a bicycle on the walk in front of your home for an hour in the morning.[19]
10. ____Hitchhiking in your neighborhood.

*4. Open-ended Statements and Stories.*    This measuring device asks students to write, or even role-play, a question, statement, topic, situation, or story that is open-ended. Analysis of the responses can assist teachers in gaining an understanding of students' feelings. Teachers can provide students with several options from which to choose, including a final, open-ended option.

**A. Example of open-ended statements**

1. What I enjoy most about this class is _____.
2. One thing that really bothers me about this class is _____.

*or*

3. Immigrants to this country are _____.
4. American involvement in the affairs of other countries is _____.

**B. Example of open-ended story** [20]

Greg is vice-president of the freshman class at a city college. There is a sit-in led by a radical group. Greg supports some of their aims, but he tries to keep his friends from taking part in the sit-in.

Later a detective asks Greg to join the radical group and report what goes on to the police. "I don't like the idea of spying on my friends," Greg says. "Besides, I think some of the changes the group wants are needed."

"If you are a good citizen, people like them couldn't really be your friends," the detective says. "It's your duty as a loyal American to help us."

Greg should:

____a. Join the radical group and report on them.

____b. Refuse to do what the detective wants him to do.

____c. Tell his friends in the group about the detective's plan to spy on them.

____d. _____

## C. Example of student evaluation of class activity*

Sample Instrument: Classroom-environment checklist

Name _____

Date _____

I. If I had to describe this activity/ unit/course, I would use the words:

(Check no more than two from this list.)

___easy

___confusing

___hard

___makes me think

___fun

___not very important

___important to me

___related to problems today

___interesting

___other (What is it? _____)

II. During the last three weeks in this class I spent most of my time:

(Check three answers.)

___listening to what was being said

___bored

___interested

___asking questions

___answering the teacher's questions

___confused

___learning a lot of things I never knew before

___wishing we could go more slowly

___wishing we could go faster

___wanting more information

___taking part

___other (What is it? ___)

III. During the last three weeks my class spent a lot of time:

(Check three answers.)

___reading

___writing answers to questions

___having whole-class discussions

___listening to the teacher

___answering the teacher's questions

___working in small groups

___taking notes

___doing role-play and/or debates

___doing projects

___other (What is it? _____)

IV. I learned the most in this activity/unit/course when I:

(Check three answers.)

___read the books

___listened to the ideas of other students in my class

___talked about my ideas with a small group

___listened to the teacher

___gave my own opinions

___asked questions

___did the written exercises

___answered questions

___discussed with the whole class

*Reprinted by permission of the National Council for the Social Studies from Whitla, *Social Education* (February 1974).

_____did small-group projects

_____other (What is it? _____)

V. What I liked best about this activity/unit/course was:

VI. What I liked least about this activity/unit/course was:

VII. During the class I find it hard to:

(Check as many as you wish.)

_____understand what I read in some books

_____take part in class discussion

_____work well in small groups

_____explain to the teacher what I was confused about

_____ask questions

_____take part in role-play and/or debates

_____express my own opinion

_____remember what I've read in the books

_____learn the names of people and places studied

_____read diagrams and charts

_____use outside source materials

_____other (What is it?_____)

VIII. To do well in this class I have to:

(Check as many as you wish.)

_____memorize all the facts in the reading materials

_____read well

_____ask questions

_____take part in discussions

_____remember everything the teacher said

_____agree with the teacher

_____have my own opinion

_____write well

_____do extra projects

_____try to be as quiet as possible

_____bring in extra information

_____answer a lot of the teacher's questions

_____use evidence to support my position

_____listen to and remember what others think

_____other (What is it? _____)

IX. In this class, my classmates and I ask:

(Check one answer.)

_____many questions

_____a few questions

_____hardly any questions

X. In this course we work in small groups:

(Check one answer.)

_____often

_____sometimes

_____never

XI. In this activity/unit/course I prefer to work:

(Check one answer.)

_____by myself

_____in a small group

_____with one big group

_____with the whole class

XII. The most important thing I have learned in this activity/unit/course is:

XIII. If I could change anything about this activity/unit/course, I would do the following:[21]

*Directions:* In each of the following statements, underscore one of the first five words that you think makes the truest statement.

1. All, Most, Many, Some, No.    Americans are better people than those of other countries.

2. All, Most, Many, Some, No.    Modern ways of doing things are better than those of the past.

3. All, Most, Many, Some, No.    People are happier today than people living in past periods.[22]

*5. Open-mindedness Scale.* The underlying assumption of this instrument is that only pupils with "closed minds" would subscribe to completely unqualified generalizations. The underscoring of either extreme position, All or No, is counted as an error.

*6. Checklists.*    Checklists can be used by teachers in conjunction with observation of students or by students for purposes of self-evaluation. The entire class may cooperate in devising a checklist and then apply it individually. Students are able to evaluate their own responsibilities and preparedness. Checklists are recording devices to be used by teachers for more objective evaluation, based on observation. They identify specific traits, and the teacher then checks whether or not these are present during the course of observing.

*7. Observation, Group Discussion, Anecdotal Records.*    Just as observation and group discussion can be used for evaluating cognitive skills, they can also be applied to affective objectives. Teachers constantly observe behavior as students relate to each other. It is important to be cognizant of both verbal and nonverbal behavior. Structuring the pattern of observation can help determine how well students function as part of a group. Here is a sample of behaviors that might be specifically looked for:

Does the student respect the ideas of others?

Does the student abide by the rules of the teacher and the group?

Does the student help fellow students?

Does the student have a sense of responsibility with regard to the property of others?

These questions and others can aid assessing affective objectives through observation of large- or small-group discussions. Another device for recording data from observations is anecdotal records. These are descriptions of specific incidents or situations regarding the behavior of individual students. Collected over a period of time they provide the teacher with a pattern of behavior and establish any changes that occur. Keeping anecdotal records for all students is time-consuming and, therefore, teachers must have some system for using such records effectively. One suggestion is to keep a notebook with the name of each student listed separately at the top of each page. Then at the end of each social studies lesson, the teacher can record short comments for only those students whose behavior warrants them. This normally involves only a few students in each lesson and does not involve a great deal of time. The types of comments should reflect specific purposes. Too often comments reflect only disciplinary problems.

*8. Interviews.* Interviews and individual conferences can be used to evaluate attitudes and values as well as cognitive skills. Very often students will express feelings in a one-to-one meeting that they would not express openly. Individual meetings present the teacher with the opportunity to effect value changes away from the watchful eyes of the entire class.

*9. Role-Playing.* Role-playing creates specific situations that enable students to act out their feelings and beliefs. Teachers can combine this with observation and recordkeeping to assess affective objectives. Problems involving human relationships can be acted out, and students should be encouraged to participate in roles that might not reflect their own backgrounds. A student who never exhibits leadership qualities might be placed in the role of a leader. The key to role-playing is that there is no prepared script and students do not rehearse any set dialogue. Teachers should encourage the expression of sincere feelings. The entire class can participate in a discussion of the handling of the problem by the participants. Questions can be asked that help in analyzing the experience. Some examples are:

> With which of the characters did you agree? Why?
>
> With which did you disagree? Why?
>
> If you had been character Y, what would you have done? Why?
>
> Which of the characters did you like best? Least? Why?

## A Summary on Evaluation

In this chapter, we have tried to show how teachers can avoid a common pitfall—they may teach very well but evaluate very poorly. Unfortunately, when this happens the teacher does not know how well learning is taking place and may easily become discouraged. These summary reminders should help:

1. Relate your evaluation to prestated objectives.
2. Communicate the objectives and criteria for evaluation to the students.
3. Use multiple evaluation techniques. Do not rely exclusively on tests.

4. Use evaluation to make midcourse corrections and for diagnostic purposes.

5. When using tests, diversify the types of questions.

6. Evaluate for affective as well as cognitive achievement.

With these reminders, teaching and evaluatory techniques can become aligned. Many changes take place in students' minds as a result of social studies learning; through the techniques suggested in this chapter, a more comprehensive and accurate picture of learning can be provided for both teacher and student.

## ENDNOTES

1. Benjamin J. Bloom, Thomas Hastings, and George Madaus, *Handbook on Formative and Summative Evaluation of Student Learning* (New York: McGraw-Hill, 1971), pp. 7–8.

2. John U. Michaelis, *Social Studies for Children in a Democracy: Recent Trends and Developments* (Englewood Cliffs, N. J.: Prentice-Hall, 1972), p. 553.

3. Benjamin S. Bloom, ed., *Taxonomy of Educational Objectives: Cognitive Domain* (New York: David McKay, 1956).

4. David R. Krathwohl, Benjamin S. Bloom, and Bertrand B. Masia, *Taxonomy of Educational Objectives: Affective Domain* (New York: David McKay, 1964).

5. Robert F. Mager, *Developing Attitude Toward Learning* (Palo Alto, Calif.: Fearon, 1968), p. 69.

6. Much of this information was adapted from *Making the Classroom Test: A Guide for Teachers* (Princeton: Educational Testing Service, 1961), p. 20, *The New York State Comprehensive Examination in Social Studies*, and E. F. Lindquist and A. N. Hieronymus, *Iowa Test of Basic Skills: Multi-Level Addition for Grades 3–9* (New York: Houghton Mifflin Co., 1964), p. 57.

7. Michaelis, p. 575.

8. Frank F. Garow, *Better Classroom Testing* (San Francisco: Chandler Publishing Co., 1966), p. 88.

9. *Making the Classroom Test: A Guide for Teachers* (Princeton, N. J.: Educational Testing Service, 1969), p. 22.

10. *New York State Comprehensive Examination in Social Studies*, January 1975, essay question 2.

11. Ibid., essay question 4.

12. Clair W. Keller, *Involving Students in the New Social Studies* (Boston: Little, Brown and Co., 1972), p. 233.

13. John M. Good, *The Shaping of Western Society: An Inquiry Approach* (New York: Holt, Rinehart and Winston, 1968), p. 39.

14. Likert, "A Technique for the Measurement of Attitudes," *Archives de Psychologie* 140 (June 1932).

15. Charles Osgood, G. Suci, and P. Tannenbaum, *The Measurement of Meaning* (Urbana, Ill.: University of Illinois Press, 1967).

16. Simon L. Howe and N. Kirschenbaum, *A Handbook of Practical Strategies for Teachers and Students* (New York: Hart Publishing Co., 1972), p. 118.

17. Board of Education of the City of New York, *Grade 12 Economics: Course of Study and Related Activities*, Curriculum Bulletin 14 (New York: Bureau of Curriculum Development, 1970), p. 385.

18. Howard Mehlinger and John J. Patrick, *Teachers' Guide to American Political Behavior* (Lexington, Mass.: Ginn and Co., 1972), worksheet 3.

19. Philip Roden, *People and the City: Teacher Tactics* (Glenview, Ill.: Scott, Foresman and Co., 1972), p. 7.

20. *Loyalties: Whose Side Are You On?* (New York: Scholastic Book Services, 1970), p. 12.

21. Janet P. Hanley, "Learning About Learning: Evaluation Strategies for Teaching About the American Revolution," *Social Education* 38 (February 1974): p. 178.

22. Lester Brown and Ellen Cook, eds., *Selected Items for the Testing of Study Skills and Critical Thinking*, National Council for the Social Studies, Bulletin 15 (Washington, D. C.: NCSS, 1971), p. 68.

## BIBLIOGRAPHY

Berg, Harry D., ed. *Evaluation in Social Studies.* Thirty-fifth Yearbook of the National Council for the Social Studies. Washington, D. C.: NCSS, 1965.

Bloom, Benjamin J., ed. *Taxonomy of Educational Objectives: Cognitive Domain.* New York: David McKay, 1956.

Bloom, Benjamin J,; Hastings, Thomas; and Madaus, George. *Handbook on Formative and Summative Evaluation of Student Learning.* New York: McGraw-Hill, 1971.

Brown, Lester E., and Cook, Ellen, eds. *Selected Items for the Testing of Study Skills and Critical Thinking.* National Council for the Social Studies, Bulletin 15. 5th ed. Washington, D. C.: NCSS, 1971.

Buros, Oscar K., ed. *The Sixth Mental Measurements Yearbook.* Highland Park, N. J.: Gryphon Press, 1965.

Ebel, Robert L. *Measuring Educational Achievement.* Englewood Cliffs, N. J.: Prentice-Hall, 1965.

Fenton, Edwin. *The New Social Studies.* New York: Holt, Rinehart and Winston, 1967.

Garrow, Frank F. *Better Classroom Testing.* San Francisco: Chandler Publishing Co., 1966.

Good, John M. *The Shaping of Western Society: An Inquiry Approach.* New York: Holt, Rinehart and Winston, 1968.

Gronlund, Norman E. *Measurement and Evaluation in Teaching.* 2nd ed. New York: MacMillan, 1971.

Howe, Simon L. and N. Kirschenbaum. *A Handbook of Practical Strategies for Teachers and Students.* New York: Hart Publishing Co., 1972.

Jarolimek, John. *Social Studies in Elementary Education.* 4th ed. New York: MacMillan, 1971.

Keller, Clair W. *Involving Students in the New Social Studies.* Boston: Little, Brown Co., 1972.

Krathewohl, David R.; Bloom, Benjamin S.; and Masia, Bertrand B. *Taxonomy of Educational Objectives: Affective Domain.* New York: David McKay, 1964.

Kurfman, Dana, ed. *Teacher-Made Test Items in American History: Emphasis Junior High School.* National Council for the Social Studies, Bulletin 40. Washington, D. C.: NCSS, 1968.

Likert. "A Technique for the Measurement of Attitudes." *Archives de Psychologie* 140 (June 1932).

Mager, Robert. *Developing Attitude Toward Learning.* Palo Alto, Calif.: Fearon, 1968.

*Making the Classroom Test: A Guide for Teachers.* Princeton, N. J.: Educational Testing Service, 1969.

Michaelis, John U. *Social Studies for Children in a Democracy: Recent Trends and Developments.* 5th ed. Englewood Cliffs, N. J.: Prentice-Hall, 1972.

Osgood, Charles; Suci, G., and Tannenbaum, P. *The Measurement of Meaning.* Urbana, Ill.: University of Illinois Press, 1967.

Roden, Philip. *People and the City: Teacher Tactics.* Glenview, Ill.: Scott, Foresman and Co., 1972.

Simon, Sidney B.; Howe, Leland W.; and Kirschenbaum, Howard. *Value Clarification: A Handbook of Practical Strategies for Teachers and Students.* New York: Hart Publishing Co., 1972.

Ten Brink, Terry D. *Evaluation: A Practical Guide for Teachers.* New York: McGraw-Hill, 1974.

# 11

•••••••••••••••••••••••••••••••••••••••••••••••••••••••••••••••••••••••••••••••••••

# Electives and Curriculum
# Considerations

•••••••••••••••••••••••••••••••••••••••••••••••••••••••••••••••••••••••••••••••••••

## WHO WRITES CURRICULUM?

"Every teacher a curriculum writer; every classroom a curriculum workshop." This very interesting message is posted across the top of the bulletin board of a faculty room in a social studies department. It points to an emphasis on the curriculum responsibilities of the teacher. There was a time when curriculum was handed down from central bureaus of the state and local school systems. Today, the individual teacher is more and more actively involved in the curriculum process.

Teachers may find themselves in schools practicing varying degrees of curriculum flexibility. The degree of flexibility will determine the extent to which the teacher will be a curriculum writer. There are three basic curriculum structures that define levels of flexibility. The first is a school in which a standard curriculum is observed. Specific material in world studies, American studies, and economics is prescribed. The student is expected to accomplish requirements in terms of Carnegie units, units of credit earned in one course studied for a complete year. Social studies is prescribed for two or three years in most high schools, leaving a year or two in which a student may enroll in social studies electives, after completing required courses. During the period of required social studies, a student may also elect to take enrichment courses. This would especially be the case in the instance of the student who is majoring in social studies.

The second curriculum structure is a school that practices the alternative-option plan. In the alternative plan, students have a choice of a course in the standard curriculum or a course that they may substitute for the standard course. For example, in a certain school, a student has the choice of taking western civilization, the standard course; or peace studies, the alternative. There may be a series of alternative modes for a standard course such as economics. It might be offered as analytical economics, economic issues, or consumer economics. These may be referred to as options. In many schools offering the option plan, three or four areas are laid out, and a student must select a certain number of courses in each area. This is shown in the four-column option plan presented in Table 11-1 below.

The third structure is the elective system, which, of course, is the most flexible. Here, a student has free choice of a wide variety of social studies offerings.

Wherever the teacher may be teaching, whether it is within the confines of the first structure or the permissiveness of the third structure, opportunities will arise to teach an elective.

## So You Want to Teach a New Course?

The teacher who wishes to deviate from a standard curriculum and introduce an elective course will find increasing opportunity to do so, because there has

**TABLE 11-1.**    *Social studies offerings*

| Column A<br>culture studies<br>3-credit requirement | Column B<br>American studies<br>2-credit requirement | Column C<br>economic studies<br>1-credit requirement | Column D<br>advanced study<br>elective |
|---|---|---|---|
| African studies | American studies | Consumer economics | Introduction to |
| Asian studies | Social pluralism | Comparative | behavioral science |
| Middle East studies | Government | economic systems | Advanced placement |
| USSR studies | Foreign policy | Analytical economics | in American history |
| Western studies | Reform movements | Economic issues | Anthropology |
| Peace studies | in American history | Economic thought | Psychology |
| Anatomy of | The Black experience | Great economists | Sociology |
| revolution | in American history | International | Black studies |
| Women in western | The Hispanic experi- | economics | Hispanic studies |
| history | ence in American | Institutional | Italian history and |
| Religion in western | history | economics | culture |
| history | The Italian experience | | Jewish history and |
| "Isms" | in American history | | culture |
| History of | The Jewish experience | | Urbanology |
| western art | in American history | | Environmental ethics |
| Latin American | Women in American | | Futurism |
| studies | history | | Field work (executive |
| Western law | Dissent in American | | internship) |
| | history | | Civil service |
| | Youth and the law | | orientation |
| | The ethnic experience | | Environmental- |
| | in American history | | improvement |
| | American values and | | project |
| | culture | | Legal studies |

been an increase in the number of school systems that offer students a certain amount of latitude in selecting courses to fulfill the total social studies requirement. Assuming that the teacher wants to propose the elective and not wait to be "tapped" to do so, he or she should begin by examining personal reasons for proposing the elective: Does the teacher want to "teach from strength?" Does he or she wish to respond to outside pressure to introduce a new subject? Or does the teacher recognize a new subject area, the study of which will fulfill a definite student need and, at the same time, carry out a major social studies objective? While many courses are introduced as a result of any one of or a combination of these demands, the demand that seems most valid is the last one. In this case, the teacher recognizes that the social studies curriculum should change as the needs of the students, as well as the needs of the community, change. The teacher feels that the constant inclusion of new courses insures a flexible curriculum.

Undoubtedly, the teacher who proposes to introduce a new course will become embroiled in a debate concerning the proposal. There will be a need to justify it to colleagues and supervisors. Students, parents, and community people may enter the debate. This is because the discipline of social studies, probably more than any other discipline, attracts controversy. The innovative teacher will be more successful in these encounters if he or she understands both sides of curriculum issues in social studies education.

Some of the major curriculum issues are best described in terms of opposing schools of thought. They are as follows:

| | | |
|---|---|---|
| emphasis on history | *vs.* | multidiscipline approach |
| structure | *vs.* | chronology |
| process | *vs.* | content |
| electives | *vs.* | integrated curriculum |

Let us examine the key arguments on each side of these curriculum issues.

The curriculum hegemony of history has faced a serious challenge in recent years. The multidiscipline approach, which attempts to integrate concepts from history with concepts from economics, geography, political science, and the behavioral sciences, has emphasized the *now* in course content rather than the historic *then*. The impetus for the multidiscipline approach came from a desire to focus attention on the pressing problems of contemporary life. This understandable desire supplies the advocates of the multidiscipline approach with their rationale for courses that stress a contemporary theme. For example, a course called "Women's Studies" might supplement or replace a standard course such as "Western Civilization." The defenders of "Western Civilization" would say that with the de-emphasis on history, social studies has become a "social stew" and that students are being deprived of an opportunity to develop a sense of history and heritage. This argument can be reconciled, and the needs of students, as described by both sides, can be fulfilled. Exhibit 11-2 contains an outline of the course "Women in Western History" that is an illustration of a thematic approach to curriculum design. This course addresses itself to a contemporary problem, while at the same time presenting a chronological survey.

Chronology has also become an issue. It has been pointed out that survey courses such as "Western Civilization," which attempt to sweep "from Plato to NATO," are too superficial. In addition, the proliferation of information, referred to as "data glut," makes it difficult for the student to sift the essential events from the less essential events. The response to chronology has been structure: Instead of learning about all the wars, students should learn about a war; instead of learning about many revolutions, students should learn the anatomy of all revolutions. This approach stresses case studies rather than the survey method. It also relies very heavily on theoretical models rather than actual events. This approach, of course, risks the possibilities of invalid analogies and excessive generalizations, unless the wary teacher helps students discern differences between the model and specific events. The course outline of an elective that stresses structure rather than chronology emphasizes the concepts that must be mastered rather than specific facts.

Very much related to the structure vs. chronology argument are the considerations surrounding process vs. content. A typical discussion between two antagonists in this curriculum debate might sound like this:

*Process Teacher:*   Our peace studies course should concentrate on conflict and theories of aggression.

*Content Teacher:*   I disagree. I think we should present a series of wars and develop each war's causes and effects.

*Process Teacher:*   I've sent away for this terrific simulation game called *Conflict.* The model on which it is based develops the causes and effects of all wars.

*Content Teacher:*   Your approach is too abstract. Students understand human events such as wars by studying the actual events.

Behind the argument of the content teacher is the belief that the concepts of history are the most important. Content, in the thinking of this teacher, is probably equated with history. The process teacher believes that concepts from the behavioral sciences, such as psychology and sociology, are equally important. To that teacher, process does not necessarily preclude content. It may well be that all social studies courses should contain a balance between content and process. A course that stresses process but does not ignore content is presented in Exhibit 11–1.

The impetus for special electives is often supplied by outside groups. An ethnic group may desire that a gap be filled in the social studies curriculum concerning a specific minority group. Women may pressure the school for women's studies. An environmental group may propose a course in environmental ethics. When a teacher responds by wishing to design and teach one of these courses, that teacher will undoubtedly become involved in the issue of electives vs. integrated curriculum. Those that request special electives feel that specific needs of groups of students should be met. The integrationists point out that all students can benefit from an injection of black-studies material (or some other minority-group material), women's-studies material, or environmental-studies material and that this material should be part of the standard course of study. In reality, both approaches exist in most schools, and they should. It is doubtful that new material would ever find its way into an encrusted curriculum without the initial enthusiasm and excitement generated by special electives. In recent history, most of the changes in curriculum began with the injection of special electives, followed by a second phase, the integration of the material into the standard courses of study.

### GETTING YOUR ELECTIVE STARTED

There may be competition among several teachers for assignment to a specific course. Which teacher should be assigned to introduce a new course? If a teacher wants to teach a new course, the teacher must demonstrate commitment to it. He or she must show a willingness to develop interest in the course among students. In the present-day curriculum marketplace, the teacher of an elective must advertise it in order to recruit students successfully. In one school, teachers met periodically with students in a group called STIR, an acronym for Student Input and Reaction. At STIR meetings, new courses were described and students were given the opportunity to propose, as well as to react to, curriculum considerations.

Commitment is also indicated by a teacher's willingness to see the course through a reasonable run. Too often courses are introduced with an expensive outlay for funds and materials, only to be dropped after the teacher's interest wanes or the teacher departs from the school. Sometimes courses are offered with little or no advanced planning. These "catalog courses" are fine public-relations devices, but frequently turn out to be learning disasters. The teacher, therefore, should indicate a willingness to plan the new course in advance.

### PLANNING A NEW COURSE

There are some initial steps to be taken in planning a new course. The teacher should contact as many people as possible, in and out of the school, who can help him or her in drawing up the course. Community lawyers could help with a legal studies course, for example. The teacher should then survey resource material in the form of textbooks and media. After the gathering stage is complete, a course of study should be designed (see Exhibits 11-1 and 11-2).

The course of study should include a development of this breakdown:

1. Objectives
2. Rationale
3. Content outline
4. Bibliography and resources

Writing the objectives in behavioral format (see Chapter 1) insures a concrete method of evaluating the new course and gives it direction and purpose. The rationale should explain the purpose for which the course is being introduced, the specific needs for which it was designed, and its uniqueness. The content outline should provide the sequence of topics, and the bibliography and resource section should supply an inventory of items that must be obtained. Through careful planning, the "newness" of the course will not be the handicap it would otherwise be.

### WHERE WILL IT ALL END?

There has been so much change in social studies curriculum design that, justifiably, many educators are worried as to whether or not social studies as a discipline will survive. Will social studies be absorbed into an interdisciplinary humanities course? Will social studies become so unrecognizable as a discipline that its importance will diminish to minor status?

This could happen if the social studies profession does not clarify its curriculum objectives. It is quite conceivable that social studies could have a continuing proliferation of options and electives. The rapid changes in our society seem to call for this, as we attempt to prepare our students for what will be and not for what is. The difficulty in predicting each student's individual needs as he or she faces the future seems to indicate that a wide choice must be offered. But, at the same time, each of these electives should respond to some master plan relating to what has been, and always will be, the societal goals of the social studies discipline. We believe that the exhibits that follow indicate a response to this master plan.

••••••••••••••••••••••••••••••••••••••••••••••••••••••••••••••••••••••••••••••••••••••••••

## EXHIBIT 11–1.   Peace Studies

••••••••••••••••••••••••••••••••••••••••••••••••••••••••••••••••••••••••••••••••••••••••••

### Rationale

This course is designed to provide students with a detailed, graphic view of the causes and consequences of war, as well as a realistic understanding of the

*Exhibit 11-1.   Peace Studies*   **255**

great obstacles that make it difficult to prevent wars. The course will attempt to deglamorize war and, instead, will emphasize the horror of war and the real danger of its reoccurrence.

Through an examination of documents and theoretical data and participation in simulation games, students will be encouraged both to evaluate the effectiveness of the world's peace-keeping machinery and to suggest alternative ways of maintaining peace. In order to reinforce these aims, students will also participate in a field trip to the United Nations.

## Behavioral Objectives

1. Students will be able to write an essay describing the kinds of atrocities committed during at least two wars and explaining the reasons why these acts occurred.

2. Students will be able to write a short story describing how they would probably be affected if a nuclear war started.

3. Students will be able to discuss, orally and in writing, the political, economic, and environmental consequences of war.

4. Students will be able to explain, orally and in writing, the arguments that were given for and against the dropping of the atomic bomb during World War II.

5. Students will be able to compare animal and human aggressive behavior orally and in writing.

6. Students will be able to form and express an opinion, both orally and in writing, regarding the question of whether people are peaceful or warlike by nature, by referring to the findings of biologists and psychologists.

7. Given lists of political and economic causes of wars, students will be able to give specific examples of these causes drawn from twentieth-century wars.

8. Using the framework of political and economic causes of wars, students will be able to compare, orally and in writing, the causes of World War I and of World War II, as well as to identify similar causes for war that exist today.

9. Students will be able to write an essay or construct a timeline describing the development of diplomacy and international law.

10. Students will be able to compare the strengths and weaknesses of the League of Nations and the United Nations, both orally and in writing.

11. Students will be able to construct a chart that describes the organization and purposes of the United Nations.

12. Students will be able to describe, both orally and in writing, why the Treaty of Versailles, and subsequent world actions, failed to prevent the outbreak of war.

13. Given examples of international crises following World War II, students will be able to identify and describe, in writing, the components of the international peace machinery that came into play in an attempt to prevent war.

14. As a final activity, students will be able to write an essay describing a peace-keeping machine of their own that would be more effective than existing methods of preventing war. In explaining why their peace machine would be a particularly good one, students will be able to give reasons why their plans would have been effective in handling crises of the past.

## Teaching aids

### Textbook

Mazour and Peoples, *Men and Nations* (New York: Harcourt, Brace Jovanovich, 1975).

### Supplementary text

Massialas and Zevin, *World Order* (Chicago: Rand McNally, 1969).

### Simulation game

Thorpe, *Conflict: A Simulation of a Disarmed World* (World Law Fund, 11 W. 42nd Street, New York, N. Y. 10036).

### Sourcebooks

Fenton, *32 Problems in World History* (Glenview, Ill.: Scott, Foresman and Co., 1964).

Feder, *Viewpoints in World History* (New York: American Book Company, 1967).

### Teacher resource book

Moore and Moore, *War and War Prevention* (Rochelle Park, N. J.: Hayden Book Company, Inc.).

*Exhibit 11-1. Peace Studies* **257**

**Films**

*Population Explosion* (Carousel Films, 1501 Broadway, Suite 1503, New York, N. Y. 10036).

*The United Nations: Organization for Peace* (Journal Films, 909 West Diversey Parkway, Chicago, Illinois 60614).

Today, every inhabitant of this planet must contemplate the day when it may no longer be habitable. Every man, woman, and child lives under a nuclear sword of Damocles, hanging by the slenderest of threads, capable of being cut at any moment by accident, by miscalculation, or by madness.

"The weapons of war must be abolished before they abolish us."
> —*John F. Kennedy*

### Course outline

Cycle I:  The Human Side — Causes and Consequence of War

Unit I:  Is war really hell?

1.  How would we be affected if a world war began today? (A personal view: Moore and Moore, *War and War Prevention*.)
2.  What are the consequences of war?
    a.  Atrocities and Casualties
        1.  The Crusades
        2.  The Thirty Years War
        3.  The Hundred Years War
        4.  World War I
        5.  World War II
            a.  The Holocaust
            b.  Hiroshima (Zevin, Unit I)
        6.  Vietnam
    b.  Political Consequences
        1.  Totalitarianism
        2.  The Glorification of War
    c.  Environmental Consequences
    d.  Economic Consequences (guns or butter?)
3.  Should our country ever use nuclear weapons? (Zevin, Unit IV)
    a.  Why did the United States drop the atomic bomb?
    b.  Who should decide if the bomb will be used?
    c.  Do you have an individual responsibility to work to prevent war?
4.  Hypothesizing Exercise — Why have there been only 200 years of peace during the last 34 centuries?
    a.  When did these periods of peace occur?
    b.  Why was peace possible at those times?

Unit II:  The Causes of War—Human Nature or Learning? Are people naturally aggressive?

1.  Are people warlike by nature?
    a.  *Tabula Rasa*
    b.  Genetics and Other Physical Determinants of Aggression
    c.  Psychology
        1.  Child Rearing
        2.  Prejudice—The Authoritarian Personality
        3.  Media and Other Societal Influences
        4.  Animal Behavior as a Model for Men (Lorenz, Storr, and Moore, p. 65)

Unit III: The Causes of War—Governments.
Are any wars just?

1.  Political Nationalism
    a.  Wars for Independence
    b.  Wars to Regain Lost Territory
    c.  Wars to Increase Power
    d.  Wars for Military Security—Defensive Wars
    e.  Wars to Spread Ideas

2.  Economic Nationalism
    a.  Wars for Treasure
    b.  Wars for Raw Materials
    c.  Wars for Trade Routes
    d.  Wars to Control Markets
    e.  Wars to Settle Excess Population

Unit IV: The Causes of War—The International System. Do military alliances and weapons build-ups help to prevent war or to start war?

1.  The Evolution of Diplomacy
    a.  Grotius
    b.  Machiavelli
    c.  The Embassy System
    d.  The "Balance of Power"
    e.  The Holy Alliance and the Congress of Europe
    f.  International Settlement of Disputes
        1.  Principles of International Law
        2.  The Hague Court
        3.  International Arbitration and Mediation (Roosevelt, Kissinger)

2.  Simulation Game—War or Peace?
    a.  What political and economic causes were there for war?
    b.  Could the war have been avoided? What steps were taken to avoid war?
    c.  What changes in the international system should be made in order to prevent war?

Cycle II: The Political Side—An Examination of the Causes of War and the Means of Preventing War

*Exhibit 11-1. Peace Studies*    **259**

Unit V: Causes of World War I

1.  The Road to War
    a.  The Fashoda Affair
    b.  The Balkan Wars
    c.  Triple Alliance, Triple Entente
    d.  The Berlin to Baghdad Railroad
    e.  Sarajevo
2.  Who was responsible for starting the war?
    a.  The "Blank Check"
    b.  The "Scrap of Paper"
    c.  The Schlieffen Plan
    d.  English Neutrality
    e.  Pan-Slavism
    f.  Revanche and Alsace-Lorraine


Unit VI: The Treaty of Versailles, the League of Nations, and the Coming of World War II.
Why did the League fail to keep the peace?

1.  "Dictat" – Did the Treaty plant the seeds of World War II?
    a.  The Fourteen Points
    b.  Failure to Adhere to the Fourteen Points
    c.  War Guilt Clause
    d.  Reparations
2.  Why did the League fail to keep the peace?
    a.  Purposes of the League
    b.  Organization
    c.  Mediation Efforts
    d.  Strengths and Weaknesses
3.  Steps Taken to Avoid War
    a.  Washington Arms Conference
    b.  London Naval Conference
    c.  Nine-Power Treaty
    d.  Little Entente
    e.  Locarno Pacts
    f.  Kellogg-Briand Pact
4.  The Road to War
    a.  Manchuria, 1931
    b.  Ethiopia, 1935
    c.  Demilitarization of the Rhine, 1935
    d.  Spanish Civil War, 1936
    e.  China, 1937
    f.  Austrian Anschluss, 1938
    g.  Munich, 1938
    h.  Nazi-Soviet Pact, 1939
    i.  Danzig, 1939

Unit VII: Preventing War
Is the present international system a "war machine" or a "peace machine?"

1.  How was the peace made? — Yalta and Potsdam
    a.  The Division of Germany
    b.  Occupation of Germany, Japan, and East Europe
    c.  War Crimes Trials
2.  The United Nations — Purposes and Structure
    a.  Strengths and Weaknesses of the U. N. as Compared to the League
    b.  What has the U. N. done to maintain the peace? (e. g., Korea)
    c.  Is the U. N. too politicized?
3.  What are the other components of the world's peace machinery?
    a.  NATO and SEATO
    b.  Warsaw Pact
    c.  The Third World
4.  What elements of the world's peace machinery were most effective in dealing with international crises?
    a.  Kashmir
    b.  Korea
    c.  Vietnam
    d.  The Cuban Missile Crisis
    e.  The Middle East Wars


Unit VIII. Alternative Means of Avoiding War

1.  The Role of the Individual in Keeping the Peace — Peace Movements Around the World
2.  Simulation Game — *Conflict* (a model for an international police force)

    *Filmstrips:*

    *The Crusades*, Multi-media Productions, P.O.B. 5097, Stanford, California 94305

    *Causes of World War I*, Education Visual Aids, Pleasantville, New York 10570

    *Prejudice*, Guidance Associates, 757 Third Avenue, New York, New York 10017

    *What Is Prejudice?* Schloat Productions, 150 White Plains Road, Tarrytown, New York 10591

    *Hitler and the Germans*, Multi-media Productions (same address as above)

*Exhibit 11-2. Women in American History*     **261**

# EXHIBIT 11-2.   Women in American History

### Keynote

We, who like the children of Israel, have been wandering in the wilderness of prejudice and ridicule for forty years, feel a peculiar tenderness for the young women on whose shoulders we are about to leave our burdens. . . . The younger women are starting with great advantages over us. They have the results of our experience; they have superior opportunities for education; they will find a more enlightened public sentiment for discussion; they will have more courage to take the rights which belong to them. . . . Thus far women have been the mere echoes of men. Our laws and constitutions, our creeds and codes, and the customs of social life are all of masculine origin.

The true woman is as yet a dream of the future.

—Elizabeth Cady Stanton, at the age of 72,
speaking to the International Council of Women, 1888

### Rationale

Women have traditionally played a significant role throughout our nation's history. Unfortunately, many of their accomplishments have often been overlooked or minimized, and women achievers have been deprived of their history and their identity. This course will serve to awaken students to the proud history of women in America and help them develop a consciousness and a frame of reference through which they can examine everyday problems confronting them. This course will trace the history of women in America from earliest times to the present.

### Behavioral objectives

The following are the more important behavioral objectives of this course:

1. Students will be able to interpret, both orally and in writing, primary and secondary sources of women's literature, as well as statistics, charts, and cartoons and, by doing so, will be able to identify the problems that have confronted (and still confront) women throughout our nation's history.

2. Students will be able to compare and distinguish, both orally and in writing, the characteristics of widespread sexual discrimination in our society's history.

3. Students will be able to explain, both orally and in writing, society's rationale for discrimination against women.

4. Students will be able to compare, both orally and in writing, the various roles allotted to women throughout our history.

5. Students will be able to develop a basis for examining today's problems by comparing them to those of the past.

6. Students will be able to demonstrate their grasp of the course by being able to interview both individuals and organizational representatives who will speak to the class.

7. Students will be able to describe, both orally and in writing, the achievements of female figures in our nation's history.

8. Students will be able to explain, both orally and in writing, ways that American women influence (and have influenced) decisions in each of the following areas: (1) economics, (2) politics, and (3) cultural activities.

9. Students will be able to defend their positions in a discussion or debate concerning the progress women have or have not made throughout our nation's history.

10. Students will be able to demonstrate their feelings about current discriminatory practices against women by writing to their elected representatives.

11. Students will be able to describe a specific incidence of injustice involving women's rights and will be able to write a piece of legislation directed towards correction of the injustice.

12. Students will be able to describe, both orally and in writing, the changes in values and in male-female roles taking place in our society.

13. Students will be able to describe, both orally and in writing, the influence of America's women's movement on the women's movements in other nations.

## Teaching aids

### Textbooks

Schneir, Miriam, ed. *Feminism: The Essential Historical Writings.* New York: Vintage Books (Random House), 1972.

Scott, Ann Firor. *Women in American Life.* New York: Houghton Mifflin, 1970.

### Audio-visual (filmstrips and cassettes or records)

*Free to Be . . . You and Me.* Music arranged by Stephen Lawrence. New York: Bell Records (Columbia Pictures), 1972.

*Masculinity and Femininity.* (2 filmstrips and 2 cassettes) New York, New York: Guidance Associates, 1969.

*Exhibit 11-2.  Women in American History*     **263**

*Women—The Forgotten Majority.* Chicago, Ill.: Denoyer-Geppert (Times Mirror).

*Women's Rights in the U. S.: An Informal History.* Barbara Welter and Dan Klugherz. Berkeley, Calif.: University of California Extension Media Center (No. 9059).

**Basic course outline**

Unit I:   Women in the New World

Introduction

1.  The Earliest American Women
    a.   The Pueblos of the Southwest*
    b.   Women in the Nomadic Tribes*
    c.   Pocahontas

2.  Women in Colonial Life (17th century)
    a.   Hardships in the Massachusetts Bay Colony*
    b.   Women's "Proper Place" in Puritan New England*
    c.   Witches and Witch Hunting in New England
    d.   The Trial of Anne Hutchinson*
    e.   A Poetic Complaint—Ann Bradstreet*

3.  Women in the Emerging Nation (18th century)
    a.   A Woman Planter—Eliza Lucas*
    b.   "Remember the Ladies"—Letters of Abigail and John Adams during the Revolutionary War Era***
    c.   A Vindication of the Rights of Women—Mary Wollstonecraft**

4.  Women in an Expanding Territory and Economy (19th century)
    a.   A Slave Woman and Her Master*
    b.   Labor in the Mills and Factories—After the War of 1812*
        1.   The Evils Suffered by Working Women—Catherine Beecher*
        2.   Factory Worker Turned Feminist—Harriet H. Robinson**
        3.   "Song of the Shirt"—Poem by Thomas Hood**
    c.   The Condition of Women***
        1.   George Sand (pen name)**
        2.   Sarah M. Grimké**
        3.   Margaret Fuller***
    d.   Women in the Cities*
    e.   Women Pioneers*
    f.   Women on the Frontier
        1.   "Calamity Jane" (Martha Jane Burke)
        2.   "Annie Oakley" (Phoebe Ann Oakley Mozee)
        3.   Laura Ingalls Wilder

(Note: A single asterisk following a theme indicates Scott's book as the main source of information; two asterisks indicate Schneir's book as the main source; three asterisks indicate both books as main sources.)

5. Education for Women
    a. A "Ladylike" Curriculum*
    b. The Need for Female Education*
    c. Planning Education for Women — Emma Willard*
    d. Fashion, Marriage, and the Intellect — Sarah M. Grimké***
    e. Training Women to be Teachers — Catherine Beecher*
    f. Doctors Elizabeth and Emily Blackwell

Unit II: The Women's Movement: The Struggle for Equal Rights
    Introduction
6. Feminism and Reform Movements (mid-19th century)
    a. The Seneca Falls Declaration of 1848***
    b. The Married Women's Property Acts of New York**
        1. Act of 1848**
        2. Act of 1860**
        3. Petitioning Legislators — Ernestine L. Rose**
    c. The Marriage of Lucy Stone Under Protest**
    d. Elizabeth Cady Stanton's Address to the New York State Legislature**
    e. "Ain't I a Woman?" — Sojourner Truth — A Freed Slave**
    f. Female Anti-Slavery Societies and the Abolitionist Movement***
        1. World Anti-Slavery Movement*
        2. Lydia Maria Child*
        3. Frederick Douglass**
        4. William Lloyd Garrison**
        5. Lucretia Mott**
    g. The Dual Battle Over the Fourteenth Amendment*
    h. Division within the Women's Movement
        1. The National Woman Suffrage Association (Stanton and Anthony)*
        2. American Woman Suffrage Association (Stone and Howe)*

7. Expanding the Women's World (late 19th century)
    a. The General Federation of Women's Clubs*
    b. Social Settlements*
        1. Jane Addams*
        2. Ellen Gates Starr*
    c. Working Women of New York
    d. Equal Pay for Equal Work — Susan B. Anthony**
    e. The United States of America vs. Susan B. Anthony**
    f. Feminist Journalists**
        1. Victoria Woodhull**
        2. Tennessee Claflin**
    g. "Womanliness" — Elizabeth Cady Stanton's Speech to the Reunited Factions of the American Women's Movement (NAWSA)**

8. Toward a New Image of Women (late 19th, early 20th century)
    a. Letter from a Radcliffe "Girl"*

(Note: A single asterisk following a theme indicates Scott's book as the main source of information; two asterisks indicate Schneir's book as the main source; three asterisks indicate both books as main sources.)

*Exhibit 11-2.  Women in American History*    **265**

    b.   The Four Hamilton Sisters*
    c.   The Family Relation ("Women and Economics")—Charlotte Perkins Gillman***
    d.   Homemaking as Well as Careers*
    e.   A Case Against Women—Francis Parkman*
    f.   Women of the Leisure Class—Thorstein Veblen**
    g.   "The Lady"—Emily James Putnam**
    h.   Senate Report—"History of Women in Industry in the United States"—Helen L. Sumner**
    i.   "Women's Share in Social Culture"—Anna Garlin Spencer**

9.  Suffrage: The Symbolic Cause
    a.   The Final Battle—Susan B. Anthony*
    b.   Critics within the Ranks—Amelia Barr*
    c.   The "Woman's Hour" Is at Hand—Carrie Chapman Catt**
    d.   "We Want Bread and Roses Too"—Poem by James Oppenheim**
    e.   A New Generation in the Suffrage Movement—*McClure's Magazine*\*
    f.   The Winning Plan—Maud Wood Park*
       1. NAWSA's Congressional Committee*
       2. League of Women Voters*
    g.   The Germ of Militancy*
       1. Alice Paul*
       2. The New Radical "National Women's Party"*
       3. The Equal Rights Amendment Campaign*

Unit III: 20th Century Themes

Introduction

10.  The New Woman of the 20th Century
    a.   The "Flapper" Generation*
    b.   "The Traffic in Women" and "Marriage and Love"—Emma Goldman**
    c.   The Economic Basis of the New Morality—Suzanne LaFollette*
    d.   Motherhood and Mankind—Margaret Sanger***

11.  The Depression and World War II
    a.   "It's Up to the Women"—Eleanor Roosevelt*
    b.   Equal Pay and the New Deal—Mary Anderson*
    c.   Women Workers in the Depression*
    d.   In Defense of the Exceptional Woman*
    e.   Women in the War Effort*

12.  The Postwar Years
    a.   Homemaking as a Career*
    b.   Attitudes Towards "Woman's Place"*
    c.   Report of the President's Commission on the Status of American Women (1963)*
    d.   Feminism Revived—Betty Friedan*

(Note: A single asterisk following a theme indicates Scott's book as the main source of information; two asterisks indicate Schneir's book as the main source; three asterisks indicate both books as main sources.)

13.   A New Era of Feminism (late 1960s to the present)
      a.   Second Class Status of Working Women*
      b.   A New Feminist Declaration of Purpose — National Organization for
           Women (NOW)*
      c.   The Birth of Women's Liberation*
      d.   Rights of Welfare Mothers*
      e.   Crucial Question Yet to Be Answered

(Note: A single asterisk following a theme indicates Scott's book as the main source of information; two asterisks indicate Schneir's book as the main source; three asterisks indicate both books as main sources.)

## BIBLIOGRAPHY

Brubaker, Dale L. *Secondary Social Studies for the 70's: Planning for Instruction*, New
     York: Crowell, 1973.
Lee, John R., Ellenwood, Stephen E., and Little, Timothy H., *Teaching Social Studies
     in the Secondary Schools*, New York: The Free Press, 1973.
Fantini, Mario D. and Weinstein, Gerald, *Toward a Contact Curriculum*, New York:
     Anti-Defamation League.
Fraser, Dorothy McClure, ed. *Social Studies Curriculum Development: Prospects and
     Problems*, 39th Yearbook, National Council for the Social Studies, Washington,
     D. C., 1969.

# 12

•••••••••••••••••••••••••••••••••••••••••••••••••••••••••••••••••••••••••

# Mainstreaming

•••••••••••••••••••••••••••••••••••••••••••••••••••••••••••••••••••••••••

The term "mainstreaming" took hold to describe the intent of legislation passed in 1975; Public Law 94–142, the "Education for All Handicapped Children Act."[1] Mandating that all children with handicapping conditions be given the most "appropriate" education to suit their individual abilities in the "least restrictive environment," the law essentially calls for placing handicapped students into classes with their "regular" peers, in a setting that is closest to "normal" when it is at all possible to do so.[2] Whether or not it is possible to do so depends upon the handicapped child's individual development, learning style, and needs. Rather than placing students in specialized classes for their entire day based on some label such as "mentally retarded" or "physically handicapped," the law calls for placements that are based on an individual child's specific needs. What this all means for those social studies teachers who fear that they will be faced with medically nonfunctioning, unteachable, or uncontrollable students, whom they may be ill-equipped or untrained to teach, may be best summarized by means of paraphrasing a current commercial. Just as a certain wine company claims it "will sell no wine before its time," so too, no child will be placed into a class until she or he is ready for it. Thus, the students social studies teachers receive are those who have been determined as being able to profit from a placement with "regular" classmates.[3]

## THE SOCIAL STUDIES ROLE IN MAINSTREAMING

Social studies educators play a special role in mainstreaming. This has been recognized in professional writing within the field. A booklet by the National Council for the Social Studies on the subject pointed to the fact that social studies is a general education subject within which many mainstreamed students will be placed.[4]

The history of special education in general, and mainstreaming specifically, deals with the issue of social studies content and, therefore, should catch the attention of social studies curriculum designers and teachers. The social studies teacher should especially take notice that the campaign for and the implementation of Public Law 94–142 is best viewed within the context of the civil rights movement. The same NCSS booklet previously cited described this special concern of social studies educators in the following way:

> If exclusion, isolation, and separation are illegal by race, then exclusion, isolation, and separation by handicapping condition must be just as injurious and illegal. An examination of this tenet applied to handicapping conditions is an excellent way to conduct a set of concept development lessons relating to such social studies topics/area/content/as: the role of minorities, the elements of social change, democracy as an evolving system.[5]

In addition to the curriculum insights that social studies teachers can provide, the authors of the NCSS booklet also draw attention to social studies teachers' particular interest in the social interaction that takes place within a social studies class between mainstreamed students and "regular" students. Teachers in all disciplines are concerned with this; however, the socialization lesson is the main learning vehicle in social studies learning, making group interrelations even more crucial. Besides, there is a relationship between content and these interactions. Certain topics related to the strivings of an ethnic minority or of handicapped students, if well presented, may improve group interactions.

The topic of mainstreaming fits this description. The authors of the NCSS booklet state:

> Children with handicapping conditions historically have been placed in isolated situations with varying degrees of geographic and emotional distance from regular classrooms. As a result the social and emotional interactions that are a part of the major socializing agency of American youth—the public schools—have not been available to handicapped youngsters.[6]

Therefore, social studies teachers might ask themselves two basic questions with regard to teaching mainstreamed students: 1) Am I paying enough attention to teaching the rationale for mainstreaming? 2) What actually is taking place in my classroom when special education students are mainstreamed, as regards the interaction among the students?

## Mainstreaming and Individualization

In an earlier edition of this *Handbook,* the necessity of individualizing instruction was stressed. It was recognized that:

> There is no single method of teaching that is good for all subject matter at all times, in all places, and for all children. Rather, . . . methods . . . are instru-

ments and must be chosen and appraised in view of the end to be reached and in light of conditioning circumstances. . . . Method(s) . . . should be adjusted to the experience and ability of the pupil.[7]

Perhaps nowhere is this principle more compelling than in the teaching of mainstreamed students in "regular" social studies classrooms.

Notice that in the preceding discussion, emphasis was put on the concept of the student's ability to profit from a social studies class setting. Handicapping disabilities are not to be confused with inabilities. All students in the mainstreamed class *can* learn. While handicapping disabilities may hinder some students from learning in a particular way (e. g., some students may have visual, auditory, or orthopedic/motor deficiencies), these conditions can usually be compensated for by adapting and employing a different learning mode. Thus, the challenge for the social studies teacher is to find out the mode in which each student has his or her greatest strength and then to provide opportunities for the student to succeed by using that strength.

## HOW DOES THE SOCIAL STUDIES TEACHER FIND OUT THE STUDENT'S STRONGEST MODALITY?

As a consequence of P.L. 94–142, subject-class teachers are provided with, and contribute to, a document known as an Individualized Educational Program, or IEP, that provides for each mainstreamed student a set of proposed educational objectives, suggested ways they are to be achieved, and suggested measurements for achievement. With this document as a starting point, the teacher may discuss with the student's special education teacher those ways the student best learns. Cooperatively, the teachers may design activities geared to take advantage of that student's strength. However, if this is done to excess, the intent of mainstreaming that student can be distorted. After all, the purpose of mainstreaming any particular student was so that he or she might profit from being in as "normal" a setting as possible. The teacher should attempt to discover mainstreamed students' best learning modalities (this should also apply to every student as well).

One relatively simple way of doing this assessment is to administer, near the beginning of the term, the preference survey reproduced below:

### PERCEPTUAL PREFERENCES*

*Mark each question either true or false.*

|  |  | True | False |
|---|---|---|---|
| 1. If I have to learn something new, I like to learn about it by: | | | |
| | a. Reading a book | _____ | _____ |
| | b. Hearing a record | _____ | _____ |

*From the book *Educator's Self-Teaching Guide to Individualizing Instructional Programs* by Rita Dunn and Kenneth Dunn. © 1975 by Parker Publishing Co.

|  | True | False |
|---|---|---|
| c. Hearing a tape recording | ___ | ___ |
| d. Seeing a filmstrip | ___ | ___ |
| e. Hearing my teacher tell me | ___ | ___ |
| f. Playing games | ___ | ___ |
| g. Going someplace and seeing for myself | ___ | ___ |
| h. Having someone show me | ___ | ___ |

2. The things I remember best are the things:

|  | True | False |
|---|---|---|
| a. My teacher tells me | ___ | ___ |
| b. Someone shows me | ___ | ___ |
| c. I learned about on trips | ___ | ___ |
| d. I read | ___ | ___ |
| e. I heard on records | ___ | ___ |
| f. I heard on radio | ___ | ___ |
| g. I saw on television | ___ | ___ |
| h. I wrote stories about | ___ | ___ |
| i. I tried or worked on | ___ | ___ |
| j. My friends and I talked about | ___ | ___ |

3. I really like to:

|  | True | False |
|---|---|---|
| a. Read books, magazines, or newspapers | ___ | ___ |
| b. See movies | ___ | ___ |
| c. Make tapes on a tape recorder | ___ | ___ |
| d. Draw | ___ | ___ |
| e. Play games | ___ | ___ |
| f. Talk to people | ___ | ___ |
| g. Listen to people talk | ___ | ___ |
| h. Go on trips | ___ | ___ |
| i. Learn new things | ___ | ___ |
| j. Study with friends | ___ | ___ |
| k. Build things | ___ | ___ |
| l. Do experiments | ___ | ___ |
| m. Take pictures or movies | ___ | ___ |
| n. Use typewriters, computers, calculators, or other machines | ___ | ___ |
| o. Go to the library | ___ | ___ |
| p. Trace things in sand | ___ | ___ |
| q. Mold things with my hands | ___ | ___ |
| r. Make scrapbooks | ___ | ___ |
| s. Write stories | ___ | ___ |
| t. Play guitar | ___ | ___ |
| u. Sew | ___ | ___ |
| v. Take things apart to see how they work | ___ | ___ |

In marking the survey, the following key is suggested:[8]

**Perceptual preferences**

*Totals:*

| Auditory | Visual | Tactile | Kinesthetic |
|----------|--------|---------|-------------|
| True | True | True | True |
| ___ | ___ | ___ | ___ |
| 10 | 10 | 10 | 10 |

*Consistency Key:*

| Auditory | Visual | Tactile | Kinesthetic |
|----------|--------|---------|-------------|
| True | True | True | True |
| 1b | 1a | 1f | 1g |
| 1c | 1d | 2h | 2c |
| 1e | 1f | 3d | 2i |
| 2a | 1h | 3k | 3e |
| 2e | 2b | 3p | 3c |
| 2f | 2d | 3q | 3h |
| 2g | 2g | 3r | 3l |
| 3f | 3a | 3s | 3m |
| 3h | 3b | 3t | 3n |
| 3j | 3o | 3u | 3v |

As a general rule, any area with a score of seven or more "true answers" reflects the modality of strength for that student. To score higher in one or more areas is an indication of how that student processes information. Combined with the information in the IEP, the teacher may then know the student's learning preferences. A learning profile for each student may then be constructed as follows:

## STUDENT STYLES PROFILE

One educator suggested setting up a chart that gives a relatively concise overview of mainstreamed students' learning styles:[9]

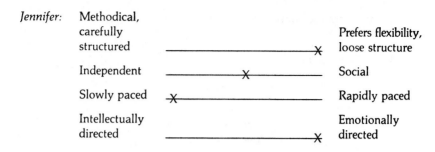

*Jennifer:*  Methodical, carefully structured — Prefers flexibility, loose structure

Independent — Social

Slowly paced — Rapidly paced

Intellectually directed — Emotionally directed

Other teacher comments, observations: Jennifer is artistic; easily tunes out school—a daydreamer; labeled EMR (Emotionally and Mentally Retarded); tactile and visual learner; cannot read at grade level.

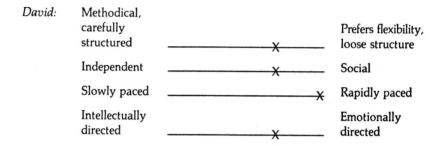

*David:*  Methodical, carefully structured — Prefers flexibility, loose structure

Independent — Social

Slowly paced — Rapidly paced

Intellectually directed — Emotionally directed

Other teacher comments, observations: All the teachers refer to David as "hyper": he has trouble concentrating on a task for more than ten minutes at a time; always wants to be the leader; shows strength in tactile and kinesthetic learning.

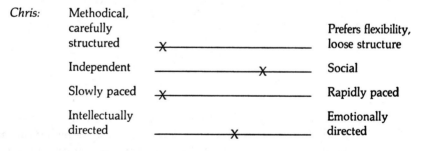

*Chris:*  Methodical, carefully structured — Prefers flexibility, loose structure

Independent — Social

Slowly paced — Rapidly paced

Intellectually directed — Emotionally directed

Other teacher comments, observations: writing and spelling are very poor—illegible and incorrect; auditory learner.

Knowing the variety of ways students learn best helps the teacher determine the type and kind of activities that need to be designed. Exhibit 12–1 details some possible activities that may be used with the topic of the American Revolution. The information that has been compiled about the students may now be used by the teacher to select those activities that are most appropriate for tapping each student's individual strength. The hypothetical student Chris, above, who prefers structure and working with others, but slowly, and primarily learns through auditory processes, would probably benefit from activities such as the meeting of the United Nations (Activity 3) or the newscast (Activity 6), because both involve oral tasks completed by working with others. Jennifer, because she is artistic and tactile and learns best visually, might benefit from working on designing the newspaper editorial page (Activity 1) or creating the bulletin-board mural (Activity 4). Matching the students' abilities to the most appropriate activity is where the true skill of the teacher lies.

"It is not advocated, however," as even the teacher who designed Exhibit 2 recognized, "that the entire course be taught using only . . . individual or small group independent work. . . . There are days when (an) . . . entire class"[10] activity will be more appropriate. The materials in Exhibit 12-2 illustrate how students can both work together and independently during the course of a single unit.

"The notion of multiple paths to learning—that each child learns in, by and through different input processes—is the basis for appropriate procedures for each child."[11] Most methods discussed throughout this *Handbook* may be used successfully with the mainstreamed students, provided that adjustments are made in the way the methods are offered to them.

To be forewarned is to be forearmed. The social studies teacher should know that the mainstreamed student is the one who simply has difficulty with processing information through one or more learning modalities, that these learning difficulties may lead to frustration and fear of failure on the part of those students, that these difficulties have various manifestations, and that they may be circumvented by stressing the learning modalities of the students' strength. Knowing this, the teacher is in a better position to create a classroom environment that will make teaching mainstreamed students a rewarding experience.

## HOW DOES THE SOCIAL STUDIES TEACHER TEACH TO THE STUDENT'S STRONGEST MODALITY?

There are basically three ways of doing this. The first is by designing independent activities for each student based on his or her best learning modality. The second is by grouping (see Exhibit 12-1). The teacher divides a content area into several types of activities, each activity stressing a different modality. For example, in a unit on the American Revolution, a teacher had one committee work on preparing a newspaper for the visually oriented student and another committee prepare a "press conference" for the auditorially oriented students.

The third way is to diversify strategies so that all four learning modalities can be utilized within one lesson in which the entire class participates. If the teacher uses a multiple-strategy approach, students who are strong in each type of learning modality get a chance to shine. The trick for the teacher is to be aware of switching modalities with the new activity. The teacher would call on the student who could best contribute to the lesson at any given time because that student's modality is being stressed.

For example, let us plan activities for a lesson on Renaissance art. You will show slides of famous paintings and call on the visually strong students to describe them. Most probably, you will want to play recordings of Renaissance music. Naturally, you will call on the auditorially strong students to express themselves by describing what it is they experienced as they were listening to the music. The tactilely predisposed students will get their chance when you have them describe what they felt as you passed around the replicas of museum artifacts which you have borrowed from the local museum. Finally, you will want to have a student role-play Michelangelo lying flat on his or her back on a desk, re-creating the manner in which the Sistine Chapel was painted. The kinesthetic learner should have little trouble describing to the class Michelangelo's agony.

Although not all lessons lend themselves as easily to all modalities as the above, opportunities exist in every lesson for imaginative diversification. In a lesson on the Industrial Revolution, a kinesthetic learner might role-play an assembly-line worker doing only the one task of making a paper hat over and over again. The student then would be asked to describe his or her feelings about the task and his or her resultant commitment to the product. Also, you can call on those students to form an archway, vault, or flying buttress with their bodies when your are teaching about the architecture of the Middle Ages. Students who learn kinesthetically can also huddle between rows of desks to re-create the feeling of trench warfare in a lesson dealing with World War I.

The tactilely oriented students would logically be the first to touch and describe a cotton plant, announcing to the class the number of seeds and then conjecturing about the problem of weaving this plant material into fiber.

Teaching to students' strengths opens up the possibility of overcoming their weaknesses. It is a point of departure from which students are led to attack their weaknesses. For example, the tactilely oriented students who were successful in describing for the class the textures of a terra-cotta cup might now be asked to risk going into a weak area by writing out a description of the textures they have just described.

## RESPONDING TO LEARNING DEFICIENCIES LIKELY TO BE ENCOUNTERED IN THE SOCIAL STUDIES CLASSROOM

While the main thrust of this chapter is to emphasize the mainstreamed student's strengths, realistically, on a day-in, day-out basis the classroom teacher is teaching to an entire class. Opportunities for teaching to the mainstreamed students' strengths may not always be present at all times within a given lesson. Therefore, the teacher must also respond to conditions of deficiency.

While most teachers can recognize those conditions known as physical handicaps (e. g., significant loss of hearing or sight), orthopedic impairments (paralysis or amputations), and neurologic impairments (cerebral palsy or epilepsy), most teachers are unfamiliar with the other types of learning disabilities that can also hinder a child's ability to learn in a particular modality.[12]

## Ia. Visual Perceptual Disorders

To simulate perceptual problems, complete the following tasks:

1. Read this paragraph:

Bonnie yas wis$_n$al percegtual grodlews. Sye has aso wearnerape lwtellibence som eof the things t het wahe reab ing wor e biff ic cult for ner are yer becifits in biscrimination, clo sume, and fipuregroumb. To nuberstanb einnoB, trink adout yo ur re acti ous whi le attengting tor eab this garapragh.

2. Draw the dashboard of your car from memory.
3. Unscramble these words: oykceh, yakenry, solubtsecroli

Although all teachers do not realize Bonnie's frustration,* every teacher will recognize her performance.

Bonnie epitomizes the "b-d, was-saw" problem: she reverses, rotates, inverts, and confuses similar letters and words. Omissions, substitutions, and guesses based on general configuration and initial consonants are common reading behaviors. Unable to note detail or concentrate on relevant visual stimuli, Bonnie constantly loses her place and has difficulty distinguishing medial vowels, medial parts, or endings of words. She cannot remember sight words, especially abstract words such as "what," "the," "there," "for," and "were."

Poor memory and visual-sequencing skills also result in poor spelling. Sometimes Bonnie's spelling answers do not even resemble the stimulus words; other times, when the teacher asks her to spell such words as "laugh," "because," "sure," "enough," and "nation," she writes "laf," "bekuz," "shur," "enuf," "nashun." When she is able to recall all the letters, she may transpose the order: she writes "thier," "huoes," and "eth" for "their," "house," and "the."

Her handwriting is characterized by reversals, inversions, and rotations, by size variation, mixture of upper- and lower-case letters, insufficient spacing between words, and inadequate letter formation.

Although Bonnie has adequate visual acuity, she cannot correctly and consistently identify, discriminate, process, or recall visual sensations.

---

*So that the reader not be frustrated as well, this paragraph reads: Bonnie has visual perceptual problems. She also has near average intelligence. Some of the things that make reading more difficult for her are her deficits in discrimination, closure, and figure-ground. To understand Bonnie, think about your reactions while attempting to read this paragraph.

**Ib. Responses to Visual Perceptual Disorders**

1. *Use a tape recording to provide focus.* The social studies teacher should be wary of the length of reading assignments. Concentration and ability to master content diminish with increased length and complexity. This applies even more to a student who has to struggle just to see the printed word in the first place. The task of comprehension is facilitated if a teacher focuses on the essence of a reading passage. This can be done by the teacher preparing a tape for a homework assignment that includes the salient excerpts from the reading selection. For example, if students were assigned to read a passage on the causes of the Spanish-American War, the tape should present the essence of the entire selection. In this case, excerpts from two documents, the Teller Resolution and the Platt Amendment, could be condensed while still providing the students with at least some insight for understanding the lesson.

2. *Give easy readings and short reading assignments.* Many students with visual-perceptual problems show improvement with persistent and patient exercise. Therefore, continually avoiding reading is not the answer. Students may be given modified reading assignments (see Chapter 6 for the techniques of simplifying materials) or be given a shortened version of an assignment in enlarged print.

**II. Auditory Perceptual Disorders**

If you have ever mistaken a ringing phone for an alarm clock, attempted to remember the names of four people to whom you were just introduced, taken notes from a college professor who lectured too rapidly, or tried to listen to an important phone conversation against the competing background noises of stereo, television, children, and a dog, you have some idea of what school is like for a child with auditory perception problems.

Although these children have acuity, they are not always able to identify, discriminate, integrate, recall, or attend to relevant sounds. In reading, they do not learn through a phonetic approach. They will hear the teacher say, "desk and dog," and "cup and top"; they cannot, however, perceive the similar initial and final consonants. They do not recognize that "map," "cap," and "tap" rhyme. They are unable auditorially to discriminate the short vowel sounds in "ham," "hem," "him," and "hum." Unable to establish the sound/symbol relationship, these students cannot sound out new words or relate them to known words. Therefore, each new word is a unique experience. Auditory synthesis and analysis present additional problems. When the teacher asks them to blend the syllables or say something they hear as "ghaspetti," "b-i-g" remains "b-i-g" or becomes "gib," "bigu," "bug," "book," or "buiga." Assignments that require these students to syllabicate or break a word into individual sounds are not done or done incorrectly.

All closure tasks are difficult for them. If they hear "—outh—akota," "—ouisiana," or "Illi—ois," they cannot fill in the missing sounds and name the states. They are the students who say "childrens," "mouses," and "foots," "Tom has aten all the ice cream," and "I am walks to the store."

These deficits in the auditory channel also interfere with their spelling and writing. If a teacher pronounces the spelling words in a different order from the study list, these students might respond with the original list. Stimulus words such as "mist," "tent," "pot," and "ship" produce responses like "mus," "ten," "pat," and "chip."

The students will ask "What did you say?" or state, "I can't remember." Easily distracted by background noises, unable to focus on relevant auditory stimuli in a noisy classroom, they find it difficult to attend to what is going on. In general, they are unable to follow oral directions, remember verbal instructions, or comprehend and write down appropriate lecture notes.

These students are learning disabled. They have adequate sensory acuity and average intellectual ability; however, they require special intervention strategies and alternate teaching approaches.

## IIb. Responses to Auditory-Motor Disorders

1. *Have other students repeat instructions and/or restate important parts differently.* The social studies teacher attempts to develop listening skills in all students. For this reason, teachers try to avoid repeating their questions or instructions; to do so would encourage students not to listen the first time. However, with mainstreamed students who have auditory problems, repetition is frequently necessary. But it need not come from the teacher: by having other students restate the teacher's question or instruction, other benefits will accrue. The mainstreamed students will be given the needed additional oral aid, while the other students are given training in being effective listeners.

2. *Provide written and printed support.* The teacher should place crucial questions and instructions on the chalkboard or on a handout. Students with auditory perceptive disorders will benefit from printed study guides. Chapter 6 discusses possible ways of preparing these guides.

3. *Use paralanguage techniques to insure attention.* Communication is not always in the use of words but the way the words are used. Students who have difficulty processing the spoken word may benefit from the reinforcement of verbal stimuli through changes in the teacher's vocal pitch, rhythm, and tone. In addition, looking briefly at the student or gently and discreetly touching the student's shoulder alerts the student to the need for an extra effort to listen intensively. Effective socialized discussion, which depends on listening, is useful in all teaching but crucial in social studies.

All students can learn. The teacher's role is to find the modality in which each student's strength lies and then to provide opportunities for using that strength. Mainstreamed students are like the so-called "regular" ones: they have areas of strength in certain learning modalities and weaknesses in others. The primary difference is that the mainstreamed students' deficiencies in certain areas are more severe. The social studies classroom is an area for diversity: in approach, topic, and methodology. Few other subjects lend themselves to such a wide variety of techniques, the use of such a variety of materials, and the ability to organize flexibly. Selecting a variety of activities appealing to each of the senses for each unit, topic, or daily lesson plan is the key to integrating the mainstreamed students successfully into the regular social studies classroom.

••••••••••••••••••••••••••••••••••••••••••••••••••••••••••••••••••••••••••••••••••••••••••••••••

## EXHIBIT 12-1.

••••••••••••••••••••••••••••••••••••••••••••••••••••••••••••••••••••••••••••••••••••••••••••••••

Unit: The American Revolution (high school)

*Objectives:*

1. Students will be able to explain at least three reasons why the American colonists felt they should engage in warfare against and seek independence from England in 1775.

2. Students will be able to explain at least three reasons why the leaders of the government in England felt their nation should engage in warfare against the American colonists in 1775.

*General Directions and Materials:*

After examining and using texts and other readings written on various levels, films, filmstrips, slides, projectors, and other teacher-made or commercially produced materials, the students will complete one or more* of the following activities according to their abilities, learning styles, interests, and pace.

---

*Students may choose to do a second activity for extra credit, or the teacher may assign a second one for students exhibiting difficulty with the first activity undertaken.

*Source:* Linda Biemer, "Mainstreaming and Secondary Social Studies" (Washington, D. C.: NEA Publications, 1981).

*Exhibit 12-1.* **279**

*Activity 1*

Using a current newspaper editorial page as a format guide, the students will prepare the editorial page for a newspaper in Boston (or New York, Philadelphia, or Charleston) in 1775 containing at least six items, including an editorial, letters to the editor, guest editorials, and political cartoons. Contributions are to be from both patriots and loyalists.

*Activity 2*

Students will present for the entire class, or record on audio- or videotape for presentation to the teacher and/or class, a series of "press conferences" during which four of the following will be questioned:

| | |
|---|---|
| 1765 James Otis | George Grenville |
| 1775 Samuel Adams | General Thomas Gage |
| 1776 Thomas Jefferson | King George III |
| 1777 George Washington | General William Howe (or John Burgoyne) |
| 1781 Benjamin Franklin | Lord Cornwallis |

A written script might also be prepared. Biographies should be made available by the teacher or the librarian.

*Activity 3*

Students will conduct a meeting of the "United Nations Security Council of 1776" to discuss the problems between England and the North American colonies. Present at the meeting will be representatives from England, France, Spain, Holland, Russia, and the North American colonies. This special session of the council will be presented live or videotaped for presentation to the class.

*Activity 4*

Students will make a bulletin-board mural either of drawings and cartoons, or in collage/montage form using magazine pictures, small wooden boats, tea, etc., explaining the cause of the American War for Independence as seen by both American patriots and by the British and the loyalists.

*Activity 5*

Students will make two comic books, one explaining the American view and the other the British view of the Revolutionary War, which are to be read by American and by English children.

*Activity 6*

Students will prepare an American national-network "evening news" and a BBC "nightly news" broadcast for six significant dates of the American revolutionary period. Dates might include December 17, 1773; April 19, 1775; and July 4, 1776.

••••••••••••••••••••••••••••••••••••••••••••••••••••••••••••••••••••••••••••••••••••••••••••

# EXHIBIT 12–2.

••••••••••••••••••••••••••••••••••••••••••••••••••••••••••••••••••••••••••••••••••••••••••••

Sample lesson plan for use in teaching about Austria in intermediate-grade social studies*

*Objectives* (as determined by the teacher):

1. Students will be able to
   a. Locate Austria on a map of Europe and on a world map
   b. Describe and identify Austria's geographical features
   c. Explain how Austria's geography in part determines its economy

*Concept:* Geographic determinism

*Generalizations:*

1. A nation's location and geographical features in part determine its economy.
2. A nation must export goods in order to import goods.

*Class procedure:* This sample lesson is divided into a prereading activity, a reading activity, reinforcement activities, and possible evaluation instruments. It also would cover three to five class periods of about forty-five minutes in an intermediate school. The authors assume that there is a wide range of reading abilities in the class and up to four mainstreamed students.

*Day 1:*

*Brainstorming activity* for full class prior to reading in text about Austria. Teacher has available a map of Europe that clearly shows where Austria is. Students may also refer to maps in their text, an atlas, and other books in the rooms.

*Source:* These lessons were prepared by Linda Biemer, State University of New York at Binghamton.

*Exhibit 12-2.*    **281**

Question teacher poses to the class: "What do you think might be true about Austria, or what do you suppose we can say about (what tentative statements can we make about) Austria from looking at these maps?" Teacher writes students' responses on overhead transparency or chalkboard as well as on a ditto master or paper to be photocopied. Teacher might ask a student who writes well to do the latter.

If a text is used, teacher would ask students to look at the pictures in the text and answer the question: "From looking at the pictures, what else do you think might be true about Austria?" In addition, teacher might show slides, a filmstrip (without cassette or record on, or if with a written narrative, without showing the narrative), or other pictures of Austria. Students would then make additional statements about Austria.

*Reading activity:* Students would next read pages in text (or different texts) on Austria in small groups, first silently, while teacher prepares, if possible, a ditto for each student containing some of the statements made earlier about Austria. There would be fewer statements on the paper for slower readers or mainstreamed students, more challenging statements for quicker students. As students work in groups, they should decide if statements are true or false. If some statements are false, students should modify them so that each statement is correct. Teacher would lead the full class in discussing some of the statements, making certain that each group is called on to give correct statements.

*Day 2:* (If the preceding activity is completed in one class period)

*Reinforcement/postreading activity:* To reinforce learning from the class activity above and to learn even more about Austria, students will next engage in small-group or individual activities about Austria. The teacher will be available to work with individuals or groups of students. Possible activities include:

a. Cloze activity for poor readers (see example below)

b. Word-hunt activity (see below)

c. Word-scramble activity (see below)

d. Sentence cards: using 3 × 5 cards prepared in advance by the teacher, students will formulate accurate sentences about Austria. Each card will contain one word relating to the topic studied. For example, cards about Austria would include the words Vienna, cows, Mozart, music, Danube, mountains, Alps, German, Germany, and Switzerland. In addition, teacher must prepare several word cards containing *the, of, and, is, The, A, a, were, are,* and punctuation cards. Each sentence must begin with a capital letter, end with a period, and contain correct internal punctuation (where appropriate). After a student develops each sentence using the cards, the teacher must approve it. The student then writes that sentence on her or his paper.

e. TV show: two students might write a script for a TV travel program. One student would be the "Austrian," the other the "reporter." They will present their show to the class.

f. Map activity: one or more students might draw a map of Austria and, using their own drawings or paper cutouts from magazines, label Austria's geographical features and products.

g. Magazine article: a student or students might write a news article on Austria for a travel magazine. Travel brochures obtained by teacher or students from a local travel agency could supplement their article.

*Day 3, 4, or 5:* (Depends on how much time is allocated to reinforcement and reading activities)

*Evaluation:* Students will be graded according to their ability to perform at their particular academic level. Their report-card grade will reflect the "real grades" they as individuals have earned. Two sixth-grade report cards, for example, might read:

Social Studies 85*
> *At bottom of report card would be written: "Susan's grade is based on her ability to learn social studies content on her level. She is currently reading at the fourth-grade level."

Social Studies 98*
> *"Sam's grade of 98 reflects his mastery of social studies content on his level. He is working on materials at the sixth-grade level."

*Possible evaluation activities:*

a. Cloze activity, word scramble, or word hunt to formulate sentences

b. Use of sentence cards to make at least ten true statements about Austria

c. Regular paper-and-pencil multiple-choice and short-essay questions, for average students

d. Challenging essay-type "creative" test for bright students.

*Cloze activity* for poor readers (or use as formative or summative test) (fifth-grade reading level)

Austria is a land next to _____. Both countries are _____. Austria has lots
            1           2

of _____. The people get _____ from the forests. They _____ the lum-
  3           4            5

ber. There are many farms, but they are _____. Lots of _____ graze there,
$\underset{6}{}$   $\underset{7}{}$

so _____ farming is an important industry. Many people visit Austria to "see
$\underset{8}{}$

the sites." We call those visitors _____. Most Austrians speak _____. The
$\underset{9}{}$   $\underset{10}{}$

most famous _____ in Austria is Vienna. Mozart was a famous _____.
$\underset{11}{}$   $\underset{12}{}$

Austria's famous river is the _____.
$\underset{13}{}$

Print either below or on a separate card or paper:

1.  the United States, England, France, Switzerland
2.  mountainous, on the ocean, islands
3.  forests, lakes, valleys
4.  fish, cotton, lumber, cows
5.  export, import
6.  dry, small, rocky
7.  horses, pigs, cows, sheep
8.  tree, dairy, fish, chicken
9.  tourists, workers, travelers, teachers
10. French, Swiss, German, English
11. city, dance, crop, cathedral
12. city, capital, empire, musician
13. Danube, Roman, Strauss, Alps

## ENDNOTES

1. For a discussion of the historical background of the movement towards mainstreaming, see Ramon M. Rocha and Howard G. Sanford, "Mainstreaming: Democracy in Action," *Social Education* 43 (January 1978), p. 60.
2. This integration of students who had previously been excluded from regular classrooms because of their supposed disabilities is seen by many educators as in the best tradition of the social studies movement. The National Council for the Social Studies relates this push to the struggle for the extension of civil rights, to the purpose of our system of free public education, and to the need to make the classroom a microcosm of the real world. For a full discussion of the rationale

behind mainstreaming, see, John G. Herlihy and Myra T. Herlihy, eds., *Mainstreaming in the Social Studies* (Washington, D. C.: National Council for the Social Studies, 1980), pp. 6–7.

3.  How children with handicapping conditions are evaluated for this determination of appropriateness is outlined in P. L. 94–142. For a description of how this determination is made, see Esther Tolkoff, "Mainstreaming," *New York Teacher*, January 18, 1981, p. 11.

4.  J. Herlihy and M. Herlihy, *Mainstreaming in the Social Studies* (NCSS Bulletin 62, Washington D. C., 1980), p. 3.

5.  Ibid., p. 6.

6.  Ibid., p. 2.

7.  Daniel M. Feins and Jack W. Entin, eds., *Handbook for Social Studies Teaching* (New York: Holt, Rinehart and Winston, 1967), p. 5.

8.  R. Dunn and K. Dunn, *Educator's Self-Teaching Guide to Individualizing Instructional Programs* (West Nyack, New York: Parker Publishing Company, 1975). Modified by Jeanne Powell, SUNY-Binghamton, February 1978.

9.  An adaptation by Linda Biemer of the State University of New York at Binghamton of P. B. Smith and G. Bentley, *Mainstreaming Mildly Handicapped Students into the Regular Classroom* (Austin, Texas: Education Service Center, 1975).

10. Linda Biemer, "Mainstreaming and Secondary Social Studies" (Washington, D. C.: NEA Publications, 1981), p. 2.

11. Herlihy and Herlihy, p. 64.

12. These descriptions of learning disabilities were taken from Mary M. Banbury, "What Are Learning Disabilities?" *New York Teacher*, March 15, 1981. Published by the AFT Teachers' Network for Education of the Handicapped.

# 13

••••••••••••••••••••••••••••••••••••••••••••••••••••••••••••••••••••••••••••••••••

# Professional Growth

••••••••••••••••••••••••••••••••••••••••••••••••••••••••••••••••••••••••••••••••••

Social studies is a dynamic discipline because it relates to an ever-changing world society. Consequently, social studies teachers cannot afford to remain static. The extent to which they improve their teaching skills and expand their perspectives in content areas is referred to in the field as professional growth. All social studies teachers are involved in this process, some perhaps more intensively than others. On the job, professional growth results from classroom visits, conferences, and self-appraisal. Outside of school, there are many experiences, such as reading and involvement in professional organizations, that help shape the teacher's views and continually alter his or her educational goals and objectives.

## SELF-EVALUATION

Undoubtedly, the best and most common way for teachers to grow professionally is through objective self-evaluation. The responses of students, the expressions on their faces in the learning situation, are indications of the teacher's performance. Systematic review of lesson plans and teaching strategies can result in the elimination of unsuccessful methods and materials and in a consideration of new directions and techniques.

One of the best methods for self-evaluation is the use of the videotape recorder. Granted that this approach has limitations, if used wisely and consistently, it does help the teacher to gain insight into his or her performance and to consider necessary adjustments and changes. The videotape recorder is most effective when the teacher concentrates on one aspect of the lesson, such as questioning or use of the chalkboard. The teacher is often the best judge in selecting which area should be the subject of an initial effort. The value of the videotape recorder is that the tape can be stored, replayed, and evaluated with later work in order to determine progress. The effectiveness of this technique, or any other self-evaluative process, is dependent upon the teacher's willingness to critically evaluate his or her work.

A more thorough treatment of self-evaluation techniques is presented in Chapter 14.

## INTERVISITATION

Related to the self-evaluation process, intervisitation is an activity similar to the "buddy system," but with a different emphasis. Whereas many teachers may react adversely to a supervisory visit, a planned visit by a colleague can often have beneficial results. As in the use of the videotape recorder, intervisitation is most effective when it focuses on a specific part of a lesson and is carried out on a sustained basis.

A teacher's visit to his or her supervisor or colleague has great value. Not only can the visitor zero in on a specific aspect of interest, but he or she can learn about classroom interrelationships.

A morale problem can develop when a younger and sometimes inexperienced teacher becomes involved in the intervisitation process. A teacher new to the profession may come away feeling intimidated, overwhelmed, or inadequate. None of us was born a good teacher. All of us would agree that it takes many years of dedicated work to become an effective teacher. In addition, many experienced teachers are anxious to learn new methods and approaches from colleagues who are recent college graduates and new to the profession. If the proper attitudes prevail, an intervisitation program can be of extreme benefit to all participants.

## SUPERVISORY VISITS

The supervisory visit can often create apprehension and a variety of ill feelings and emotions. These negative aspects can be overcome if the supervisor and the teacher meet before the lesson and work out the objectives of the visit. Generally, the supervisor is interested in overall classroom presence, lesson organization, and a specific aspect of the teacher's performance. Many times, the supervised lesson or specific practices that were noted are called to the attention of the department because of their value to all. If conducted in the proper spirit, the supervisory visit can be a beneficial experience.

## IN-SCHOOL CONFERENCES

If the teacher is involved in organizing a conference, he or she should seek assistance from colleagues and make the presentation as pragmatic as possible. Departmental and general faculty conferences can be extremely worthwhile if planned with faculty input and then adequately reinforced or followed up. Many people are interested in education and many organizational representatives are willing to participate in conferences. Many colleges and universities offer guest lectures from among their staff. Two important suggestions that can be helpful are:

1. Establish a theme for several conferences. For example, a series of conferences devoted to a current social studies controversy would be worthwhile.

2. Develop and distribute material that will be useful for the classroom situation. Explain how the materials have been used, and supply an evaluation that demonstrates various options and alternatives that fit individual needs.

Involved teachers must learn how to balance activities and plan for using limited time. Teachers are sometimes overwhelmed with afterschool work and are frustrated because they cannot participate in all of the worthwhile activities that could enhance their teaching.

## Reading

One of the joys of teaching social studies is that teachers are rewarded for reading. The more they read, the more insight they gain. Continuous reading is essential for the effectiveness and professional growth of all social studies teachers. The materials that teachers choose to read should be determined by their interests, the subjects they teach, the needs of their classes, and current national and international developments. It is just as important for teachers to read the latest in science fiction bestsellers as it is for them to read the latest in historical scholarship. The latter apprises them of the latest scholarship in a particular area of historic controversy. The former gives them an idea of what their students are interested in and how they view the world.

Two suggestions regarding reading are, in a sense, self-evident. One is that reading be balanced so that the teacher can present both sides of an issue. For example, Toland's book *The Rising Sun* should be read to counter the view presented by Bergamini in *The Imperial Conspiracy*. Secondly, included in the teacher's list of periodicals should be magazines and publications that are published by recognized professional organizations, such as the National Council for the Social Studies and the American Historical Association. These publications help teachers to keep up to date on the latest developments in the field and to evaluate new texts, audiovisual materials, and other features that serve to advance their work. Once again, content and pedagogy must be emphasized and related.

**Professional Organizations**

Every year social studies teachers are asked to join any number of professional organizations. Some are content-based, such as the American Historical Association, and others are education-based, such as the National Council for the Social Studies. In addition, these organizations are sometimes subdivided into regional or local groups, which are looking for membership and support. Obviously, a teacher can't join all the groups. A teacher should select the organizations he or she feels will best suit individual needs.

A professional organization can serve teachers in many ways. It represents their specific subject areas or disciplines on a national or state level and speaks for them with authority to those in government. At meetings and conventions, described below, teachers are made cognizant of the latest trends in their field. In addition, they are afforded the opportunity to exchange views and ideas regarding social studies education with colleagues.

To take full advantage of the opportunities for professional growth offered by these organizations, it is worthwhile for a teacher to do more than just pay dues — to become actively involved in the organization. This involvement automatically places the teacher in the mainstream of the latest developments in the field. (See list of organizations at the end of this chapter.)


## CONVENTIONS

A technique recently demonstrated by a sixth-grade geography teacher from Illinois at a convention in Boston became the basis for a series of lessons in an urban-studies elective class in a select New York City high school. Conventions offer a great deal to the interested and discerning teacher. They offer him or her the opportunity to exchange ideas and views with colleagues in many different areas; to gain insight into the teaching and social conditions that prevail beyond his or her own base of operations, to obtain firsthand information about the new methods and experimental work in social studies, and to gain insight into new subject and curricular innovations. Important political and educational leaders speak and participate in enlightening programs on current issues in the nation and in social studies. Usually, publisher's representatives, audiovisual vendors, and others offering educational materials will be there to explain and demonstrate their wares. Although attendance at conventions can be costly, there is no question as to their value in broadening the vistas of the teacher. In addition, many costs involved in attending professional conventions are tax-deductible.


## IN-SERVICE COURSES AND WORKSHOPS

In-service courses and workshops are usually offered to fill an apparent need. They offer teachers the opportunity to develop an awareness of a problem area and to work towards practical solutions in resolving those problems. For example, many teachers recognize the value of using simulation games in their classes. A workshop on this new technique can provide them with the experience and confidence necessary to use it in their teaching.

In large metropolitan areas such as New York, unique opportunities are afforded social studies teachers to attend in-service courses offered by organizations such as the *New York Times*, the Asia Society, or the Metropolitan Museum of Art. These are normally rewarding and excellent programs.

A teacher who has expertise in a particular area, such as the use of audiovisual instructions materials, might consider giving an in-service course. The interchange that often results between the instructor and the teacher can benefit all parties.

### Postgraduate School

Many teachers are required to take courses for increment credit. Most of them take courses because they are interested in advancing their craft. Although many colleges and universities are in the forefront of innovative approaches in the social studies, teachers should not neglect courses in those content areas that were lacking in their undergraduate sequence. The decision as to which courses a teacher should take should be made by a realistic assessment of what will be most beneficial in enhancing his or her performance.

### Travel and Exchange Programs

The nature of their work provides teachers with the time to travel. Photos in textbooks or slides are of value but cannot compare with the personalized photos, slides, and anecdotal experiences of a teacher who has visited the place being discussed.

There are many organizations that offer excellent programs for the teacher. The U. S. Office of Education and various state education departments sponsor travel and exchange programs and also serve as a source of information regarding travel and exchange programs under the auspices of organizations such as the English Speaking Union or various universities.

## GUIDE FOR PROFESSIONAL GROWTH

Participation in any travel or exchange program is usually one of the most rewarding experiences that a social studies teacher can have and such experiences usually translate themselves into more effective classroom teaching.

As in any other work, the teacher's job is what he or she makes it. Teaching can be a great source of joy and excitement. Making it such requires involvement, participation, and interest. Review the list of questions that follow. They can serve as a guide that will ultimately result in professional growth and a vital experience.

1. Of which professional organizations are you a member?
2. Which magazines in the field of education do you read?
3. How have you participated in educational organizations?
4. What have you contributed to department or faculty meetings?
5. To which community groups do you belong?
6. What have you written?
7. What books of a professional nature have you read?
8. Which periodicals do you read regularly?
9. Which pupils have you guided?
10. What professional courses have you taken or given?
11. Of what value are your travels?
12. What innovations in teaching have you tried?
13. What professional help have you given to a colleague or a prospective teacher?
14. What new teaching methods have you tried recently?

Professional growth is a continuous development that makes social studies teaching an exciting and vital profession. The involved teacher enjoys expanding personal horizons. Attendance at meetings and conventions, the purchase of professional books and materials, and membership in professional organizations are generally recognized by the Internal Revenue Service as tax-deductible items. The social studies teacher should keep a carefully documented account of the expenses incurred.

Many professional ideas can be formulated by working and learning with others. Belonging to a political party or running for office can be more meaningful than reading about political candidates. The social studies teacher's political activity is certainly a vital way of developing professionally. Involvement in community-action programs and social causes can be both a learning and a teaching experience. Many social studies educators derive professional satisfaction by assuming leadership roles in the home and/or the school community. They have become a force in improving education as a social institution. When a teacher reads a novel, takes a trip to California, joins a union and/or professional group, or writes a letter to the editor, he or she is engaging in a process of professional growth. Why not take advantage of these opportunities to develop as a better educator and a more significant human being?

## Social Studies and Social Science Service Organizations*

The African-American Institute, School Services Division, 833 United Nations Plaza, New York, NY 10017

American Assembly, Columbia University, New York, NY 10027

American Association of University Women, Sales Office, 2401 Virginia Avenue, N. W., Washington, DC 20037

American Civil Liberties Union, 132 W. 43rd Street, New York, NY 10036

American Committee on Africa, 198 Broadway, New York, NY 10038

American Federation of Labor and Congress of Industrial Organizations, 815 16th Street, N. W., Washington, DC 20006

American Friends Service Committee, Inc., 1501 Cherry Street, Philadelphia, PA 19102

American Geographical Society, Broadway at 156th Street, New York, NY 10032

American Italian Historical Association, c/o St. Charles Seminary Center for Migration Studies, 209 Flagg Place, Staten Island, NY 10304

American Jewish Committee, Institute of Human Relations, 165 E. 56th Street, New York, NY 10022

The American Legion, National Headquarters, 700 N. Pennsylvania Street, Indianapolis, IN 46206

American Library Association, American Association of School Librarians, 50 E. Huron Street, Chicago, IL 60611

American Medical Association, 535 North Dearborn Street, Chicago, IL 60610

American Newspaper Publishers Association, The Newspaper Center, 11600 Sunrise Valley Drive, Reston, VA 22091

Anti-Defamation League of B'nai B'rith, 823 United Nations Plaza, New York, NY 10017

Association for Asian Studies, One Lane Hall, University of Michigan, Ann Arbor, MI 48109

Atlantic Council of the United States, 1616 H Street, N. W., Washington, DC 20006

Carnegie Endowment for International Peace, 11 Dupont Circle, N. W., Washington, DC 20036

Center for Inter-American Relations, 680 Park Avenue, New York, NY 10021

Center for War/Peace Studies, 218 E. 18th Street, New York, NY 10003

Committee for Economic Development, 477 Madison Avenue, New York, NY 10022

The Conservation Foundation, 1717 Massachusetts Avenue, N. W., Washington, DC 20036

European Community Information Service, Suite 707, 2100 M Street, N. W., Washington, DC 20037

Foreign Policy Association, School Services Division, 205 Lexington Avenue, New York, NY 10016.

Freedom House, Willkie Memorial Building, 20 West 40th Street, New York, NY 10018

Institute of International Education, 809 United Nations Plaza, New York, NY 10017

International Council for Educational Development, 680 Fifth Avenue, New York, NY 10019

*For a more complete listing of social studies and social-science service organizations, you may want to consult the *Encyclopedia of Associations*, Denise S. Akey, editor, published by Gale Research Company, Detroit, MI, 48226.

International Friendship League, 22 Batterymarch Street, Boston, MA 02109

Japan Society, Inc., 333 East 47th Street, New York, NY 10017

Joint Council on Economic Education, 1212 Avenue of the Americas, New York, NY 10036

League of Women Voters of the United States, 1730 M Street, N. W., Washington, DC 20036

The Middle East Institute, 1761 N Street, N. W., Washington, DC 20036

National Audubon Society, 950 Third Avenue, New York, NY 10022

National Committee on U.S.-China Relations, Inc., 777 United Nations Plaza, Room 9B, New York, NY 10017

National Conference of Christians and Jews, 43 West 57th Street, New York, NY 10019

National Geographic Society, 17th and M Streets, N. W., Washington, DC 20036

National Parks Association, 1701 18th Street, N. W., Washington, DC 20009

National Wildlife Federation, 1412 16th Street, N. W., Washington, DC 20036

Planned Parenthood-World Population, 810 Seventh Avenue, New York, NY 10019

The Population Council, One Dag Hammarskjold Plaza, New York, NY 10017

Population Reference Bureau, Inc., 1337 Connecticut Avenue, N. W., Washington, DC 20036

Public Affairs Committee, Inc., 381 Park Avenue South, New York, NY 10016

Sierra Club, 530 Bush Street, San Francisco, CA 94108

Social Science Education Consortium. 855 Broadway, Boulder, CO 80302

Social Science Research Council, 605 Third Avenue, New York, NY 10016

The Twentieth Century Fund, 41 East 70th Street, New York, NY 10021

United Nations Association of the United States of America, 300 East 42nd Street, New York, NY 10017

World Law Fund, 777 United Nations Plaza, New York, NY 10017

# 14

●●●●●●●●●●●●●●●●●●●●●●●●●●●●●●●●●●●●●●●●●●●●●●●●●●●●●●●●●●●●●●●●●●●●●●●●●●●●●●●●●●

# Professional Evaluation

●●●●●●●●●●●●●●●●●●●●●●●●●●●●●●●●●●●●●●●●●●●●●●●●●●●●●●●●●●●●●●●●●●●●●●●●●●●●●●●●●●

The previous chapters have presented methods and techniques for the effective teaching of social studies. In this era of educational accountability, supervisors and teachers, both new and experienced, must be concerned with means of measuring and evaluating what is actually happening in the classroom. To what extent, and how successfully, are the methods and techniques of effective teaching being applied? What impact is actually being made upon the students? What growth or change is taking place on the part of the teacher and of the student?

It is the purpose of this chapter to present some well-established and widely used methods of professional evaluation, as well as some new, still little-used instruments of evaluation, that measure a wide range of activities and objectives involved in the social studies classroom.

The need for professional evaluation for the purposes of accountability and as an aid in teacher change and growth and in the maintenance of the professional status of the teacher is evident. The "what" and the "how" of evaluation are more complex.

The most frequently used, and perhaps the oldest, means of evaluating classroom performance is through an observation report by the supervisor. The observation report may be a short narrative on the general impressions and observations of a classroom visit, or it may be a detailed checklist, covering a wide range of specific aspects of teacher and pupil performance.

The following checklist, Table 14-1, is presented as a guide. It provides a means for the teacher to determine to what extent he or she is using the methods and techniques presented in the previous chapters. It is offered as a means of insuring that the fundamental requirements of learning are present. Later in the chapter, attention is given to the nuances that are sometimes more difficult, yet essential, to evaluate.

It must be stated that such checklists are not meant to be adhered to slavishly but should be used as applicable, in differing classroom situations, as

**TABLE 14-1.**  *Observation checkoff*

| Teacher | | Class | Room | Period |
|---|---|---|---|---|
| Topic | | Type of Lesson | Date | |

| | Poor | Fair | Good |
|---|---|---|---|
| | 1  2 | 3  4 | 5  6 |

A.  *The Lesson*

| | Poor | Fair | Good |
|---|---|---|---|
| 1. Motivation | ____ | ____ | ____ |
| 2. Aim | ____ | ____ | ____ |
| 3. Topic | ____ | ____ | ____ |
| 4. Development | ____ | ____ | ____ |
| 5. Integration with other skills | ____ | ____ | ____ |
| 6. Relevance | ____ | ____ | ____ |
| 7. Medial summary | ____ | ____ | ____ |
| 8. Timing of lesson | ____ | ____ | ____ |
| 9. Individualization of instruction | ____ | ____ | ____ |
| 10. Homework assignments | ____ | ____ | ____ |
| 11. Use of materials (A–V, etc.) | ____ | ____ | ____ |
| 12. Use of chalkboard | ____ | ____ | ____ |
| 13. Final summary | ____ | ____ | ____ |
| 14. Outcomes | ____ | ____ | ____ |

B.  *The Pupils*

| | | | |
|---|---|---|---|
| 1. Pupil participation | ____ | ____ | ____ |
| 2. Pupil interest | ____ | ____ | ____ |
| 3. Pupil questions | ____ | ____ | ____ |
| 4. Pupil interaction | ____ | ____ | ____ |
| 5. Pupil behavior | ____ | ____ | ____ |
| 6. Pupil initiative | ____ | ____ | ____ |
| 7. Evidence of good work habits | ____ | ____ | ____ |

C.  *The Teacher*

| | | | |
|---|---|---|---|
| 1. Teacher preparation | ____ | ____ | ____ |
| 2. Evidence of teacher's scholarship | ____ | ____ | ____ |
| 3. Teacher's questions | ____ | ____ | ____ |
| 4. Teacher's use of language | ____ | ____ | ____ |
| 5. Teacher's voice and/or diction | ____ | ____ | ____ |
| 6. Teacher's attire | ____ | ____ | ____ |
| 7. Teacher's animation | ____ | ____ | ____ |
| 8. Ability to manage the class | ____ | ____ | ____ |
| 9. Judicious use of praise | ____ | ____ | ____ |
| 10. Teacher's handwriting on board | ____ | ____ | ____ |

**TABLE 14-1.** *(Continued)*

| D. The Room | Poor<br>1  2 | Fair<br>3  4 | Good<br>5  6 |
|---|---|---|---|
| 1. Heat and ventilation | —— | —— | —— |
| 2. Lighting | —— | —— | —— |
| 3. Decorations | —— | —— | —— |
| 4. Materials in evidence | —— | —— | —— |
| 5. Atmosphere | —— | —— | —— |
| 6. General condition of room | —— | —— | —— |

## Description

### A. The Lesson

1. _____
2. _____
3. _____
4. _____
5. _____
6. _____
7. _____
8. _____
9. _____
10. _____
11. _____
12. _____
13. _____
14. _____

### B. The Pupils

1. _____
2. _____
3. _____
4. _____
5. _____
6. _____
7. _____

### C. The Teacher

1. _____
2. _____
3. _____
4. _____
5. _____
6. _____
7. _____
8. _____
9. _____
10. _____

**TABLE 14-1.**    *(Continued)*

D.  *The Room*
1.  _____
2.  _____
3.  _____
4.  _____
5.  _____
6.  _____

well as geared to differing teacher personalities. If an instrument of evaluation creates a rigid mold and stifles teacher creativity, then it loses its basic purpose.

It may help beginning teachers if, before the observation, they ask their supervisors which items on the checklist will be especially important in classroom visits.

Teachers may wish to establish their own checklists, using their own criteria for effective teaching. The pages that follow can help teachers to do objective self-observation to measure classroom performance against their own checklists.

In the teacher-supervisor conferences that generally follow an observation visit, the supervisor will point out the most positive and/or negative aspects of the lesson observed.

Most people are sensitive about criticism, no matter how constructive it may be. Yet the teacher-supervisor conference offers the teacher an opportunity that could prove extremely useful. In this day and age, when it is often difficult to obtain anything but a superficial response from other people, the teacher will find that many supervisors are willing to come forward with a detailed reaction to the teacher's lesson. A sincere reaction in modern life is indeed a rarity. The teacher should get the most out of it! He or she will derive maximum benefit from these conferences by way of a healthy exchange with the supervisor. The chance for this type of exchange is enhanced if the teacher comes prepared to discuss the goals and objectives that are guiding him or her. If they are muddled, the supervisor could help to clarify them. The teacher might be asked about what the class has done and where he or she and the class are heading. He or she might ask for specific details that define his or her strengths and deficiencies so that he or she can build on the former to overcome the latter. The teacher might also ask about materials and alternative methods of teaching the same lesson. Professional pilots ride "shotgun" with each other periodically for the purpose of providing constructive criticism. When postobservation conferences are conducted in this spirit, everyone in the learning process comes out ahead.

The following excerpts from the files of supervisors are reprinted here as a means of illustrating how the specific methods and techniques dealt with in earlier chapters can be or should be used in the classroom.

## 1. Inquiry method

Dear_____:

The students in your class were asked to read a statement made by John Brown during his trial for his Harper's Ferry Raid in October of 1859. This was an account of John Brown's final speech in court after his conviction.

After the students read the account, you asked them to describe the tone of his speech. After each student gave a response, you asked them to substantiate their statement by reference to a specific part of the speech. You then instructed your students to analyze President Lincoln's appraisal of John Brown.

Throughout this discussion, analysis and evaluation, _____, your co-teacher in the Humanities Program, participated with the rest of the class and helped to relate aspects of what was under discussion to what he had previously done with the class in the area of speech analysis.

As was indicated in our post-observation conference, _____ was involved with an analysis of persuasive speeches with this particular group. During the lesson, an attempt was made to show contemporary parallels between Mr. Lincoln's speech and the Republican Party's attempt to disassociate itself from blame. After the class had analyzed an editorial from a newspaper of the times, an hypothesis was formulated which went as follows: The Republican Party was more concerned with preserving the union than with abolition. One of the final activities of this lesson was an analysis of a campaign poster stating, "The Union: It Must and Shall Be Preserved."

During the course of our post-observation conference, we discussed some of the following excellent aspects of this lesson:

1. *Student interest and participation.* Throughout the lesson, due to your excellent preparation and careful correlation with _____, your students were involved and interested and functioned on a very mature and sophisticated level. Although there were two classes in the room together, students had an opportunity to express their views and to substantiate their opinions.
2. *An inquiry and discovery-type lesson.* Through your attempt to formulate a working hypothesis, you were able to have your students understand a major issue involved in the Civil War. Rather than hearing from you that President Lincoln and the Republican Party were most concerned with preserving the Union, your students were able to substantiate this hypothesis through the readings.

We also discussed the following aspect of this lesson which is in need of your careful consideration: in your attempt to move the lesson on, you at times cut off part of the discussion and imposed too much of your own will. In other words, there was too much talk by the teacher and not enough reliance on the very capable discussion and analysis of your students. It might be interesting for you to try to use a tape recorder to understand better the point that I have just made. If you would like, we can make the necessary arrangements.

In conclusion, this was a very worthwhile lesson due to your careful preparation, your excellent teamwork with _____, and your concern with using methods and techniques that enhance the social studies program. You once again have demonstrated that you are willing to experiment and make social studies the exciting subject that it is.

## 2. Value learning

Dear_____:

At the beginning of the period, you stated that your class had just completed reading the book *DIBS,* which dealt with a six-year-old boy who was very bright but had many emotional problems. You asked the class, "Why was he such a good candidate for therapy?" You also asked, "Do you think people with less severe problems benefit from therapy?"

There followed an excellent discussion and analysis of these two questions, with the responses on a very mature level. After this motivational discussion, you referred to an article by Carl R. Rogers entitled, "What It Means to Become a Person." The students were asked to refer to their textbook *Introduction of the Behavioral Sciences,* and you then proceeded to ask a series of questions dealing with why some people present a false facade. You then distributed two rexographed sheets. One was entitled *"Freud's View of the Defense Mechanism,"* and the other contained a series of definitions related to defense mechanisms.

The first rexographed sheet contained a series of short case studies which illustrated seven different kinds of defense mechanisms (repression, reaction formation, projection and rationalization, fantasy, fixation, and regression). You then wrote on the chalkboard the following problem: "How do we avoid confronting problems directly?" For the remainder of the period, you used the case studies and the definitions to analyze and evaluate each of the seven defense mechanisms. Towards the end of the period, as a summary question, you posed the following problem: "Is it good, bad, or irrelevant to use defense mechanisms?"

During our postobservation conference, we discussed many aspects of this lesson and of your part in the behavioral-sciences program. The following is a summary of some of the excellent aspects of this lesson:

1. *Materials.* Your use of materials from the textbook, the pocketbook *DIBS,* and the rexographed material, was extremely worthwhile. Your students were able to read, analyze, and discuss important and complex topics based upon information which they had available.
2. *Use of case studies.* The use of case studies to illustrate the definitions was extremely worthwhile. Your students were able to understand better Freud's theories of defense mechanism in a very mature yet simple manner.

We also discussed one aspect of this lesson on which I believe you should reflect and make necessary improvements. There was too much teacher-student interreactions and not enough student-student discussion and reaction.

In this kind of lesson, you could have taken a more passive role and permitted your students to get involved in evaluating and reacting to each another's responses. This is a higher level of discussion, for which I believe you are ready.

In conclusion, this was an excellent lesson due to your careful preparation, use of excellent materials, and your concern for making the behavioral-sciences program a meaningful one that contains important content and ideas and helps develop positive attitudes and understanding on the part of your students.

### 3. Planning

*Lesson description.*   The teacher began the lesson by talking in Chinese. The students inferred correctly that he was talking about Chinese foods. An assignment was written on the board utilizing the format of a Chinese-American menu — Plan A and Plan B, giving the students a choice between writing an essay about Chinese cooking or answering directed questions on the same topic. No reading, suggested or required, was assigned. The teacher then began to explain utensils that he had brought from his home — a wok, cleaver, and portable electric brazier, together with various foodstuffs — water chestnuts, scallions, rice, eggs, oil, and chicken. He explained the relationship of Chinese cooking to Chinese geography; the lack of abundant fuel and meat were the main emphasis. This, he explained, resulted in a cooking style that requires only minimal time and supplemental use of vegetables. He then involved the students, who, following his instructions, demonstrated how to use the cleaver and the technique of stir frying. The students then enjoyed their Chinese cooking, actually "licking the bowl."

*Lesson analysis.*   The teacher is to be commended for sharing his expertise in Chinese cooking with his students. His obvious enthusiasm for the subject was contagious. This is another demonstration of how our social pluralism classes have contributed to the generally happy tone of our school. The underlying concept of ethnic understanding through shared cultural experiences is always praiseworthy. The assignment was differentiated and a direct application of the lesson. In a subsequent lesson it is suggested that the teacher develop the relationship of this type of cooking to Chinese philosophy by pointing out the relationship of the precepts of Taoism (stressing "essence" and quick inspiration) to the Chinese chef's desire to preserve quickly the flavor (essence) of a food object.

### 4. Media

*Lesson description.*   The lesson began with a discussion on modern Kenya and the troubles of adjustment. A study sheet was distributed containing the study questions under two headings: Masai Herdsman and Tradition and Customs. Some of the questions were "How do the herdsmen obtain nourishment without killing the cattle?" and "What factors would a Masai regard as important in deciding whether or not to give up his nomadic life to settle on a government land grant?" A ten-minute nonnarrated 16 mm film on the Masai was then shown. After the film showing, the class answered the questions on the study sheet in a sustained discussion. At the close of the lesson, the students were reminded to view the "Tribal Eye" program on the educational television channel.

*Lesson analysis.*   Educational media are being used in a masterful way by this teacher. By utilizing a nonnarrated film, the students became more intellectually involved than if the information had been spoon-fed to them. The film acted as a document in the inquiry mode of teaching. The teacher attempted to invite the students to raise hypotheses concerning the conflict of tradition and change in Africa. This objective would have been more easily achieved if the excellent question on nomadic life vs. government land grant had been raised at the beginning of the lesson.

*Lesson summary.*    The marvelous reaction of the class to this teacher (90 percent of the class took part in the summary discussion) is testimony to this teacher's planning and thoughtful use of educational media. The students in the class came face to face with self-realization and cultural understanding through the sharing of the daily activities of another society.

### 5. Professional growth

At the close of the current school year, we take note of the extensive contributions you have made in the area of curriculum development. You wrote the course of study in three courses: Bicentennial History of the American People, American Culture and Values, and Environmental Ethics.

In addition, you attended a weekend conference on advanced placement, cosponsored the Bicentennial Club, and organized our school's exhibit at the Learning Cooperative Dissemination Conference, for which our school won an award.

For these and many other contributions, our department has to be extremely grateful to you.

## CHANGING BASES FOR THE EVALUATION OF SOCIAL STUDIES INSTRUCTION

In recent years, the evaluation of teacher performance has become a complex and sometimes controversial process. Extensive application of the behavioral sciences to both teaching and supervision has led to some changes in the understanding of what constitutes effective teaching and in the methods of evaluating teaching. In addition, the emphasis on creating individual learning environments for particular student needs has necessitated the use of many models of acceptable procedures.

Teachers have sometimes been directed to select a mode of instruction in order to be characterized as effective teachers. Therefore, a teacher may have been proud to be referred to as an "inquiry teacher" or "developmental teacher" or by some other stylish label. This kind of teacher self-image placed the emphasis on style rather than on process. With the realization that personal interactions should be given primary emphasis, new instrumentation had to be developed to gauge interactions rather than format.

The stress on self-directed learning, continuous growth, and the affective domain in the classroom has been applied to new methods and techniques for teacher evaluation. There are several basic similarities in these recent methods: (1) they attempt to provide a more objective picture of what is happening in the classroom, (2) they involve the teacher to a much greater extent in the process of his or her evaluation and change, and (3) they provide more "scientific" scales of measurement or some form of systematic analysis.

For those teachers, whether novices or long experienced, who have the courage and endurance to face objectively their classroom performance and to undertake whatever change they feel is desirable, the following methods of teacher self-evaluation may be of great help.

## NEW SYSTEMS OF OBSERVATION AND ANALYSIS

### 1. Interaction Analysis

Although earlier work and studies have been done in this area, Ned Flanders's work is particularly distinctive because it crystallizes a long line of effort into specific form, usable not only for research but for private inquiry and self-improvement.

Flanders's methods for evaluating classroom climate are based on the theory that a sensitive recognition and acceptance of students' feelings, coupled with a judicious but generous use of individual support and backed by responsiveness to student ideas and the ability to build upon them, will lead to greater responsiveness in students, a more fluent generation of ideas, and greater autonomy. In the long run, this will result in not only a better affective climate, but also in greater cognitive productivity.

What interaction analysis measures most directly is the amount and proportion of time teachers and pupils spend in various categories of verbal behavior and the nature of that verbal behavior. With the use of videotapes or audiotapes, teachers can make their own observations and analyses. If such media are not available, two or more teachers can work together observing each other.

Classroom interaction analysis is particularly concerned with the influence pattern of the teacher. Its purpose is to record a series of acts in terms of predetermined concepts. The concepts refer to the teacher's control of the students' freedom of action. Flanders's system attempts to distinguish those acts of the teacher that increase students' freedom of action from those acts that decrease students' freedom of action. The system of categories is used by the observer to separate those acts that result in compliance from those acts that invite more creative and voluntary participation. At the same time, the observer is prevented from being diverted by the subject matter, which is irrelevant to the purpose.

Interaction analysis is concerned primarily with verbal behavior because it can be observed with higher reliability than most nonverbal behavior. It is assumed that the verbal behavior of the teacher is an adequate sample of his total behavior—that is, that the teacher's verbal statements are consistent with his or her nonverbal gestures.

In providing an objective and systematic way of analyzing some of what goes on in the classroom, the Flanders system can help to reduce the inconsistencies between the teacher's intentions and his or her actions. Interaction analysis can be used in conjunction with microteaching, or it can be coupled with audio- or videotaping.

*The Categories.*   There are ten categories in the system, as shown in Table 14-2. Seven are assigned to *teacher talk* and two to *student talk*. The tenth category covers pauses, short periods of silence, and talk that is confusing or noisy.

Of the seven categories assigned to teacher talk, categories 1 through 4 represent indirect influence, and categories 5, 6, and 7 direct influence. Indirect influence encourages participation by the student and increases freedom of action. Asking a question (category 4) is an invitation to participate and to ex-

---

**TABLE 14-2.**   *Summary of categories for interaction analysis*

1.* *Accepts feeling:* accepts and clarifies the feeling tone of the students in a nonthreatening manner. Feelings may be positive or negative. Predicting or recalling feelings is included.

2. *Praises or encourages:* praises or encourages student action or behavior. Jokes that release tension, but not at the expense of another individual; nodding head, or saying "mm hm?" or "go on" are included.

3. *Accepts or uses ideas of students:* clarifying, building, or developing ideas suggested by a student. As teacher brings more of his or her own ideas into play, shift to Category 5.

4. *Asks questions:* asking a question about content or procedure with the intent that a student answer.

---

5. *Lecturing:* giving facts or opinions about content or procedures; expressing his or her own ideas, asking rhetorical questions.

6. *Giving directions:* directions, commands, or orders with which a student is expected to comply.

7. *Criticizing or justifying authority:* statements intended to change student behavior from nonacceptable to acceptable pattern; bawling someone out; stating why the teacher is doing what he or she is doing; extreme self-reference.

---

8. *Student talk—response:* talk by students in response to teacher. Teacher initiates the contact or solicits student statement.

9. *Student talk—initiation:* talk by students, which they initiate. If "calling on" student is only to indicate who may talk next, observer must decide whether student wanted to talk. If he or she did, use this category.

---

10. *Silence or confusion:* pauses, short periods of silence, and periods of confusion in which communication cannot be understood by the observer.

---

*There is no scale implied by these numbers. Each number is classificatory; it designates a particular kind of communication event. To write these numbers down during observation is to enumerate—not to judge a position on a scale.

press ideas, opinions, or facts. The more general a teacher's question, the greater the opportunity for the student to assert his or her own ideas.

When the teacher accepts, clarifies, or uses constructively students' ideas and opinions, (category 3), they are encouraged to participate further. Often teachers act as if they did not hear what a student said; to acknowledge and make use of an idea is a powerful form of recognition. To praise or encourage student participation directly (category 2) is to solicit even more participation by giving a reward. Flanders maintains that the ability to use the feeling tone of a student's response constructively, to react to feeling and clarify it (category 1), can often mobilize positive feelings in motivation and successfully control the negative feelings that may otherwise get out of control. All of the actions in categories 1 through 4 tend to increase student participation and to give students the opportunity to become more influential.

Direct influence increases the active control of the teacher and often stimulates compliance. The lecture (category 5) focuses the attention of the students on ideas chosen by the teacher. To give directions or commands (category 6) is to direct the activities of the class with the intent of obtaining compliance. Category 7 refers to criticizing student behavior or justifying the teacher's use of authority. Direct influence tends to increase teacher participation and to establish restraints on student behavior.

The division of student talk into categories 8 and 9 provides an automatic check on freedom of student action within the system of categories. Ordinarily, a pattern of direct teacher influence is associated with less student talk, which generally consists of responses to the teacher (category 8); and a pattern of indirect influence is associated with more student talk, which is often initiated by the students (category 9).

Flanders cautions that the system of categories is designed for situations in which the teacher and the students are actively discussing school work. It is an inappropriate tool when verbal communication is discontinuous, separated by fairly long periods of silence, or when one person is engaged in prolonged lecturing or in reading aloud to the class.

*The Procedure.*    The observer sits in the classroom in the best position to hear and see the participants. At the end of each three-second period, he or she decides which of a prescribed set of numbered categories best represents the communication events just completed. The observer writes down this category number while simultaneously assessing communication in the next period and continues at a rate of about twenty to twenty-five observations per minute, keeping the tempo as steady as possible. The notes should be a sequence of numbers written in a column, so that the original sequence of events is preserved. Occasionally, marginal notes can be used to explain the class formation or any unusual circumstances. When there is a major change in class formation or in the communication pattern, as when the activity of the class changes, the observer draws a double line and indicates the time. In situations in which two-way communication does not exist, the observer should stop and make a note of the exact time at which spontaneous interaction lapsed and the reasons for the interruption.

The coded data is entered into a matrix, as shown in Figure 14-1, and results in a teacher "I/D ratio" — the ratio of indirect to direct verbal behavior.

*Recording Data in a Matrix.*   There is a method of recording a coded sequence of events in the classroom in such a way that certain facts become readily apparent. It consists of entering the sequence of numbers into a ten-row by ten-column table, or matrix (see Figure 14-1). The generalized sequence of teacher-pupil interaction can be examined readily in this matrix. The following example shows how an observer might classify what happens in a classroom and how the observations are recorded in the matrix.

A fifth-grade teacher is beginning a social studies lesson. The observer has been sitting in the classroom for several minutes and has begun to get some idea of the general climate before beginning to record. The teacher says to the class, "Boys and girls, please open your social studies books to page 5." (Observer classifies this as a 6, followed by a 10 because of the period of silence and confusion as the children try to find the page.) The teacher says, "Jimmy, we are all waiting for you. Will you please turn your book to page 5?" (Observer records a 7 and a 6.) "I know now," continues the teacher, "that some of us had a little difficulty with,

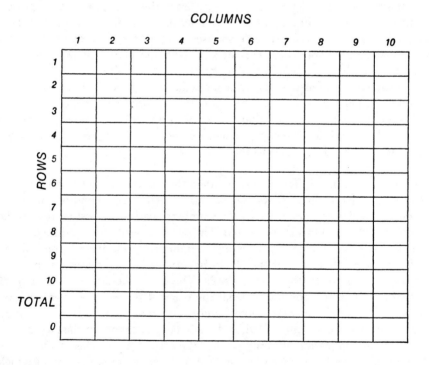

FIGURE 14-1.   *The Flanders system of interaction analysis*

and were a little disturbed by, the study of this chapter yesterday; I think that today we are going to find it more exciting and interesting." (Observer records two 1's, reacting to feeling). "Now, has anyone had a chance to think about what we discussed yesterday?" (Observer records a 4 for the question.) A student answers, "I thought about it, and it seems to me that the reason we are in so much trouble in Southeast Asia is that we haven't really had a chance to learn to understand the ways of the people who live there." (Observer records three 9's.)

The teacher responds by saying, "Good, I am glad that you suggested that, John. Now let me see if I understand your idea completely. You have suggested that if we had known the people better in Southeast Asia, we might not be in the trouble we are in today." (This is classified as a 2, followed by two 3's.)

The observer has now classified the following sequence of numbers in this fashion:

|  |  |  |
|---|---|---|
| | 10 | } First pair |
| | 6 | |
| Second pair } | 10 | |
| | 7 | } Third pair |
| Fourth pair } | 6 | |
| (The use of a 10 at the | 1 | |
| beginning and end of | 1 | |
| the sequence is explained | 4 | |
| in the discussion that | 9 | |
| follows.) | 9 | |
| | 9 | |
| | 2 | |
| | 3 | |
| | 3 | |
| | 10 | |

Tabulations are now made in the matrix to represent pairs of numbers. Notice in the listing above that the numbers have been marked off in pairs. The first pair is 10-6, the second pair is 6-10, etc. The particular cell in which a pair of numbers is tabulated is determined by using the first number in the pair to indicate the row and the second number in the pair the column. Thus, 10-6 would be shown by a tally in the cell formed by row 10 and column 6. The second pair, 6-10, would be shown in the cell formed by row 6 and column 10. The third pair, 10-7, is entered into the cell, row 10 and column 7. Notice that each pair of numbers overlaps with the previous pair, and each number, except the first and the last, is used twice. It is for this reason that a 10 is entered as the first number and as the last number in the record. This number is chosen because it is convenient to assume that each record began and ended with silence. This procedure also permits the total of each column to equal the total of the corresponding row.

The tabulations in the matrix can be checked for accuracy by noting that there should be one less tally in the matrix than there were numbers entered into the original observation record.

The matrix provides the observer with a convenient device for analyzing the summarized teacher-pupil interaction data. By studying the matrix, the observer will be able to identify those cells in which there is a heavy buildup of tallies, as well as those in which there are no tallies.

The use of Flanders's system for self-evaluation can be time-consuming and difficult. It involves a thorough learning of the categories, practice, and the use of a tape recorder; however, the teacher may find that the resulting change in the climate of the classroom and in the attitudes of the students make the effort more than worthwhile.

## 2. Audiotaping and Videotaping

These electronic aids introduce a wholly new element, making it possible to preserve at least part of the fleeting process of the classroom and to subject it later to multiple analyses. There are systems that enable the teacher to turn on the audio or video recorder and then carry on his or her own self-analysis. Such a system may provide teachers with prototype films and some other form of directive as to skills they are to practice and then provide them with systematic guides to the analysis of their procedures.

For those teachers who cannot use the relatively time-consuming approaches to self-evaluation described thus far, the new trends in systematic analysis and evaluation of teacher-student classroom behavior provide some simple instruments for analysis of the feedback obtained from audiovisual media. Table 14-7 offers a scale of measurement for important aspects of classroom behavior and can be used for self-analysis as well as for observer and/or student feedback.

If the teacher is concerned with the amount and kind of student participation in the classroom, the observation guide shown in Table 14-4 zeroes in on this aspect of classroom climate.

Few teachers believe that they project an authoritarian or unfriendly image. The observation guide in Table 14-3 can help teachers to see themselves as the camera sees them and as the tape recorder hears them.

## 3. Classroom Intervisitation

If teachers want to observe other teachers at work and are willing to be observed themselves, intervisitation and cooperative analysis and evaluation of teacher-learning situations constitute a type of experience that promotes teacher growth. Your supervisor is likely to respond quickly to a request from several

**TABLE 14-3.** *Observation guide: part 4, directing*

An important area of classroom management concerns the giving of directions. Observers should make note of the way in which directions are given in the classroom, by the teacher and by members of the class. Questions are offered below to guide the observer in studying this area of classroom behavior.

| | Most or much of the time | Some of the time | Very little of the time | Not at all | No chance to observe/ Didn't notice |
|---|---|---|---|---|---|
| 1. Does the teacher give directions as commands (e. g., Do this! Erase the board!)? | | | | | |
| 2. Does the teacher give directions by saying, e. g., Please do such and such! or Why don't you close the door? Would you do such and such? | | | | | |
| 3. Does the teacher criticize students when commands are not followed? | | | | | |
| 4. Does the teacher give directions in a neutral, indifferent, and operational way? | | | | | |
| 5. Does the teacher offer suggestions to the students on possible courses of action (e. g., We could read from our books today or have a discussion about the story)? | | | | | |
| 6. Does the teacher ask students for suggestions about the direction they would like to take? | | | | | |

teachers for the opportunity to observe and evaluate each other. The following is an illustration of how the problems of programming and scheduling intervisitations were worked out in a large city high school.

It was decided to make Mondays a film day for all social studies students. All classes of social studies meeting during the same period on that day would assemble in a large visual-aids room. Because there were six periods during the day, six different instructors on any Monday would assume responsibility for discussions accompanying the films. Because many teachers would be present each period, every member of the department would get a chance to see, over a period of time, every other member of the department handle a teaching situation. Because there

**TABLE 14-4.** *Observation guide; part 5, participation*

This observation guide pertains to student participation in the classroom and to the teacher's use of group dynamics. Observers should pay special attention to participation patterns and to the different groupings a teacher might make use of in the course of a lesson. Questions follow to aid the teacher's observation of the classroom.

|  | Most or much of the time | Some of the time | Very little of the time | Not at all | No chance to observe/ Didn't notice |
|---|---|---|---|---|---|
| 1. Is classroom discourse dominated by the teacher? | | | | | |
| 2. Is classroom discourse dominated by the students? | | | | | |
| 3. Do students have to be called on to answer questions? | | | | | |
| 4. Do students volunteer answers, ideas, and comments? | | | | | |
| 5. Do students talk to each other – answer or react to each other's ideas? | | | | | |
| 6. Do a majority of the students contribute to the discussion or question-and-answer period? | | | | | |
| 7. Do a few students occupy the discussion (i. e., a few students – the same ones – do most of the talking)? | | | | | |
| 8. Do most of the students seem attentive? | | | | | |
| 9. Is the class excited and talkative (i. e., about the topic at hand)? | | | | | |
| 10. Do the students gossip in informal cliques in the classroom? | | | | | |
| 11. Do the students discuss the lesson or express their ideas to their neighbors? (Can you overhear ideas exchanged between neighbors while the lesson is going on?) | | | | | |
| 12. Are the students asked to form groups of their own choosing to solve problems, make something, work up a report, etc.? | | | | | |

was no pressure of any kind to imitate anyone or follow any set of procedures, individual teachers experimented in various ways, from traditional question and answer lessons to panels of students and committee work. The result was a stimulating experience for all members of the department who share experiences, observe each other informally, confront similar problems and gain from each other's efforts. (Wiles, Kimball, *Supervision for Better Schools* [3rd ed., Englewood Cliffs, N. J.: Prentice-Hall, 1967], p. 254.)

Classroom intervisitation need not take place on a department-wide basis. Two or more teachers who are willing to forego nonassigned time and who have acquired some of the skills and tools of evaluation can work together toward mutual growth and change.

## 4. Guided Self-analysis

For those teachers seeking a systematic means of self-evaluation for all the methods of effective teaching presented in the previous chapters, we recommend guided self-analysis (GSA).

GSA is another means by which teachers can make careful and objective analyses of their own teaching behaviors as recorded on videotape. The GSA system, designed by Theodore Parsons, has been tested in New York City classrooms and found to be helpful for those teachers who wish to do their own self-analysis and interpretation of a recorded sequence of teaching behaviors. The GSA system was designed particularly for self-evaluation of the inquiry method of teaching. However, several of the schedules can be adapted for use in any teaching situation.

The system consists of several programs of carefully sequenced interaction codes by means of which the individual teacher analyzes a videotape made in his or her own classroom and comes to a more objective understanding of personal teaching behaviors. Each program of interrelated codes (or schedules) directs the teacher's attention to an important educational objective.

The schedules help the teacher to define and identify specific categories of teaching behaviors and to express them in quantitative terms. The teacher is asked to represent these graphically and is provided with guidelines for interpreting their meaning.

As the teacher employs the successive coding schedules to analyze a tape made in the classroom, he or she constructs a profile of personal teaching behaviors. This profile can be compared with profiles of other teachers or with an earlier one the teacher has made.

In its current form, Parsons's program consists of six schedules. Though each schedule may be used independently, their impact is enhanced by the cumulative insights that result when they are used together.

Schedule A directs the teacher's attention to the types of questions that he or she asks of pupils. The teacher is asked to classify these questions and to consider the relationship between them and the thinking that pupils must do in order to provide satisfactory responses.

With Schedule B, the teacher is asked to classify responses according to whether they promote or inhibit further thinking. The teacher is then helped to interpret the relationship between questions strategies and response patterns.

Schedule C helps the teacher analyze classroom talk and determines the relative percentages of time devoted to questions and responses, to instruction, to classroom management, and to behavior management.

Schedule D provides a means of "mapping" the pattern of communication between teacher and pupil. This map adds to a teacher's self-profile as it reveals the extent to which he or she intervenes in pupil statements, dominates the classroom with his or her own talk, controls the flow of talk, or is permissive in allowing pupils to work through their own thoughts.

Schedule E directs attention to another important aspect of teaching for inquiry. This schedule helps the teacher to assess the extent to which he or she utilizes the experiences of pupils in the process of building new concepts and principles.

Schedule F focuses attention on the nature of pupil responses to questions. This schedule maps the congruency between the levels of thinking required by the teacher and that produced by the pupils.

While Flanders's interaction-analysis categories system for codifying pupil-teacher interaction totally disregards the content matter being taught, Parsons states:

> Although there is no substantial research literature available on the subject, it is possible that there is a relationship between the curriculum content being taught and strategies for working with pupils. In view of this it seems desirable to plan your tapings so that you can monitor your teaching strategies by subject area as well as by the size of your group. We suggest, therefore, that you make your first series of tapes in a particular subject area, e. g., reading and/or social studies.

It was once said that "to question well is to teach well." While there is much more to teaching than questioning, it is true that the best teachers make effective use of questions. With the assumption that all teachers are concerned with improving their questioning techniques, we will present, in some detail, the means for analyzing one's questioning strategy given in Parsons's Schedule A.

When using Schedule A, the teacher is asked to identify each teacher-posed question and code it into one of five categories. These categories will help him or her to map questioning strategy and to determine its potential capability for promoting the development of thinking skills in pupils. Each time the teacher categorizes a question, he or she will have to focus attention on the amount and complexity of thinking required for pupils to produce a verbal response. He or she will code questions according to whether they are *rhetorical*, therefore, requiring no overt evidence of pupil thinking; *information*, requiring recall or recognition; *leading*, requiring pupils to assemble clues provided by the question itself in order to organize an answer; or *probing*, requiring complex organization and analysis. The fifth category, *other*, is used to discriminate questions that are not lesson-related.

Table 14-5 is a portion of an actual taped lesson illustrating coded teacher-posed questions.

**TABLE 14-5.** *Guided self-analysis, Schedule A, Teacher question code*

| | | |
|---|---|---|
| *Teacher:* All right. What are some other kin names they use? | Information | Pupils are asked to recall previously learned information. |
| *2nd Pupil:* They call their cousins brothers and sisters. | | |
| *Teacher:* Fine. | | |
| *3rd Pupil:* Adults call nieces and nephews daughters and sons. | | |
| *Teacher:* Good. Do we use the same names for these relatives? | Information | Pupils are asked to recall a practice from their own experience. |
| *3rd Pupil:* No. They're different. | | |
| *Teacher:* If our terms for the same relatives are different, then there must be a reason. Why do you think the Cheyenne use different terms than we do for the same relations? | Probing | Pupils are asked to explain a phenomenon. They must choose, from previously learned concepts and principles, those that are appropriate to explaining terminology differences. |
| *4th Pupil:* Maybe they don't know which children belong to which parents, so they just fake it. | | |
| *Teacher:* But they do know. What are some other reasons a person would call someone they know not to be their brother by the same name they use for their real brothers? | Leading | Teacher provides clues that guide pupils to the desired answer. Pupil is asked to give an example that fits the precise conceptual requirements supplied by the teacher. |
| *5th Pupil:* I call my Mom's friend "Aunt Maud" but she isn't really my aunt. | | |
| *Teacher:* Good! Good! Good! Why? | Probing | Pupil is asked to explain a phenomenon. The teacher expects the pupil to discover or remember concepts and principles that might explain why the term "aunt" is appropriate to the situation. Instead the pupil merely recalls an immediate cause for her own actions. The teacher does not probe further. |
| *5th Pupil:* Because my Mom tells me to. | | |
| *Teacher:* You know, I had a neighbor I used to call "uncle" when I was little. How many of you do the same thing? Lots of people do. | Rhetorical | No opportunity provided to answer. |
| *6th Pupil:* In our church everyone calls everyone else brother or sister. | | |

Table 14-6 illustrates the coding form used to record types of teacher-posed questions. This form can be used when teachers view their own videotapes.

The coding form provides a clear, graphic representation of the types of questions asked during the lesson. It also provides a means of recording the sequence of those questions. The coding form will enable teachers to assess their questioning strategies and to determine the extent to which their questions stimulated pupils to think critically.

Each dot in the coding form below represents a teacher-posed question. A total of thirteen questions was asked. The first dot indicates that the teacher asked an information-type question. This was followed by another information question (second dot) and then a rhetorical question (third dot). The sixth question the teacher posed was a probing question. This question was preceded by an information question and followed by a leading question. The sample coding form is a record of the classroom dialogue.

Students have been found to be surprisingly honest and reliable in their judgments of classroom performance. While a few in any group may be excessively positive, negative, or simply smart-alecky, groups of students — whole classes — have shown themselves capable of giving valuable and trustworthy feedback. Teachers should not shy away from evaluation by their students.

Table 14-7 uses items typical of concern in pupil-teacher interaction as a tool in measuring pupil perceptions of a class period. Teachers may wish to revise the questions to reflect their own classroom situations more closely or use them in conjunction with other tools that elicit certain student perceptions of the teacher's behavior. The authors have found that this form has been used effectively in grades as low as the fourth and, occasionally, the third.

In assessing pupil-teacher interaction, a teacher might wish to obtain some feedback on the proportion of behaviors aimed at the whole class and the proportion aimed at individuals. He or she might want to know how much time is spent in negative comments related to social control or to work. Perhaps he or she wants to compare the number of dependency responses with the number of contributions. Perhaps he or she wants to see how the pupils

**TABLE 14-6.**  *Guided self-analysis sample coding form*

|  | 1 | 2 | 3 | 4 | 5 | 6 | 7 | 8 | 9 | 10 | 11 | 12 | 13 |
|---|---|---|---|---|---|---|---|---|---|---|---|---|---|
| Other |  |  |  | • |  |  |  |  |  |  | • |  |  |
| Rhetorical |  |  | • |  |  |  |  | • |  |  |  |  |  |
| Information | • | • |  |  | • |  |  |  |  |  |  |  |  |
| Leading |  |  |  |  |  |  | • |  | • | • |  |  |  |
| Probing |  |  |  |  |  | • |  |  |  |  |  | • | • |

**TABLE 14-7.**    *Pupil perceptions of a class period*

Think about the last hour of class. About how much time would you say was spent in each of the following activities? Draw a circle around the answer you think best tells how much time was spent. *There are no right or wrong answers.*

*How much time? (Circle one)*

1. The *teacher* talking to the *whole class* – telling, answering, or asking something          a lot    some    a little    none

2. The *teacher* talking to *individual pupils* – telling, answering, or asking something          a lot    some    a little    none

3. *Pupils* talking to the *teacher* – telling, answering, or asking something.          a lot    some    a little    none

Now think about what you yourself did during the last class hour. Write in the number you think is right. Make the best guess you can.

4. My teacher told or asked me things or answered my questions _____ times.

5. I told or asked my teacher things or answered my teacher's questions _____ times.

6. I told or asked other pupils things or answered their questions _____ times.

7. During the last class hour, my teacher told or asked me things or answered my questions

           a. _____ much more than most other pupils
*check*    b. _____ a little more than most other pupils
*one*      c. _____ a little less than most other pupils
           d. _____ much less than most other pupils.

8. I volunteered to say things or do things during the class hour

           a. _____ much more than most other pupils
*check*    b. _____ a little more than most other pupils
*one*      c. _____ a little less than most other pupils
           d. _____ much less than most other pupils

9. When my teacher told or asked me something, it was

           a. _____ only about my work
*check*    b. _____ mostly about my work, but a little about my behavior
*one*      c. _____ mostly about my behavior, but a little about my work
           d. _____ only about my behavior

10. When telling me to do something, my teacher was

           a. _____ very pleased
*check*    b. _____ satisfied
*one*      c. _____ somewhat dissatisfied
           d. _____ quite dissatisfied

have perceived what has been done by comparing what the observer has seen with what the pupils have perceived. Another important thing for the teacher to look for is whether he or she is behaving differently towards girls than towards boys. Research has shown that teachers often indicate more satisfaction with girls than with boys.

## IN CONCLUSION

Despite the stress on skills and techniques, common sense seems to indicate that what a teacher *is,* is as important to his or her teaching as anything the teacher *does.* Over a period of years, researchers have been studying the differences between "good" and "poor" practitioners. They have not found the distinctive differences they expected in what these people knew or in the methods they used. The monograph summarizing these investigations (*Florida Studies in the Helping Professions,* Gainesville, Fla.: University of Florida Press, 1969) states that the more effective teachers were concerned with people rather than things and with perceptual meanings rather than facts and events. They saw other people as able, friendly, worthy, and helpful. They saw themselves as adequate rather than lacking, as dependable and worthy, as wanted rather than unwanted. They saw their teaching task as freeing rather than controlling, as larger and more involved, and as an encouraging process rather than a process of achieving goals.

Perhaps, then, the greatest need for evaluation lies in teachers' genuine insight into themselves, their ability to "lay themselves on the line," and a developing awareness of how they affect others. There are unobtrusive, less jarring ways of moving towards such understanding than a weekend workshop or a two-week T-group. A careful use of interaction analysis, for instance, is a sensitizing experience. Teachers can learn to see themselves more validly and see how others respond to them. What may seem like bare skills training in the art of asking open-ended questions – and maybe pushing and probing a bit further and really hearing the responses – can be a sensitizing experience.

> Professional evaluation, then, is not something to be feared or dreaded – a critical judgment handed down from on high by super-ordinates; but rather a challenging variety of opportunities for classroom teachers to work with supervisors, peers, students, and on their own, in order to grow professionally as they meet their own needs, and those of their students.

## BIBLIOGRAPHY

Amidon, E., and E. Hunter. *Improving Teaching: The Analysis of Classroom Verbal Inspection.* New York: Holt, Rinehart, and Winston, 1966. An easy-to-read introduction to a modified form of Flanders's interaction analysis.

Bruner, Jerome S. *Toward a Theory of Instruction.* Cambridge, Mass.: Harvard University Press, 1966. Attempts to synthesize what is known about teaching into a coherent theory with a strong base in John Dewey and the Gestalt school of psychology.

Ehman, Lee, Howard Mehlinger, and John Patrick. *Toward Effective Instruction in Secondary Social Studies.* Boston: Houghton Mifflin Co., 1974. Complex and intellectual, this is a social studies "methods" book available with abundant suggestions for teaching and for evaluating teacher-student performance.

Flanders, Ned A. *Analyzing Teaching Behavior.* Reading, Mass.: Addison-Wesley, 1970. A comprehensive methodology for studying the classroom using interaction analysis by its originator.

Fox, R., M. Luszki, and R. Schmuck. *Diagnosing Classroom Learning Environments.* Chicago: Science Research Associates, 1966. Clear and concise methods for studying classrooms, but particularly useful for the examples it gives of questionnaires and polling devices suitable for collecting student reactions to life at school.

Good, Thomas L., and Jere E. Brophy. *Looking Into Classrooms.* New York: Harper and Row, 1973. An approach to diagnosing classroom interaction, which the authors view in terms of pupil-teacher dyads.

Hyman, Ronald T., ed. *Teaching: Vantage Points for Study.* Philadelphia: J. B. Lippincott Co., 1974. Compilation of articles covering nearly every aspect of this field; particularly good for learning more about diagnostic tools and classroom evaluation methods.

Hyman Ronald T. *Ways of Teaching.* 2nd ed., Philadelphia: J. B. Lippincott Co., 1974. A very solid coverage of many "methods" of teaching, including questioning, discussion, role-playing, sociodrama, the Socratic approach, and others.

Joyce, Bruce R., Marsha Weil, and Rhoda Wald. *Three Teaching Strategies for the Social Studies.* Chicago: Science Research Associates, 1972. A brief, readable, and useful introduction to role-playing and simulations, with devices offered to assess the impact of each "strategy" on students.

Massialas, Byron, and Jack Zevin. *Creative Encounters in the Classroom.* New York: John Wiley and Sons, 1967. An introduction to the inquiry method oriented toward social studies teachers with plentiful examples of lessons and transcripts of student reactions — analyzed and evaluated.

Rosenshine, Barak, and Naomi Furst. "Current and Future Research on Teacher Performance Criteria," *Research on Teacher Education: A Symposium,* ed. B. Smith. Englewood Cliffs, N. J.: Prentice-Hall, 1971. A critique of past studies and a call for new ones that is pointed, frank, and somewhat despairing of concrete progress.

Sanders, Norris M. "Changing Strategies of Instruction: Three Case Examples," *Social Studies Curriculum Development,* chap. 5. Thirtieth Yearbook of the National Council for the Social Studies, ed. Dorothy Fraser. Washington, D. C.: NCSS, 1969, pp 139–73. Ways social studies instructors can vary their presentations and enrich their classroom behavior patterns by the author of the well-known *Classroom Questions.*

Skinner, B. F. *Technology of Teaching.* New York: Appleton-Century-Crofts, 1968. The application of stimulus-response theory to instruction, including its analysis and evaluation by one of the masters of "behaviorism."

# Index